WILLIAM CARLOS WILLIAMS,
THE ARTS, AND LITERARY TRADITION

WILLIAM CARLOS WILLIAMS,
THE ARTS, AND
LITERARY TRADITION

Peter Schmidt

Louisiana State University Press
Baton Rouge and London

10   9   8   7   6   5   4   3   2   1

Designer: Sylvia M. Loftin
Typeface: Goudy Old Style with Gill Sans Italic
Typesetter: Composing Room of Michigan
Printer: Thomson-Shore, Inc.
Binder: John H. Dekker & Sons, Inc.

The author gratefully acknowledges the University of Michigan Press for permission to reprint passages from "First Surrealist Manifesto," by André Breton; Madame André Breton and Philippe Soupault for permission to publish passages from "La Glace sans tain" in *Les Champs magnétiques*, © Editions Gallimard 1968; and Wittenborn Art Books, Inc., for permission to cite passages from Robert Motherwell's *The Dada Poets and Painters* (New York, 1954). William Carlos Williams' manuscript "Rome" is cited with the permission of The Poetry / Rare Books Collection, University Libraries, SUNY at Buffalo. Passages from William Carlos Williams' *Collected Poems, Vol. I, 1909–1939* (1987), edited by A. Walton Litz and Christopher MacGowan, copyright 1986 by New Directions Publishing Corporation, and William Carlos Williams' *Collected Later Poems* (1950) copyright 1944, 1948, 1949, 1950 by William Carlos Williams, © 1963 by the Estate of William Carlos Williams, are reprinted by permission of New Directions Publishing Corporation and Carcanet Press Limited. Passages from the following works are also reprinted by permission of New Directions Publishing Corporation: *The Autobiography of William Carlos Williams.* Copyright 1951 by William Carlos Williams. *The Embodiment of Knowledge.* Copyright © 1974 by Florence H. Williams. *Imaginations.* Copyright © 1970 by Florence H. Williams. *Interviews.* Copyright © 1976 by the Estate of William Carlos Williams. *Paterson.* Copyright © 1946, 1948, 1949, 1951, 1958 by William Carlos Williams. *Pictures from Brueghel.* Copyright © 1949, 1951, 1953, 1954, 1955, 1956, 1957, 1959, 1960, 1961, 1962 by William Carlos Williams. *Selected Letters.* Copyright 1957 by William Carlos Williams. Passages from Ezra Pound's *Translations.* Copyright © 1954, 1963 by Ezra Pound. All Rights Reserved. Reprinted by permission of New Directions Publishing Corporation and Faber & Faber Ltd.

Chapters One and Five appeared, in somewhat different form, as "Some Versions of Modernist Pastoral," *Contemporary Literature*, XII, No. 3 (Summer, 1980), 383–406, and "Dada, *Paterson*, and Epic Tradition," *William Carlos Williams Review*, VIII, No. 2 (Fall, 1982) 1–14, respectively.

Library of Congress Cataloging-in-Publication Data

Schmidt, Peter, 1951—
    William Carlos Williams, the arts, and literary
tradition.

    Bibliography: p.
    Includes index.
    1. Williams, William Carlos, 1883–1963—Criticism
and interpretation. 2. Williams, William Carlos,
1883–1963—Knowledge—Art. 3. Williams, William Carlos,
1883–1963—Knowledge—Literature. 4. Art and literature—
United States—History—20th century. 5. Influence
(Literary, artistic, etc.) I. Title.
PS3545.I544Z879   1988   811'.52   87-32483
ISBN 0-8171-1406-5

For my father

CONTENTS

ILLUSTRATIONS

ACKNOWLEDGMENTS

I would like to acknowledge the good advice and criticism of some of the many people who influenced me during the decade this book took to shape itself, from my days as a student to my teaching at Swarthmore College and my work editing the *William Carlos Williams Review.* David Young, David Walker, and Stuart Friebert at Oberlin College first taught me how to read modern poetry critically, and J. C. Levenson, Ray Nelson, David Levin, Gordon Braden, Ralph Cohen, Robert Langbaum, Paul Barolsky, Marjorie Balge, and Jeff Cox at the University of Virginia helped me extend, qualify, and complicate my learning. L. S. Dembo, Thomas Gardner, Catherine Rasmussen, and Debra Shostak of *Contemporary Literature* readied an early version of Chapter One for publication.

More recently, numerous friends at Swarthmore and elsewhere have been invaluable in teaching me the art of rethinking, including Lisa Aaron, Susan Snyder, Thomas Blackburn, Harold Pagliaro, Philip Weinstein, Chuck James, Craig Williamson, Nat Anderson, Abbe Blum, Constance Cain Hungerford, Kaori Kitao, Rachel Blau DuPlessis, Walter Benn Michaels, Wai-chee Dimock, Mark Seltzer, Steve Youra, Mary Poovey, Michael Fried, Emily Mitchell Wallace, Thomas Whitaker, Theodora Rapp Graham, Paul Mariani, Marjorie Perloff, Robert Bertholf, Henry Sayre, Stephen Cushman, Cecelia Tichi, and Lisa Steinman. Swarthmore College and the National Endowment for the Humanities assisted at crucial times with research support, and two editors at Louisiana State University Press, Elizabeth Carpelan and Catherine Landry, have ably helped prepare the manuscript for the printer. Finally, as someone who has made the transition from revising with scissors and a stapler to revising with a mouse, I would like to thank John von Neumann for helping invent word processing.

ABBREVIATIONS

A   *The Autobiography of William Carlos Williams* (1951; rpr. New York, 1967)

CLP   *The Collected Later Poems of William Carlos Williams* (1950; rpr. New York, 1963)

CP1   *The Collected Poems of William Carlos Williams, Volume I: 1909–1939*, eds. A. Walton Litz and Christopher MacGowan (New York, 1986)

EK   *The Embodiment of Knowledge*, ed. Ron Loewinsohn (New York, 1974)

I   *Imaginations*, ed. Webster Schott (New York, 1970). Contains *Kora in Hell: Improvisations* (1920); *Spring and All* (1923); *The Great American Novel* (1923); *The Descent of Winter* (1929); *A Novelette* (1932); and other prose

Int   *Interviews with William Carlos Williams*, ed. Linda W. Wagner (New York, 1975)

IWWP   *I Wanted to Write a Poem*, ed. Edith Heal (Boston, 1958)

P   *Paterson* (1946–58; rpr. New York, 1969)

PB   *Pictures from Brueghel and Other Poems* (New York, 1962)

RI   *A Recognizable Image*, ed. Bram Dijkstra (New York, 1978)

SE   *Selected Essays* (1954; rpr. New York, 1969)

SL   *The Selected Letters of William Carlos Williams*, ed. John C. Thirlwall (1957; rpr. New York, 1985)

Y   *Yes, Mrs. Williams* (New York, 1959)

WILLIAM CARLOS WILLIAMS,
THE ARTS, AND LITERARY TRADITION

PREFACE

Everything
is a picture
to the employing eye
that feeds restlessly to
find peace.
—William Carlos Williams
"The Fault: Matisse"

Q. Are you conscious, in your own writing, of the existence of a 'usable past'. . . ?
A. Yes, most assuredly, I am conscious in everything I write of a usable past, a past as alive in its day as every moment is today alive in me: Work therefore as different from mine as one period can be different from another, but in spite of that preserving between the two an identity upon which I feed. In all work in any period there is a part that is the life of it which relates to whatever else is alive, yesterday, today, and forever. To discover that in past work makes that work important to me. How can we say that the work of Henry James is more relevant to the present and future of American writing than the writing of Walt Whitman, or vice versa? The only question of any relevance in either case is, Was that work alive to its own day? If so then it is alive every day. If it was a palpable denial of its own day then—if I can discover it as such—out with it. I want to look in a work and see in it a day like my own, of altered shapes, colors, but otherwise the same. *That* I can use to reinforce my senses and my intelligence" (*Int,* 82).

In an essay entitled "Love and Service" dating from the early years of this century, 1910–1915, William Carlos Williams made an assertion about the goal of modern art that speaks with uncanny prescience to recent debates about the future of art (and criticism) now that the authority of Modernism has waned. It is both a quintessential statement of the Modernist goal of newborn purity in the arts and a radical questioning of the value of such a goal: "Then lest we mistake our signs for the reality let them be ever new, forever new for only by forever changing the sign can we learn to separate from it its meaning, the expression from the term, and so cease to be idolators" (EK, 182). Like the claims of so many other manifestos written around the turn of the century, Williams' statement rings with visionary optimism about being able to remake his culture's visual and verbal forms, its "signs." To do this, Williams implies, makers of art should interrogate their methods and return to first principles, discarding those features that are external to their medium in order progressively to purify and "modernize" their work. Thus, Williams believed, writers had to rediscover that their art was words on the page, linguistic signs before they became systems of representation referring to the world, just as painters needed to rediscover the tactility of paint and the flatness of the painted surface. In the words of Stéphane Mallarmé regarding the Modernist revolution in painting, "The scope and aim of Manet and his followers. . . is that painting shall be steeped again in its cause." Much other writing on Modernism in art and literature reveals similar premises, whether it be Williams' essays on how Marianne Moore and Gertrude Stein taught him the virtues of seeing and hearing words for "themselves," with "a curious immediate quality quite apart from their meaning" (I, 345), as if each syllable had been cleaned of the dirt of everyday use and reminted, or Clement Greenberg's famous dictum that Modernism in the arts meant that each art was required "to determine, through the operations peculiar to itself, the effects peculiar and exclusive to itself." In each case, the goal seems to be to discover a lost point of origin for each art outside history, a place of first principles that, when correctly recovered, will allow the art to reform itself and (ultimately) the world it represents.[1]

Williams' statement about the Modernist sign, however, also reveals a deep ambivalence about it: he calls such reverence for the

1. The Mallarmé and Greenberg quotations are discussed in the introduction to T. J. Clark's The Painting of Modern Life: Paris in the Art of Manet and His Followers (Princeton, 1984), 3–22, which contains a fine discussion of the contradictory principles of Modernism in the arts and literature, as do the essays in Brian Wallis (ed.), Art After Modernism: Rethinking Representation (New York, 1984), one of the best of the recent collections published on the subject. See also Ron Loewinsohn's excellent introduction to Williams' The Embodiment of Knowledge (New York, 1974), for further analysis of Williams' understanding of the paradoxes of representation in art and literature.

potential purity of signs nothing less than "idolatry," the worship of a
false god. All signs must be "forever" made new apparently because
each sign is inherently imperfect, mediating and deflecting the "real-
ity" to which it is supposed to refer. Heresy of heresies, Williams even
seems to value the reality behind the sign more than the sign itself:
he explicitly warns against mistaking "our signs for the reality."
Moreover, he defines reality as the product of a complex social and
political process, dependent upon both the private "expression" that
a sign's user seeks to make public and the public "meaning" that signs
are given whenever the act of communication occurs. Admittedly,
such meanings can only be articulated using further signs, a fact of
which much has been made in recent theoretical writings on semiot-
ics and the arts. But Williams' essential point here is a different one:
one can't fully understand systems of representation if one follows
Modernist theory and finds the essence of all discourse to be signs
merely about signs. The essential act of representation, Williams
implies, is the presentation of what is taken to be *content*, not form,
what he elusively calls "expression" and "meaning."

This is not to argue that Williams' essay (or any of his other
writing) implies that content is all-important and form provisional,
or that he naïvely believes that "reality" is definable without signs.
In Williams' eyes, either of these positions would be only another
form of idolatry. Rather, he urges that there be a perpetual explora-
tion of the complex paradoxes of representation, where "meaning"
cannot be rigidly aligned with the author's intended "expression," or
with the play of the "terms" or signs themselves, whether linguistic
or visual or musical, or with the referential values a creator's au-
dience gives his or her work. Signs must be "forever new" so that we
are forced to be sensitive to what signs veil as well as what they
reveal, to the ways the words *expression, meaning,* and *signs* are prob-
lematic cultural constructs, shaped by a specific historical period, a
particular idiom, even as the artist struggles to reshape them. In
contemporary terms, Williams marks the fact that art may at most
attain a "beginning" within historically bound materials, never a
point of "origin" transcending history.[2] As Williams said in the essay
"Waste and Use," also from 1910–1915: "But when man begins to be

2. For two meditations on the important difference between a "beginning" and an "ori-
gin," see Edward Said, *Beginnings: Intention and Method* (New York, 1975), and Michel
Foucault, "Nietzsche, Genealogy, History," in Donald F. Bouchard (ed.), *Language, Counter-
memory, Practice: Selected Essays and Interviews* (Ithaca, N.Y., 1977), 139–64.

an idolator before the simple, knowledge rescues him by presenting the complicated, for the disillusion which he must continually have, but the value is the indestructible and unchanged, the perfection" (*EK*, 191). (Like the previous quotation, this one shows that Williams is about equally divided between desiring and doubting the goal of finding a transcendental point of origin—"the perfection"— for art. Even his syntax is contradictory.)

Williams' skepticism about the Modernist quest for purity in the arts is of course hardly his alone. All of the major Modernist artists were also drawn to "impurity," whether in the form of seeking out "vulgar" or different subject matter that was new to the medium but "long since impregnated with humanity" (Guillaume Apollinaire's term describing the new materials used in Cubist collage), or in merging art forms, or in seeking out a political and social impact that challenged what was thought proper for the arts to signify. And all of the major Modernists, however much they labored to perfect their craft, also shared something of Williams' disdain for idolatry, whether it was in the form of the worship of art for art's sake or the worship of the art of conspicuous consumption. (Consider Ezra Pound's *Hugh Selwyn Mauberley*, or T. S. Eliot's *The Waste Land*, or the role of Leopold Bloom in James Joyce's *Ulysses*.) This truth about Modernism is something that we have come to appreciate much more thoroughly with hindsight, with the recent diminishing authority of Modernist "New Criticism" in the arts and literature and the new interest in exploring how the act of representation never occurs within a historical vaccuum, never is "pure" or wholly "new."[3]

For some reason that is not clear to me, Williams criticism has generally been slower than, say, Pound or Wallace Stevens or Hilda Doolittle criticism to reinterpret its subject from perspectives other than those sanctioned by Modernism. Perhaps this has been because until the 1970s Williams' work was not securely a part of the canon of Modernist work, at least as far as many academics were concerned. (For some, of course, it still isn't.) Apparently the most efficient way that critics of Williams could argue for his centrality was by defining his qualifications in more or less acceptably formalist ways. This pattern in Williams criticism is less clear when we consider critics

---

3. Guillaume Apollinaire, "Aesthetic Meditations on Painting: The Cubist Painters," trans. Mrs. Charles Knoblauch, *Little Review*, IX (Autumn, 1922), 44.

who discuss the body of Williams' fiction, drama, criticism, and experimental prose as well as his poetry. But the formalist bent of criticism of Williams emerges quite sharply when readings of what is generally taken to be the heart of Williams' work—his lyrics and the epic *Paterson*—are considered. This is hardly an accident; Modernist criticism has always been more adept at discussing the lyric, which (like Modernism itself) aspires to transcendental origins, than it has been analyzing other genres.

Williams' career as a poet has typically been divided into four phases: an early, immature phase (to 1913, approximately); an "Imagist" phase (1914 through 1921), in which Williams discovered modern American subject matter; an "Objectivist" phase (1922 through 1950), in which he discovered that his true subject was words themselves, the American idiom and the poem-as-object; and a late phase (from 1951 until his death in 1963), in which, according to some critics, he was finally able to record the "dance" of thought itself, while according to others he mostly fell off from the high Modernist standard his earlier work had set. Such chartings of Williams' poetic career reveal a fundamentally Modernist bias: they read the career as a heroic evolution toward the discovery of "pure" poetry, a moment when the subject of a poem comes to be primarily about the moment of its own making. Such criticism places poems like "The Red Wheelbarrow," "This Is Just to Say," or "Composition" at the heart of Williams' work and is in fundamental agreement with the interpretation of Williams' lyrics first made in the early 1930s by the poet Louis Zukofsky, who to describe his friend's work coined the term *Objectivist* that many recent critics schooled like Zukofsky in Modernist criticism have found so useful. The readings this criticism of Williams' work has produced are indispensable and often eloquent; they have taught us much about the intellectual sophistication of his methods, the continual inventiveness of his technique, and the importance of his choice of founding his poetry on an explicitly *native* idiom, as Dante and Chaucer did in their day. But the time has come to ask what is lost as well as gained by such a division of Williams' poetry into historical phases, particularly the Imagist and Objectivist ones. It may be that Williams' development as a writer of poems shows as much multiplicity as his overall oeuvre, so that instead of speaking of a fairly linear evolution of his lyric art phase by phase we could explore the ways in which Williams often seems to be investigating simultaneously several rather contradictory (or at least divergent) modes of writing poetry, without necessarily assigning a hierarchy of importance or value among these modes.

I am continually astonished that the man who wrote the fastidious "The Red Wheelbarrow" also wrote the sprawling poem "To Elsie" in the same year (1923), or that his *Collected Poems, 1921–1931* (1934)—the most unjustly underrated volume of poems in all of Williams' work—could include new poems as different in mood, movement, and subject as "Nantucket," "The Cod Head," "April" from the sequence "Della Primavera Trasportata al Morale," "This Is Just to Say," "The Sea-Elephant," and "Hemmed-In Males." How can we account for the rich diversity of these poems? Certainly a classification such as Objectivist won't help us, hallowed though the word is through its association with Zukofsky. It may be that the eclecticism practiced by critics who discuss Williams' career as a whole is an appropriate model for those commentators like myself who for reason of space and depth have restricted themselves to just a part of Williams' plenteous world.

This book focuses on Williams' lyrics from 1913 to 1963, his epic *Paterson* (1946–1958), and his experimental prose, especially *Kora in Hell: Improvisations* (1920). I have sought to be interdisciplinary in my approaches to these materials, relying on interpretive methods associated with art history and American Studies as well as literary criticism.

My discussion of Williams and the visual arts is selective rather than synoptic. Instead of giving an overview of Williams' contacts with artists and works of art (something that has been done well by other critics), I focus on the three movements in the arts that influenced Williams most profoundly during his formative years—Precisionism, Cubism, and Dada—to discriminate among several distinct theories and methods informing his poetry and experimental prose after 1913. My rationale in focusing on these three movements has been to avoid the two extremes that have characterized scholarship on the topic of Williams and the arts. Much of the early research unearthed biographical information and examined poems by Williams that appeared to be based on particular paintings or photographs. But necessary as this was, it now seems too naïvely empirical and impressionistic. It generated almost as many influences for Williams as he had friends in the art world and has led some critics to assume that Williams' interest in the arts inspired him to discard or at least downplay certain literary techniques such as simile and meta-

phor in favor of supposedly more "visual" modes of writing. Recent
scholarship on the topic has become more tightly structured, but in
my opinion it has gone over to the other extreme and become too
consistent and abstract, as if overly compensating for the limitations
of the earlier criticism on this subject. Two recent studies of Williams
and the arts, for example, assume that Williams' greatest poems share
a single innovation—either the "poetics of indeterminacy" or a
graceful kind of concrete poetry (a "visual text").[4] As I read
Williams' poetry and experimental prose, however, I am most struck
by the variety, not the consistency, of his theories and methods of
writing, and by the fact that such pluralism is reflected in the art
world that Williams knew, particularly among the Precisionists,
Cubists, and Dadaists.

More efforts need to be made integrating art historical and literary
criticism in Williams studies. Absorbed by the new information on
Williams' interest in the arts that has been unearthed over the last
two decades, scholars of Williams have to some degree over-
emphasized the importance of those art historical sources by treating
them in an overly isolated context. What is now needed are explora-
tions of how even during the decade in which Williams wrote *Spring
and All* he sought to integrate ideas from the visual arts with what in
1939 he called "the usable past"—the full range of both American
and European literary tradition. Accordingly, in this book I argue
that in general Williams used the inspiration he gained from the arts
not to write poems about pictures or even to create a visual poetics,
but to return to and renew specifically *literary* traditions and modes.
Additionally, I try to place Williams' work in a broad cultural context
that allows us to see what kinds of cultural work those literary genres
were expected to perform.

Many critics have mentioned the powerful influence of John Keats
on Williams' early work, and scholars have also recognized the im-
portance of other European writers such as Paul Valéry, Theocritus,
Homer, and Sappho for Williams' very late writings. The influence of
Ralph Waldo Emerson and Walt Whitman has been chronicled, as
has Williams' relation to Anglo-American and Continental Mod-
ernism. Yet the question of Williams' relation to literary tradition
remains very much a volatile one. This is true partly because schol-

4. Marjorie Perloff, *The Poetics of Indeterminacy: Rimbaud to Cage* (Princeton, 1981); Henry
Sayre, *The Visual Text of William Carlos Williams* (Urbana, Ill., 1983).

arship on Williams' mature work has generally focused on American influences and partly because the few studies that have emphasized Williams' mature use of the European literary tradition have uncovered a vein so rich it has just begun to be mined for what it is worth.

To discuss the role played by the American and European literary traditions that Williams thought were "usable" for him, I have again opted for a selective rather than synoptic approach. Whenever I discuss an influence from the visual arts I also trace how that influence led Williams back to a specific literary tradition, to particular authors and literary modes. When Williams was influenced by Precisionism and Cubism, for example, he sought as early as 1915 to use what he learned to revitalize the topics and poetic forms associated with pastoral lyrics and the sublime (irregular) ode. And when he sought to assimilate Dadaist ideas, he used them not only to produce his own versions of Dadaist "automatic" writing—his *Kora in Hell, The Great American Novel,* and *Spring and All* are the most important literary works to come out of the New York Dada movement—but also to explore the implications of Emerson's and Whitman's assumption that originality and inherited literary forms are incompatible.

The result is a study that does not read Williams' poetic career chronologically, in terms of phases, except when this seems most sensible. Instead, I follow Williams' development within several different modes of writing for as long as his growth there seems interesting—from 1913 to the 1940s for the chapter on the modern American utopian strain in Williams' pastoral lyrics, for example, or from 1915 to 1929 for Williams' experiments with automatic writing. My intent is not to provide a new set of fixed categories to impose on Williams' career ("Precisionist," "Cubist," or "Dadaist" can be made to be as cumbersome a label as "Imagist" or "Objectivist," after all) but to be able to follow several things at once, to range back and forth over the course of Williams' career, tracing the histories of several clusters of ideas. This kind of pluralism yields insights that a more linear approach to Williams' work cannot. As Williams said at the end of his draft of *The Embodiment of Knowledge* (1928–1930), "by such pluralism of effort in each several locality a 'reality' is kept; in plural—and so verified" (*EK,* 150).

The last two chapters of the book and the epilogue show to what degree I think Williams integrated these different earlier modes of writing in his later work. I read the heterogeneous text of *Paterson* as the provocative "sum" (*P*, 3) of the Precisionist, Cubist, and Dadaist poetics that Williams had been developing since 1913. Critics have begun to talk about the theory and practice of the collage form as it applies to *Paterson*, but I argue that just as there are a variety of ways in which the arts influenced Williams' earlier work, so there are several versions of the collage aesthetic in *Paterson*, all contributing to the rich tension between "closed" and "open" form that readers of the poem have praised. I also place my discussion of *Paterson* within a literary as well as art historical context, seeking new conclusions about the way Williams' collage methods allow him to renew epic tradition even as he seems to question it.

In Williams' last decade of writing, the influence of certain aspects of Precisionism, Cubism, and Dada may still be discerned. In particular, Williams' earlier experiments with using Cubism to recreate the sublime ode provide an invaluable context for discussing his odes of the mid-1950s written in "variable" measure, the three-step, "triadic" line. In those late odes, Williams sublimely absorbed and merged many different *kinds* of lyrics—including the Horatian *carpe diem* ode, Edmund Spenser's "Epithalamion," Keats's odes, the dramatic monologue, and various kinds of pastoral poetry, including the elegy and the inscription lyric. But the result of using these many different sources is significantly different from that of Williams' earlier Cubist odes in ways that give us special clues about how to read these late poems. Once again, my goal has not been to multiply labels but to discover how various the lyric gists are that give Williams' late odes their special radiance.

Other American Modernists such as Eliot, Stevens, Pound, and Doolittle have recently had their work assessed within the context of earlier American and European literature, rather than just Modernism. A similar broadening of the terms of discussion has begun in Williams studies and continues with this book. The reader should take the book's title to refer not merely to what Williams learned from the visual arts but to how he learned to *read*—to treat literary texts, paintings, photographs, and everyday events he witnessed as cultural documents ready for interpretation and criticism. In the words of Williams' essay "Love and Service," these materials were the "signs" whose meanings he sought, whose energy he employed. And as Emerson had demanded in "The American Scholar," this new poet on the American scene proved to be a creative reader, not an idolatrous one.

ONE/SOME VERSIONS OF MODERNIST PASTORAL
Williams and the Precisionists

> The present is a void, and the American writer floats in that void because the past that survives in the common mind of the present is a past without living value. But is this the only possible past? If we need another past so badly, is it inconceivable that we might discover one, that we might even invent one?
>
> Discover, invent a usable past we certainly can, and that is what a vital criticism always does.
>
> —Van Wyck Brooks, "On Creating a Usable Past"

Because Precisionism was a native American movement, it was for Williams the most congenial source of inspiration in the visual arts, and its presence in his work became the most pervasive and long-lasting of all visual arts influences on him. From painters like Charles Demuth and Charles Sheeler and photographers like Alfred Stieglitz, Williams learned how much psychological and cultural drama could be implied by a sharply focused, seemingly literal depiction of a scene rather than calculated attempts to create atmosphere, narrative, and symbolism. Inspired by the Precisionists' revisions of the current conventions of photography, Williams strove to make his own poetic language more visually precise and less overtly symbolic and "literary." Most important, the Precisionists developed an ideology of the American urban pastoral that influenced Williams' choices of subject matter and point of view, particularly his exploration of the proper relation between human beings and modern industrial technology.

Williams' contact with Stieglitz and the Precisionists was first documented by James Guimond and Bram Dijkstra, and recently more information has been unearthed by Mike Weaver, Dickran Tashjian, and others. In general, however, these critics document biographical influences but do not use the new information that they have found to give us new readings of Williams' works. After more than a decade of research into Williams' contacts with Precisionism, it is time to consolidate what is known of the movement's influence on Williams and to place that information within a larger, more traditional literary context.

Such a consolidation means testing to see whether premises and techniques that are identifiably Precisionist show up in Williams' poetry and prose and, if so, whether they are at all revised in the process. It also means comparing the influence of Precisionism with that of three literary influences important to Williams at the time. The first of these is Imagism as defined by Ezra Pound between 1912 and 1916. Several of its tenets are remarkably similar to those of Precisionism, yet Precisionism's treatment of the image differed from Imagism in ways that were vitally important to Williams, especially since he felt that doctrinaire Imagism was too limited for what he wanted to do. A second influence on both Williams and Precisionism at this time was Emersonian transcendentalism, the guiding force behind Precisionism's myth of America as a potential industrial Arcadia. The study of Precisionist art ultimately led Williams to reconsider the relevance of transcendentalism. A third influence on Williams was European pastoral poetry. At first glance, it is surprising that Williams would allow such an influence, for after making friends with members of the American avant-garde after 1915 he became embarrassed by the imitative, European-sounding poetry in his first two books of verse. But a study of how Williams adapted Precisionist ideas shows that Williams' conception of the relation between art and literature and tradition and avant-garde is far more complex than we might guess from reading such slogans as his boast in *Kora in Hell* (1920) that "nothing is good save the new" (I, 23). Precisionism's new versions of pastoral in the arts led Williams to believe that he could renew the pastoral tradition in literature as well.

Accordingly, in this chapter I first attempt to synthesize what we know about the Precisionist movement's influence on Williams and then discuss how Precisionism may be used both to give us new readings of selected Williams poems and to place those poems back within a distinctively literary as well as art historical context.[1]

1. See James Guimond, *The Art of William Carlos Williams* (Urbana, Ill., 1968), 42–64, for the best introductory discussion of the influence of the Precisionists Charles Demuth and Charles Sheeler on Williams. Other materials on this topic include Bram Dijkstra, *Cubism, Stieglitz, and the Early Poetry of William Carlos Williams: The Hieroglyphics of a New Speech* (Princeton, 1969); Mike Weaver, *William Carlos Williams: The American Background*

The term *Precisionist* properly applies only to painters such as Georgia O'Keeffe, Demuth, and Sheeler who were directly influenced by Stieglitz, Paul Strand, and other "straight" photographers associated with the magazine *Camera Work* and Stieglitz's gallery at 291 Fifth Avenue. Because these painters and photographers share many of

---

(Cambridge, England, 1971), 55–64; Dickran Tashjian, *Skyscraper Primitives: Dada and the American Avant-Garde, 1910–1925* (Middletown, Conn., 1975); Tashjian, *William Carlos Williams and the American Scene, 1920–1940* (New York, 1979); James E. Breslin, "William Carlos Williams and Charles Demuth: Cross-Fertilization in the Arts," *Journal of Modern Literature*, VI (1977), 248–63; Paul Mariani's indispensable biography, *William Carlos Williams: A New World Naked* (New York, 1981), especially pp. 116–347; Perloff, *The Poetics of Indeterminacy*, 109–54; William Marling, *William Carlos Williams and the Painters, 1909–1923* (Athens, Ohio, 1982); and Sayre, *The Visual Text of William Carlos Williams*. For readings of "straight" photography and Precisionism in the context of American art, see Milton W. Brown, "Cubist-Realism: An American Style," *Marsyas*, III (1943–45), 138–60; Brown, *American Painting from the Armory Show to the Depression* (Princeton, 1955); Martin L. Friedman, *The Precisionist View in American Art* (Minneapolis, 1960); *Charles Sheeler* (Washington, D.C., 1968), particularly Friedman's "The Art of Charles Sheeler: Americana in a Vacuum," 33–57, and Charles Millard's "The Photography of Charles Sheeler," 80–89; Barbara Novak, *American Painting of the Nineteenth Century: Realism, Idealism, and the American Experience* (New York, 1969), 270–76; Jonathan Green (ed.), *"Camera Work": A Critical Anthology* (Millertown, N.Y., 1973); William Innis Homer, *Alfred Stieglitz and the American Avant-Garde* (Boston, 1977); Rosalind Krauss, "Stieglitz/*Equivalents*," *October*, XI (Winter, 1979), 129–40; Abraham A. Davidson, *Early American Modernist Painting, 1910–1935* (New York, 1981), 13–73; John Pultz and Catherine B. Scallen, *Cubism and American Photography, 1910–1930* (Williamstown, Mass., 1981); Beaumont Newhall, *The History of Photography From 1839 to the Present* (Rev. ed.; New York, 1982), 141–97; Karen Tsujimoto, *Images of America: Precisionist Painting and Modern Photography* (San Francisco, 1982); Betsy Fahlman, *Pennsylvania Modern: Charles Demuth of Lancaster* (Philadelphia, 1983); Sidney Lawrence, "Clean Machines at the Modern," *Art in America*, LXXII (February, 1984), 127–41, 166–68; and Gail Levin, "American Art," in William Rubin (ed.), *"Primitivism" in Twentieth-Century Art: Affinity of the Tribal and the Modern* (2 vols.; New York, 1984), II, 452–73. The work of Williams and the Precisionists should also be placed within the context of broader developments in American cultural history. See especially Lisa M. Steinman, *Made in America: Science, Technology, and American Modernist Poets* (New Haven, 1987), and Cecelia Tichi, *Shifting Gears: Technology, Literature, Culture in Modernist America* (Chapel Hill, N.C., 1987). Williams' literary heritage is cogently discussed by James Breslin, "Whitman and the Early Development of William Carlos Williams," *Publications of the Modern Language Association*, LXXXII (1967), 613–21; Breslin, "William Carlos Williams and the Whitman Tradition," in Philip Damon (ed.), *Literary Criticism and Historical Understanding: Selected Papers from the English Institute* (New York, 1967), 151–80; Breslin, *William Carlos Williams: An American Artist* (1970; rpr. Chicago, 1985); Stephen Tapscott, *American Beauty: William Carlos Williams and the Modernist Whitman* (New York, 1984); and Carl Rapp, *William Carlos Williams and Romantic Idealism* (Hanover, N.H., 1984). Other cultural histories relevant for understanding the nationalism and idealism implicit in the Precisionists' program are: Leo Marx, *The Machine in the Garden: Technology and the Pastoral Ideal in America* (New York, 1964); Richard Hofstadter, *The Progressive Historians: Turner, Beard, Parrington* (New York, 1968); John F. Kasson, *Civilizing the Machine: Technology and Republican Values in America, 1776–1900* (New York, 1977); T. J. Jackson Lears, *No Place of Grace: Antimodernism and the Transformation of American Culture, 1880–1920* (New York, 1981); Cecelia Tichi, "William Carlos Williams and the Efficient Moment," in Jack Salzman (ed.), *Prospects*, VII (1982), 267–79; Tichi, "Twentieth Century Limited: William Carlos Williams' Poetics of High Speed America," *William Carlos Williams Review*, IX (1983), 49–73; Christopher Knight, "On Native Ground: U.S. Modern," *Art in America*, LXXI (October, 1983), 166–74; and Warren Susman, *Culture as History: The Transformation of American Society in the Twentieth Century* (New York, 1984).

the same premises, however, it is possible to discuss them together under one rubric.

The first premise, which gave the movement its name, was that images ought to be rendered as precisely as possible. In photography, this meant that when the photographs were taken, both foreground and background were to be focused as sharply as the camera's technology allowed. And when the negatives were developed, they had to be printed "straight," achieving effects by varying the chemical development process, not by retouching by hand.[2] Precisionist painting, though done by hand, strove for a "photographic" rather than a "painterly" surface like that of the Impressionists, and it had an overall sharp focus, a depth of field no camera could match. Objects in the background of a landscape were depicted as sharply as those in the foreground, and all had the clarity of a still life.

The Precisionists revised the genres of still life and landscape in other ways too. Stieglitz and Sheeler continued America's tradition of monumental landscape photography, but in their pictures buildings soared instead of mountains and sublime power was expressed with clouds of steam or smoke as well as rain (see Illustration 1).[3] Moreover, after they sharpened their focus, they often went a step further and made the picture's foreground its principal dramatic focus. In Stieglitz's *Two Towers—New York* and *Spring Showers*, for example, a tree in the foreground shoots up across most of the picture plane. Later Stieglitz photographs were even more radical, literally superimposing the two traditionally separate genres of still life and landscape. In *Apples and Gable*, a gable of Stieglitz's Lake George house rises behind the apples, which hang on a branch jutting across the photograph; in *Dancing Trees*, the landscape can be made out only by peering through the intertwining trunks that dominate the foreground. Such a superposition of still life and landscape had no counterpart in American painting until it was adopted by Georgia O'Keeffe—but it was immediately noticed and used to great advantage by Williams.[4]

2. For the particulars of the "straight" photographic printing process, see Newhall, *The History of Photography*, 167.

3. For more information on this tradition, see Weston Naef and James Wood, *Era of Exploration: The Rise of Landscape Photography in the American West, 1860–1885* (New York, 1975); Sidney Tillim, "The Ideal and the Literal Sublime: Reflections on Painting and Photography in America," *Artforum*, XIV (May, 1976), 58–61; and Joel Snyder, *American Frontiers: The Photography of Timothy H. O'Sullivan, 1867–1874* (Philadelphia, 1981).

4. *Spring Showers*, *Apples and Gable*, and *Dancing Trees* are in Dijkstra, *Cubism, Stieglitz, and the Early Poetry of William Carlos Williams*, Plates IX, X, and XII. *Two Towers* is illustrated in Marianne Fulton Margolis (ed.), *Camera Work: A Pictorial Guide* (New York, 1978), 126. *Spring*

Alfred Stieglitz, *City of Ambition*, 1910, photographic print, 34 × 26 cm, Alfred Stieglitz Collection, 1949.836 © 1987 The Art Institute of Chicago. All Rights Reserved.

Precisionism's most famous principle held that each picture, regardless of its subject matter, was primarily a portrait of emotion itself—an objective correlative. Stieglitz's name for this is more colloquial than Eliot's: objects may become "Equivalents" for human feelings. Distrusting narrative's ability to convey emotion, the Precisionists tried to remove any suggestion of narrative from their work and placed sharply detailed objects at the center of their compositions, believing that the tangible thing, its unique texture, could articulate the intangible most eloquently. Stieglitz at first applied the term *Equivalent* only to his photographs of clouds begun in the 1920s, relatively late in his career, but he soon became sure that "in reality all my photographs are Equivalents," and it makes sense to use this term to discuss the Precisionists' aims.[5]

The most cogent definition of what Precisionist art was trying to accomplish was published by Stieglitz's fellow photographer Strand, in the essay "Photography and the New God" in the November, 1922, issue of *Broom*, a little magazine to which Williams contributed. Strand's article was inspired by Stieglitz's important show at the Anderson Galleries in 1921. He stressed, first, that photography gave the artist a unique opportunity to capture an identifiable *moment* in time. The camera is a "machine" that has added a "new factor" to plastic expression in the arts, "the element of differentiated time. The camera can hold in a unique way, a moment." Photographs haunt us because they make us feel as if an actual fragment of the past and its light rays have once again become present, rather than merely being represented. Secondly, Strand emphasized that the camera in the hands of an artist depicts the invisible as well as the

---

Showers and *Two Towers* appeared in *Camera Work*, October, 1911, and October, 1913, respectively. For an example of O'Keeffe's innovative use of the still life, see her *Ram's Head With Hollyhock* (1935), *Pelvis with Moon* (1943), and *Pelvis III* (1944), illustrated in *Georgia O'Keeffe, Georgia O'Keeffe* (New York, 1976), Plates 70, 73, and 74, respectively. In 1915, influenced by Picasso, Juan Gris developed the same idea independently of Stieglitz in his *Still Life Before an Open Window: Place Ravignan*. This and a later work, *The Open Window* (1917), were owned by Walter Arensberg, and Williams surely studied them at his apartment and drew his own conclusions. A later "open window" painting by Gris was reproduced in *Broom*, I (January, 1922), where Williams saw it; he included an enraptured description of it in *Spring and All* (I, 107–11; see Weaver, *William Carlos Williams*, 41). For the provenance of the first two Gris works cited above, see Daniel-Henry Kahnweiler, *Juan Gris: His Life and Work*, trans. Douglas Cooper (New York, 1969), 314–16; they are illustrated on pp. 99 and 270 respectively. The *Broom* "open window" painting of Gris that figures in *Spring and All* is reproduced in Sayre, *The Visual Text of William Carlos Williams*, 32.

5. Dijkstra, *Cubism, Stieglitz, and the Early Poetry of William Carlos Williams*, 101–102. The best discussions of Stieglitz's term are by Pultz and Scallen, *Cubism and American Photography*, 1–34, and by Krauss, "Stieglitz/*Equivalents*."

visible. Stieglitz did what all photographers should strive to do, to capture "that moment when the forces at work in a human being become most intensely physical and objective."[6]

In seeking to find Equivalents for emotion, the Precisionists felt that that artist's own presence must be "objective" and impersonal. This fourth premise—that the ideal artist is as selfless as a lens—means that the emotions implied by the photograph's subject, texture, and structure are to be communal rather than private. Precisionist art concentrated on rendering what it takes to be the universal aspects of an emotion—the brute confidence in American technology expressed by Sheeler's industrial paintings, for example, or the awe and melancholy in Stieglitz's photographs of clouds—and it tended to suppress elements in the subject that could point to idiosyncrasies in the artist's individual psyche. Ideally, Equivalents were to be self-portraits of an age (and the photographic process itself), not an individual. Thus photography for Strand "achieves as pure a synthesis of objectivity as can be found in any medium." By implication, however, painting or poetry could also be "objective" in the Precisionists' sense (see Illustration 2).

The fifth premise of Precisionism is highly nationalistic and reflects America's growing sense of itself after the turn of the century as the world's leading industrial power. Although Stieglitz's group had been among the first to introduce trends in modern European art to America, they saw the new art as a challenge to produce a radically new American art, one that captured the unique qualities of America's past and present just as avant-garde European art expressed the time and place from which it came. Strand's personal declaration of independence, written in 1917, spoke for all: "America has really been expressed in terms of America without the outside influence of Paris or their dilute offspring here. . . . This renaissance found its highest aesthetic achievement in America, a small group of men and women worked with honest and sincere purpose, some instinctively and few consciously. . . . [T]his innocence was their real strength."[7]

Declaring their freedom from European academic traditions, the Precisionists sought for an alternative in American culture. They found it in Emerson's and Whitman's celebration of "innocence" and the spiritual values inherent in technology—and in America's own

6. Paul Strand, "Photography and the New God," *Broom*, III (November, 1922), 252–58.
7. Paul Strand, "Photography," *The Seven Arts*, No. 10 (August, 1917), 525.

Charles Sheeler, *City Interior*

history of technological inventiveness, from rural crafts to modern industry. They soon transformed that history into a picture of industrial America as a modern Arcadia whose high technology they believed exemplified the virtues of efficiency, beauty, and individual responsibility no less eloquently than America's rural crafts had once done. The art historian Martin Friedman thus argues that Precisionism was a self-conscious "extension of an objective and literal native American style [in painting]. The homage it pays to utilitarian objects and the surroundings of daily life relates it to the sober homilies of the American primitive painters."[8]

The nationalistic idealism of Precisionist theory is best shown in Strand's 1922 essay "Photography and the New God." The new God for Strand is modern technology, which has an Adamic superiority over nature: "men consummated a new creative act, a new Trinity: God the machine, Materialistic Empiricism the Son, and Science the Holy Ghost." The priest for this new god and his religion ought to have been the scientist, but Strand felt that World War I proved that he had abdicated his responsibility to act morally: "Having created the new God, [the scientist] has permitted himself to be used to every step and for every purpose. . . . Printing presses or poison gas, he has been equally blind or indifferent to the implications in the use or misuse of either, with the result that the social structure which he has so irresponsibly helped to rear, is to-day fast being destroyed by the perversion of the very knowledge contributed by him." Strand proposes that the figure who can now teach us how to use the machine correctly is the artist, especially the photographer, because of all artists he exemplifies "the unqualified subjugation of a machine to the single purpose of expression."[9]

The Precisionists' celebration of technology is thus neither a lauding of technology for its own sake nor a naïve belief that machinery is always used morally. It is rather a celebration of the *mind* that may invent and govern machinery. Strand ends his essay by sharply disassociating the Precisionists from the European Futurists, another group of avant-garde artists fascinated with new inventions. "We are not . . . particularly sympathetic to the somewhat hysterical attitude of the Futurists toward the machine. We in America are not fighting, as it may be natural to do in Italy, away from the tentacles of

8. Friedman, *The Precisionist View in American Art*, 22. Friedman uses the phrase "modern Arcadia" on p. 36 to describe Sheeler's painting *Classic Landscape*.
9. Strand, "Photography and the New God," 252–53, 255.

a medieval tradition towards a neurasthenic embrace of the new God. We have it with us and upon us with a vengeance, and we will have to do something about it eventually. Not only the new God but the whole Trinity must be humanized lest it in turn dehumanize us."[10] For Strand, the mind must master the machine, not the reverse. Moreover, this quotation shows that Precisionism's idealism was linked to its nationalism. Everything that the Precisionists wrote implies that the virtues they associated with machines and their users were more fully embodied in the United States than anywhere else.

In practice, of course, Precisionist art was not necessarily so optimistic. Only the art of Sheeler always favorably compares twentieth-century industry with the preindustrial cultures (such as that of the Shakers) that the Precisionists admired. Stieglitz, Demuth, and Strand could be as evangelical, but as we shall see they all also produced work that either directly or indirectly subverted the Precisionists' Arcadian ideal. Still, for all the artists associated with the movement, Precisionism's ideology was meant to be prescriptive, a credo proclaiming how things ought to be in the urban world, not a description of things as they actually were. However important the movement's documentary goals were, its underlying impulse was optative and idealistic. The Precisionists saw themselves as rediscovering an autonomous American cultural tradition that would finally prove that America could create an aesthetic rivaling Europe's. Their Equivalents, along with their attendant experiments with sharp focus, scale, rural and urban subjects, and an "objective" role for the artist, were developed with such an end in mind.

Marianne Moore once stated, "The welded ease of [Williams'] compositions resembles the linked self-propelled momentum of sprocket and chain."[11] Throughout Williams' career, his prose consistently defined all the essential ideals of Precisionism, from its fascination with modern machinery and its conception of the Equivalent to its moral and nationalistic idealism. As early as the prologue to Kora in Hell (1920; written 1917–1918), Williams claimed he would reject narrative and a frequent use of similes and metaphors in favor of a literal version of Precisionism's sharp focus: "The coining of similes is a pastime of very low order. . . . Much more keen is that power

10. Ibid., 257.
11. Marianne Moore, "A Vein of Anthracite," in Patricia C. Willis (ed.), The Complete Prose of Marianne Moore (New York, 1986), 345.

which discovers in things those inimitable particles of dissimilarity to all other things. . . . The associational or sentimental value is the false. Its imposition is due to a lack of imagination, to an easy lateral sliding" (I, 105, 102). Precisionist "straight" photography seems to have inspired this passage's very figures of speech. The poet's imagination must not be distracted from paying close attention to the object in front of his eye; he must take care to present its identifying features, its "particles of dissimilarity," as precisely as the eye and the camera lens can. And just as Stieglitz's and Strand's photographs treated their subject matter as an implied rather than a stated simile or metaphor for inner states of being, so Williams in the lyrics influenced by the Precisionists rejected the flamboyant use of metaphor and simile. As we shall see, however, this is *not* to say that tropes are absent from Williams' Precisionist poems but only that in general their use is understated and restrained. Figures of speech are often carefully suggested rather than declared, and they reward the reader only after the poem's literal, visual details—its "particles"—have been mastered.

The short essays that Williams wrote for his magazine *Contact* between 1920 and 1923 further show his consolidation of Precisionist ideas. Announcing the purpose of the first issue, Williams explained the name of his little magazine as follows: "We do not seek to 'transfer the center of the universe' here. We seek only contact with the local conditions which confront use. We believe that in the perfection of that contact is the beginning not only of the concept of art among us but the key to the technique also."[12] *Contact* here involves communication between American artists and each artist's responsibility to be in touch with the history of the place in which he or she lives. It so happens, however, that *contact* is also the word used to describe straight photographic procedures that created contact prints using the platinum or gelatin-silver processes.[13] Using Precisionist photography as an analogy, therefore, Williams reasons that only when artists learn how properly to expose themselves to the "local conditions" will they produce important work. The key to finding the proper technique—for a writer as well as a photographer—is to find ways to "perfect" the moment of contact between mind and matter, the photographic plate and "local condi-

12. *Contact*, I (1920), 10. The entire set of *Contact* has been reproduced by the Kraus Reprint Corporation, New York, 1967.
13. See Newhall, *The History of Photography,* 123–24, 142, 153.

tions." In choosing to call his little magazine *Contact*, Williams alluded to the inspiration the Precisionists gave him even as he makes the word his own.

In the second issue of *Contact*, Williams carried further the nationalistic strain of his statement in the first number of *Contact*, approvingly quoting the thesis of an essay on American art by the philosopher John Dewey that had recently appeared in the magazine *The Dial:* "We are discovering that the locality is the only universal." And in the third issue, Williams, like the Precisionists, found a model for the modern avant-garde artist in America's history of technological innovation: "It has been by paying naked attention first to the thing itself that American plumbing, American shoes, American bridges, indexing systems, locomotives, printing presses, city buildings, farm implements and a thousand other things have become notable in the world. Yet we are timid in believing that in the arts discovery and invention will take the same course. And there is no reason why they should unless our writers have the inventive intelligence of our engineers and cobblers."[14] By the fourth issue of *Contact*, Williams' definitions of the American artist's correct relation to Europe and to his own country had gained an aphoristic polish. References to Precisionist photographic techniques continue to inform his figures of speech.

> CONTACT has never in the least intimated that the American artist in preparing his position "should forget all about Europe." On the contrary the assertion has been that he should acquaint himself with everything pertaining to his wish that he can gather from European sources. . . . [T]he profit from French work begins when the student realizes that it is a special, a foreign, a peculiar growth, in its best examples every part discoverably related to some local turn of color or contour. . . . If Americans are to be blessed with [similarly] important work[,] it will be through intelligent, informed contact with the locality which alone can infuse it with reality.[15]

In *Spring and All* (1923), Williams returned to the concept of the Equivalent that he had sketched in his prologue to *Kora in Hell*. Aided by his own discussions of the perfection of "contact" and by Strand's definition of Stieglitz's Equivalents in his 1922 *Broom* essay, Williams defined the paradoxical relation between the particular and the universal that is at the heart of the Precisionist conception of the image: "In the composition, the artist does exactly what every eye must do with life, fix the particular with the universality of his own

14. *Contact*, II (1921), 7; *Contact*, III (1922), 15.
15. *Contact*, IV (1922), 18.

personality" (*I*, 105). In other words, the poet, like the photographer, ought to make sure that his personality is as "universal," as "objective," as possible. He does this, however, not by conforming to his audience's expectations of how his subject matter should be treated. That would be falsely universal appeal. Rather, he presents the object more precisely and powerfully than ever before. This new vision of the object, the Precisionists hoped, would be a truly universal or objective way of viewing: it would show the artist's audience what it might see but was overlooking because it had been trapped within conventional, historically bound ways of seeing.

The Precisionists' Equivalent and their paradoxical definition of the objective or universal personality of the artist undoubtedly reminded Williams of Ezra Pound's Imagist and Vorticist maxims of 1912–1916, which Williams knew well: "Direct treatment of the 'thing' whether subjective or objective"; "To use absolutely no word that does not contribute to the presentation"; "The natural object is always the *adequate* symbol"; "An 'Image' is that which presents an intellectual and emotional complex in an instant of time"; and "In [an Imagist or Vorticist poem] one is trying to record the precise instant when a thing outward and objective transforms itself, or darts into a thing inward and subjective."[16] The artists in Stieglitz's circle developed their concepts of direct treatment and objectivity on their own, without taking any cue from Pound. Williams critics have frequently noted that Williams was influenced by Imagism and struggled (like Pound) to apply its precepts to longer, more complex poems.[17] But because of Williams' contact with Stieglitz's circle, he could get particularly American versions of many of these ideas and could be assured that the American avant-garde would be as fruitful a source of inspiration for his art as Pound's "Imagisme" and Europe. Imagism gave Williams specific aesthetic models, including its emphasis on compression, still moments, and the drama made possible by ending a poem with a single, well-turned trope (such as Pound's diagrammatic comparison in "In a Station of the Metro" linking passengers' faces streaming by in a crowd to "petals on a wet, black

16. Ezra Pound, *Literary Essays of Ezra Pound* (New York, 1968), 3–5; Pound, *Gaudier-Brzeska* (1916; rpr. New York, 1970), 89.

17. For two adept discussions of Williams' use of Imagist principles, see Rapp, *William Carlos Williams and Romantic Idealism*, 81–101; and Suzanne Juhasz, *Metaphor and the Poetry of Williams, Pound, and Stevens* (Lewisburg, Pa., 1974), 13–49. Also relevant are Guimond, *The Art of William Carlos Williams*, 31–40; and Hugh Kenner, *The Pound Era* (Berkeley, Calif., 1971), 145–91. Kenner's is the best discussion to date of Imagism proper and of Pound's transformation of it into Vorticism.

bough"). But Precisionism also taught Williams how to use such still moments and central tropes in a more understated way than Pound's Imagist theory could account for, and Williams' use of its ideas and techniques should not be discussed separately from those that were being developed after 1913 by the American Precisionist photographers and painters.

The Precisionists' belief in the universal symbols and the innate superiority of American technology and ideals was of particular value to Williams for another reason. It had a rich American tradition: its sources lay not in European art but in the thought of Emerson and the Puritan typological tradition that Emerson's thought transforms.[18] At the beginning of *Nature* (1836), for example, Emerson sharply discriminated between inherited and original vision: "Our age is retrospective. . . . The foregoing generations beheld God and nature face to face; we through their eyes. Why should we not also enjoy an original relation to the universe?" In this passage, Emerson's diction is resolutely universal, but he is also alluding to the Puritans' establishing a church and a state in the New World to reflect as precisely as possible their vision of divine and natural laws. For him, the Puritans' voyage across the Atlantic was *the* representative example of seeking an original relation to the universe. All later efforts must be measured against theirs. And in the most famous passage from *Nature* Emerson defined such a vision as being not only original but truly universal; it purges away the decadent subjectivity of the individual and his society: "All mean egotism vanishes. I become a transparent eyeball; I am nothing; I see all; the currents of the Universal Being circulate through me; I am part or parcel of God." Behind the Precisionists' quest for "objectivity" thus lies Emerson's Universal Being and his vision of America's destiny to build and record the history of a new Eden in the New World.[19]

Emerson would probably have had grave doubts about the subservience of the photographer's camera to what he called elsewhere in *Nature* the "apparition" of visible things. But the Precisionists did

18. For general discussion of Emerson in the context of the typological tradition and for a definition of the tradition itself, see Perry Miller, *Errand into the Wilderness* (Cambridge, Mass., 1956), 1–15, 184–203; Ursula Brumm, *American Thought and Religious Typology*, trans. John Hoaglund (New Brunswick, N.J., 1970), 20–33, 86–108; and Sacvan Bercovitch, *The Puritan Origins of the American Self* (New Haven, Conn., 1975), 136–86. See also Carl Rapp's superb discussion of Williams' debt to Emerson, "Emerson as Precursor," in Rapp, *William Carlos Williams and Romantic Idealism*, 53–77.

19. Stephen Whicher (ed.), *Selections from Ralph Waldo Emerson* (New York, 1957), 21, 24.

not have doubts; they felt that their Equivalents captured the linea-
ments of the spiritual as well as the material. Indeed, Strand's defini-
tion of the Equivalent (and Pound's of an Image) seem to echo
passages in *Nature* such as this one: "Every natural fact is a symbol of
some spiritual fact. Every appearance in nature corresponds to some
state of mind, and that state of mind can only be described by
presenting that natural appearance as its picture."[20] For Williams,
the power of the Precisionists' ideas was proof of the continuing
vitality of his transcendentalist heritage. Early in his career, in his
"Five Philosophical Essays" (1910–1915), he had sounded a thor-
oughly Emersonian note:

> In me is beauty such as nature elsewhere never dreamt of, here in myself
> waiting for expression. I no longer see trees but beauty in form of trees and thus
> a new life. All nature now becomes a symbol for me to use. . . . [T]hrough the
> discovery of a more and more nearly completely expressive form, which is
> beauty in the same terms, it is possible for man to approach nearer and nearer
> to perfection. . . . Nature's final command is: "Do not waste." Insofar as life is
> to do, it is: "Do not waste time." Insofar as life is to see, it is: "Do not waste
> space." Thus we see that life is to confine our energy and for us to expand our
> view. Which, again, shows that a perfection is the object of our activity, any
> perfection concentrated into a minimum of elements constituting it[,] for in
> perfection there is no waste. . . . This "command of nature"; this universal
> abstract principle we name economy. (*EK,* 164, 168, 186)

If Emerson taught Williams that all natural forms should be ex-
pressive, it was the Precisionists who completed his education on this
topic and taught him (as Emerson and Whitman also believed) that
tools and machinery could be so as well. In Strand's words in "Pho-
tography and the New God," the photographer subjugates the ma-
chine to "the single purpose of expression." Both natural and man-
ufactured things could be celebrated for their concentrated
"economy" of form precisely fitted to purpose.

The transcendentalist heritage was of course concurrently being
rediscovered by many intellectuals other than Williams and the art-
ists in Stieglitz's circle, and such reassessments of nineteenth-century
American history are profoundly relevant for any understanding of
the cultural context of the Precisionists' and Williams' Modernism.
The fundamental aim of the Precisionists was to define which ele-
ments in American history could provide the best means for inspiring
and controlling her industrial development. The same task was the
goal of many contemporary American historians.

20. *Ibid.,* 32.

Initiated by Frederick Jackson Turner's essay "The Significance of the Frontier in American History," read at the World's Columbian Exposition in Chicago in 1893, Brooks Adams' *The Law of Civilization and Decay* (1895), and Henry Adams' *The Education of Henry Adams* (1918), the discussion as it developed in the second decade of the new century identified the Puritan work ethic and the frontier as the two crucial determinants of American history up to the 1890s. In Turner's striking words, "the existence of an area of free land, its continuous recession, and the advance of American settlement westward, explain American development." Like Turner, the Adams brothers knew that if this thesis were correct, the closing of the frontier in the late 1880s would have as profound an effect on American culture as the opening of it did. The Adamses were pessimistic about America's ability to adapt to an urban age of closed boundaries. Henry Adams wondered what the effects would be if the habits that the frontier engendered in American life—its violence, its faith in unlimited expansion, and its "acceleration"—were applied to urban industrial expansion, as cities exponentially increased their population densities and their expenditure of natural resources. Brooks Adams claimed that with the closing of the frontier the fate of American culture had now become inextricably linked to that of Western culture as a whole, which he felt to be entering a phase equivalent to the decadence of Roman civilization, without the prospect of a "stream of Barbarian blood" that would create a new civilization to follow.[21]

After 1910 (and especially in the 1920s) these sobering analyses were reinterpreted by a new generation of social critics to offer a sweeping reevaluation of America's past and a reassessment of the role that industrialism could play in her present and future. Many critics associated with the New or Progressive history, such as Van Wyck Brooks, Charles Beard, Waldo Frank, Harold Stearns, and Lewis Mumford, along with other cultural commentators such as Walter Lippmann, criticized the excesses of recent American industrialism by uncovering their origins in America's Puritan and frontier heritage. Puritan theology and the rigors of frontier life had conspired, they felt, to create the first civilization in history in which

21. Frederick Jackson Turner, *The Frontier in American History* (New York, 1920), 1. For Henry Adams' use of the term *acceleration*, see Ernest Samuels (ed.), *The Education of Henry Adams* (Boston, 1973), 489–98. The Brooks Adams citation is from *The Law of Civilization and Decay* (London, 1896), 349.

intellectual and cultural life was mistrusted rather than valued. In Stearns's words, "contempt for mere intellectual values has of course been strengthened by the native pioneer suspicion of all thought that does not issue immediately into successful action."[22] Vigorous mental creativity was thought to be expressible solely in material ways, in the world of commerce and power, the man's sphere, while "culture" in America was relegated to the sphere of ministers, women, and aesthetes, becoming merely a matter of leisure, decoration, and private sentiment. The Progressivists' analysis drew its power from the linkage of two apparently disparate aspects of the Gilded Age—the rise of sentimental, genteel culture on one hand and the rise of monopoly capital on the other.

In 1926, Mumford offered one of the most articulate views of what Puritanism and the frontier had wrought:

> The effect of the pioneer habits upon our culture has become a commonplace of literary criticism during the last half-generation; the weakness of this criticism has been the failure to grasp the difference in origin between the puritan, the pioneer, and the inventor-businessman. The puritan did indeed pave the way for the extroverts that came after him; but what he really sought was an inner grace. The pioneer debased all the old values of a settled culture, and made the path of a dehumanized industrialism in America as smooth as a concrete road; but it was only in the habits he had developed, so to say, on the road, that he turned aside from the proper goal of the Romantic movement, which was to find a basis for a fresh effort in culture, and gave himself over to the inventor-businessman's search for power. All three, puritan, pioneer, and businessman, came to exist through the breakdown of Europe's earlier, integrated culture; but, given the wide elbow room in America, each type tended to develop to its extreme.[23]

If such anti-intellectualism continued to operate even after the frontier had closed, Mumford and others believed, it would be impossible to make a genuine (rather than merely a genteel) culture out of industrialism—a culture that would guide rather than merely serve the interests of those in power. A host of possible solutions to this dilemma was offered, from Lippmann's belief expressed in *Drift and Mastery* (1914) that the new forms of governmental education and economic centralization could bring the new "discipline" that would be required to govern earlier excesses, to Frank's and Mumford's homages to what they took to be the heroic antimaterialism of the

22. Harold Stearns, "The Intellectual Life," in Stearns (ed.), *Civilization in the United States* (New York, 1922), 145.
23. Lewis Mumford, *The Golden Day: A Study of American Experience and Culture* (New York, 1926), 73–74.

writers of the American Renaissance, the period Mumford called "The Golden Day."

As Warren Susman has ably shown, the majority of these writers sought to retain certain preindustrial Puritan and frontier values even while they criticized many of their consequences.[24] Lippmann, Stearns, and Mumford sought to discriminate between self-reliance and self-indulgence, inventiveness and opportunism, practicality and mere materialism. And their clarionlike calls to analyze and redirect America's development contrast sharply with the pessimistic irony that pervades the texts of the Adamses. This new confidence unites even such disparate figures as Lippmann and, say, Frank, who otherwise would be thought, quite rightly, to have little in common.

Of all the cultural historians of this period, John Dewey was most influential for the Precisionists and Williams.[25] Dewey published an important series of articles in journals such as *The New Republic* and *The Dial* just when the Precisionists were formulating their aesthetic. Indeed, an aphorism from one of those articles advocating definitively American subject matter for art, "the locality is the only universal," became a credo of Williams'. Like Williams and the Precisionists, Dewey was determined to investigate to what extent America's preindustrial values could provide examples of "perfection" for her urban, industrial future.

At the heart of Dewey's critique of American middle-class culture was the distinction he drew between colonial Puritanism and the fundamentalist Christian evangelical movements of the nineteenth century. In his view, the latter were much more responsible than the former for American materialism and anti-intellectualism. Even more important, he stressed that one of the founding strengths of American culture was its essential pragmatism, its "experimental spirit." The frontier, like the Puritan work ethic, could be seen as an instrumental cause of America's virtues as well as its vices. Echoing Emerson's essay "Circles" and the "Commodity" section of *Nature*, Dewey claimed in "Pragmatic America" (1922) that "be the evils what they may, the experiment is not yet played out. The United

24. Susman, *Culture as History,* 7–26, 39–49.
25. Two important discussions of Dewey's relevance for Williams and the period are Lisa Steinman's "Once More, With Feeling: Teaching *Spring and All,*" *William Carlos Williams Review,* X (Fall, 1984), 7–12; and Mike Weaver's *William Carlos Williams: The American Background,* 32–35. Dewey's essays may be found in Joseph Ratner (ed.), *Character and Events: Popular Essays in Social and Political Philosophy* (2 vols.; London, 1929).

States are not yet made. . . . Commerce itself, let us dare say it, is a noble thing. It is intercourse, exchange, communication, and distribution, sharing what is otherwise excluded and private."[26] The Precisionists' belief in the potentially ethical virtues of production and commerce had essentially the same premises.

Dewey's position had its roots in "American Education and Culture" (1916), in which he stressed that the genteel forms of classicism and medievalism popular in the Gilded Age were a pathetically inadequate attempt to escape from the contradictions in American culture created by old frontier values and the new industrialism. "To transmute a society built on an industry which is not yet humanized into a society which wields its knowledge and its industrial power in behalf of a democratic culture requires the courage of an inspired imagination. . . . In short, our culture must be consonant with realistic science and with machine industry, instead of a refuge from them."[27] Dewey's equation of the modern industrial landscape with the frontier is particularly telling: he saw the industrial landscape as a new wilderness of beauty and violence waiting to be settled or "humanized," and implied that the same virtues that allowed the original colonists to survive in the New World—their willingness to experiment, their spiritual pragmatism—would now be necessary to transform the new urban world.

At the heart of Dewey's thought in these essays is a rich series of contradictions that horatory abstractions such as "humanized," "democratic," and "inspired imagination" tend to suppress. Dewey was most cogent when recommending changes, least cogent when suggesting how they were to be carried out. He completely ignored, for example, the question of how an economy dominated by large corporations could possibly be made "democratic" if it had already become essentially "feudalized."[28] But the ways Dewey's work embodied and then tried to reconcile the tensions in American culture are profoundly instructive, for the same tensions and strategies drove much of the art of Williams and the Precisionists—especially their attempts to invent a modernist and urban form of pastoral art.

However accurately Williams' prose reflects Precisionist theories, the fact remains that he does tend to ignore differences between the visual and verbal arts when he discusses how those ideas might be

26. Ratner (ed.), *Character and Events*, II, 545–46.
27. Ratner (ed.), *Character and Events*, II, 500, 502.
28. Ratner (ed.), *Character and Events*, II, 547.

embodied in literature. His poetry, on the other hand, does not. Williams appears to have had an intuitive knowledge of what visual ideas were and were not translatable into a verbal "expressive form" equivalent to theirs. He shows equal adroitness applying Precisionist thinking to traditional pastoral subjects, such as flower poems, and to new urban scenes.

A case in point is the contrast between his commentary on "Chicory and Daisies" (1915) and the poem itself. In his prologue to *Kora in Hell*, Williams says that he gave the poem "over to the flower and its plant," focusing on its "color and form," and so constructed his praise of it as "to borrow no particle from right or left" (I, 19). One critic applauded this statement, claiming that such a sharp but limited focus was "a necessary and logical correlative to [Williams'] attempts at approximating the visual and emotional unity of painting in poetry," but then also admonished Williams for still seeking "some recourse to extraneous (literary) commentary."[29] Despite such a remark, however, the visual details of Williams's poem are relatively scarce; we are given only chicory's "sky-blue" color and lack of foliage. The poem is neither a picture poem nor merely a precise recording of the plant's visual appearance—two of the more obvious traps that a literary style influenced by the visual arts could fall into. The qualities of the plant that are stressed are almost without exception nonvisual:

>Lift your flowers
>on bitter stems
>chicory!
>Lift them up
>out of the scorched ground!
>Bear no foliage
>but give yourself
>wholly to that!
>Strain under them
>you bitter stems
>that no beast eats—
>and scorn grayness!
>Into the heat with them:
>cool!
>luxuriant! sky-blue!
>The earth cracks and
>is shriveled up;
>the wind moans piteously;
>the sky goes out
>if you should fail.
>
>(CP1, 65)

29. Dijkstra, *Cubism, Stieglitz, and the Early Poetry of William Carlos Williams*, 58–59.

Williams has a naturalist's interest in the features that enable chicory to adapt to the scorched land on which it grows. Unlike the daisy, whose pliable stem can be destroyed, chicory's stiff and bitter stems protect it. Such details are as much a part of what Williams would call the plant's "inimitable particles of dissimilarity" as its "color and form," and he includes them even though a photograph could not. To this end Williams employs venerable literary devices such as personification and hyperbole. He personifies chicory throughout the poem with heroic verbs such as "lift," "bear," "strain," and at the close claims that the earth "cracks" and is "shrivelled up." Rather than being "Precisionist" or "photographic" in a simplistic way, Williams' poem interweaves many different ways of defining the plant's uniqueness—visual and conceptual, scientific and literary.

One poem by Williams that does appear to be a careful transcription of a visual experience is "Young Sycamore" (1927). As Bram Dijkstra has shown, it is probably based on a photograph by Stieglitz entitled "Spring Showers."[30] Dijkstra praises the poem as a literal record of the eye's "linear movement" as it takes in the photograph. A second reading, however, shows that the poem is hardly without personification or metaphor: through carefully chosen verbs and adjectives, Williams suggests that Stieglitz's sycamore is also a tree of life, starting from youth's "round and firm trunk" and then thinning gradually until the branches are drained of life's sap, "bending forward" like the bodies of the old (CP1, 266–67). The eye's movement thus merges with the inner eye's vision of time's passage. Literary devices remain central to the poem's technique; although Williams' tropes are understated, they remain the means by which he transforms his tree into an Equivalent in words.

Another feature of the Equivalent that Williams adopted is the ability to evoke universal or "objective" emotions. In "The Pot of Flowers" (1923), for example, a poem in Spring and All based upon Demuth's watercolor Tuberoses, the movement of the poet's eye also traces an inner trajectory, from the excitement of the "contending" flowers with their nervous riot of color, to the more "modest" green of the plant's lower leaves, to the reserved, meditative pleasures of the dark earth, clay pot, and moss. (This contrast is also enacted by

30. Illustrated in Dijkstra, Cubism, Stieglitz, and the Early Poetry of William Carlos Williams, Plate IX. Dijkstra discusses both poem and photograph on pp. 189–91. The best discussion of the poem is by J. Hillis Miller, The Linguistic Moment From Wordsworth to Stevens (Princeton, 1985), 385–89.

the poem's rhythms and line breaks, which dart back and forth
rapidly in the first part of the poem and then slow to the stately
concluding lines: "and there, wholly dark, the pot / gay with rough
moss" [*CP1*, 184].) Such a change in rhythm and mood, though,
does not mean that Williams is judging his earlier mood, nor that an
inner, repressed event from his past has suddenly emerged into the
present. Rather, by organizing the poem around opposed extremes of
feeling, Williams emphasizes the equal value of both—they
heighten each other's value just as colors are heightened by contrast,
or light by dark. And his acts of observation do not encourage us to
search for hidden, private causes motivating them; rather, the poet
seems to have allowed the object to have entirely taken over his
consciousness. In Williams' Precisionist lyrics, the poet usually
speaks with an intimate but impersonal voice, the voice of Every-
man, and the poem's action is suspended in time to be repeated
within the reader each time the poem is read.[31]

Stieglitz's experiments with combining the still life and the land-
scape are also reflected in Williams' work. The four flower studies he
published in *Sour Grapes* (1921), "Daisy," "Primrose," "Queen-
Anne's-Lace," and "Great Mullen," are especially interesting for
their sense of scale. "Daisy," for example, moves from a rapid over-
view of "Spring . . . / gone down in purple," "weeds . . . high in the
corn," a clotted furrow, and a branch heavy with new leaves, to a
close-up of the poem's flower: "One turns the thing over / in his hand
and looks / at it from the rear: brownedged, / green and pointed
scales / armor his yellow" (*CP1*, 160–61). Along with these visual
devices in the poems, Williams introduces metaphor, personifica-
tion, dramatic debate, and apostrophe, and varies their tone from
the restrained, dignified voice of "Queen-Anne's-Lace" to the gro-
tesque shouting match of "Great Mullen."

In "Queen-Anne's-Lace," literal and figurative description have
been carefully joined, rather than simply juxtaposed as in "Daisy."
And the poem's breadth of focus is breathtaking—it is a still life, a
landscape, a time-lapse photographic sequence. As if the poet were a
botanist and we, his best students, Williams shows us how the stem
splits into a cluster of stems radiating upward, each supporting a
white flowerette that, edging the others, compose the flower's lacy

---

31. *Tuberoses* is illustrated in Dijkstra, *Cubism, Stieglitz, and the Early Poetry of William
Carlos Williams*, Plate XX. See also Breslin, "William Carlos Williams and Charles Demuth."

head. When Williams personifies the plant, his rhetoric carefully preserves its unique structure; the sun is a male who creates a lover for himself touch by touch: "Each part / is a blossom under his touch / to which the fibres of her being / stem one by one." Williams then rapidly accelerates the pace of the poem, so that we see the field becoming populated in spring and the lovers increasing the momentum of their lovemaking, until the field is covered with the flowers' white, the woman's body with her lover's touch. Then, suddenly, winter appears to have come again, leaving nothing in the field:

> stem one by one, each to its end,
> until the whole field is a
> white desire, empty, a single stem,
> a cluster, flower by flower,
> a pious wish to whiteness gone over—
> or nothing.
> (*CP1,* 162)

Pumping blood into Emerson's rather cerebral equation of natural and spiritual facts, Williams' "Queen-Anne's-Lace" follows Whitman and shows them to be signs of sexual facts as well. Metaphor, personification, and mythmaking accompany literal description, and the still life's landscape is emptied or filled within the leap of a line of verse.

Many of Williams' lyrics also share the Precisionists' idealized, Arcadian vision of modern industry. Williams paid homage to Sheeler's *Classic Landscape,* a portrait of the Ford Motor Company's River Rouge Plant, in his poem "Classic Scene" (1937). The poem picks a different setting but captures Sheeler's spirit by carefully recording the height of the powerhouse's smokestacks, the industrial colors (red, buff, and gray), the construction materials (brick and aluminum), and the relation of the buildings to each other. Williams emphasizes both the kinetic and the potential energy of the plant; one burner is inactive, as the "passive" smokestack shows. However, Williams does not hesitate to use literary devices to heighten the poem's effect. The powerhouse becomes a giant "chair," and its aluminum stacks are gods reposing on a throne, "commanding" the labor of their subjects. Only the suggestion that the shacks are "squalid" goes against this mood (*CP1,* 444–45). Here, Williams inches closer to the half-ironic attitude toward industry that Demuth exhibited in paintings like *My Egypt,* with its suggestion that Ameri-

can industry has all the benevolent despotism of an Egyptian phar-
oah.[32] In general, though, Williams, like Sheeler, means us to take
his adjective *classic* quite seriously—to believe that the monumental
power and nobility of previous civilizations have been reborn in
America.

"Fine Work with Pitch and Copper" (1935) is less monumental
than most of Sheeler's or Demuth's urban landscapes, for it involves
local construction workers rather than the vast structures of high
technology and focuses on the men themselves as Sheeler and De-
muth rarely do. Nonetheless, the poem includes the Precisionists'
clear, "fleckless" light, as well as their respect for number, edge,
arrangement, and material:

> Now they are resting
> in the fleckless light
> separately in unison
>
> like the sacks
> of sifted stone stacked
> regularly by twos
>
> about the flat roof
> ready after lunch
> to be opened and strewn
>
> The copper in eight
> foot strips has been
> beaten lengthwise
>
> down the center at right
> angles and lies ready
> to edge the coping
>
> One still chewing
> picks up a copper strip
> and runs his eye along it
>
> (CP1, 405–406)

Not only does this poem argue that work and pleasure, precision and
freedom, may coexist: its very form embodies their union. The sen-
tences are unabashedly utilitarian, with the flat rhythms and imper-
sonal voice of technical manuals and certain kinds of journalism. But
Williams breaks his lines and groups his words into such strict pat-
terns that we suddenly find poetry in what we might have cast off as
prose. Listen to the sweet sibilants of stanza two, miming the job they
describe, or consider how Williams' line and stanza breaks depict the

---

32. Tashjian, *William Carlos Williams and the American Scene,* 68–69. See also Tashjian's
fine analysis of "Classic Scene" and *Classic Landscape, ibid.,* 81–85.

way good laborers divide a task into its elementary components to increase efficiency. It is as if one of Whitman's long, looping lines celebrating workmen—such as these from "Song of the Broad-Axe," Part 3: "The bricks one after another each laid so workmanlike in its place, and set with a knock of the trowel-handle, / The piles of materials, the mortar on the mortar-boards, and the steady re-plenishing by the hod-men"—had been cut up and carefully aligned, each segment precisely made plumb to the next.[33]

But the most important feature the poem shares with the Preci-sionists (and with Whitman) is its confident identification of men with their jobs. Williams compares the workers resting during lunch to sacks of sifted stone, and this startling simile at first may appear ironic, perhaps a comment on how industry dehumanizes. But no other details in the poem will support such a reading, and it appears instead that the workers, like their stone, have become "sifted" and purified by labor. They give themselves up to their work as the sacks give up their contents, or as an artist devotes himself to his craft. The poem's last stanza makes us see that they are artists who achieve their identity through their work; the poem shifts its focus from the com-munal *they* in the first line to the singular worker-artist in the last stanza. Aesthetic intelligence is as much a part of this man's labor as the lunch hour is a part of his working day. Optimistically treating America's urban energy as a rhythmic unit of work, morality, and pleasure, and viewing the artist as an integral part of a working community rather than an exile from it, "Fine Work with Pitch and Copper" is Williams' most eloquent portrait of the Precisionists' en-visioned industrial Arcadia. Published in 1935, in the midst of the Depression, this poem honoring roofers is also a survival manual, a construction of shelter.

That Williams could be so optimistic in 1935 may not seem credi-ble. Yet even in the poems that venture beyond the rather narrow boundaries of the Precisionists' urban Utopia, Williams still retains their work ethic. "An Early Martyr" (1934), for instance, bluntly attacks American institutions, but describes its martyr-hero in this manner: "Let him be / a factory whistle / That keeps blaring— / Sense, sense, sense!" (*CP1*, 378).[34] Another poem from the De-pression, "The Poor" (1938), was published in *The New Republic* one

33. Walt Whitman, *Leaves of Grass*, ed. Emory Holloway (New York, 1926), 157.
34. Compare with Joe Stecher, the hero of Williams' novel *White Mule* (Norfolk, Conn., 1937), who makes similar statements about the moral value of factory labor when managed efficiently and fairly.

year after the same magazine had taken his "Classic Scene." Its subject matter is closer to some of the naturalistic, discordant street scenes of Stieglitz or Strand than to any work by Sheeler or Demuth.[35] Williams documents "every stage and custom / of necessity" in poverty: hand-me-down clothes; "new brick tenements"; an older building's cast-iron balcony panel "showing oak branches / in full leaf" and recalling better days; and the strident collage of different architectural styles that is the American city: "It's the anarchy of poverty / delights me, the old / yellow wooden house indented / among the new brick tenements." Williams is also delighted by the pride he finds among the people. In an "unfenced age," the tenement land shows that it is carefully kept; the poem ends celebrating one old man who stubbornly sweeps the sidewalk:

> his own ten feet of it
> in a wind that fitfully
> turning the corner has
> overwhelmed the entire city
>
> (CP1, 452–53)

The line "his own ten feet of it" is the only unenjambed line in the poem. Like the old man, it triumphantly stakes out its boundaries amid the poem's flurry of energy. In the beginning of the poem, Williams celebrates the poor's "anarchy," their improvisational energy in the face of difficulties. But by the end of the poem, anarchy is associated not with the poor but with the "fitful" wind, Williams' symbol for the economic forces—chiefly, greed and the loss of a proper work ethic—that the poem suggests caused the Depression. Heroically struggling against these vices stand the forces of virtue and industry, as represented by the old man sweeping the precise ten feet of sidewalk in front of his property. No longer figures of "anarchy," the poor hurt most strongly by the Depression are now seen to be the last bastions of frugality, limits, enclosure, and order.

"Classic Scene" and "The Poor" show that Williams' vision of pastoral included several different strains of Precisionist thought, including the idealized vision of Sheeler and the ambivalent views of the modern city in Stieglitz's, Strand's, and Demuth's work—some-

35. See particularly Stieglitz's views of men at work in photographs like *Excavating, New York* (1921) (illustrated in Margolis [ed.], *Camera Work*, 100), or Strand's portraits of the city as an architectural collage in *Truckman's House* (illustrated in Tashjian, *William Carlos Williams and the American Scene*, 75), and *Photograph—New York* (in Margolis [ed.], *Camera Work*, 139). *Excavating* and *Photograph* appeared in *Camera Work*, October, 1911, and June, 1917, respectively.

times celebratory and sometimes foreboding. Williams' pastoral lyrics have a still more complex pedigree, however, for from the three "Pastoral" poems in *Al Que Quiere!* to his later translation of Theocritus' first *Idyl,* Williams shows an extensive knowledge of *literary* pastoral traditions as well. Studying the presence of such traditions in Williams' work not only allows us to define how Williams criticizes the Precisionist aesthetic even as he adopts it; it also demonstrates why Williams' interest in the visual arts invigorated rather than hindered his interest in literary tradition.

Consider the best of the three poems entitled "Pastoral" in *Al Que Quiere!,* "When I Was Younger." The poem begins with a compressed, modern version of the traditional pastoral debate between the values of the city and the country, with the poet rejecting a career (to "make something of myself") for life with those excluded from power.[36] On the back streets of an American city, Williams sees a "roof out of line with sides / the yards cluttered / with old chicken wire, ashes, / furniture gone wrong." Yet Williams discovers surprising harmony with nature, even in an urban slum; the dissonant list of clutter in the poem's middle is drawn together and gracefully unified: "all, / if I am fortunate, / smeared a bluish green / that properly weathered / pleases me best / of all colors." The unity Williams discovers is "weathered," open to nature's changes, and "proper," implying an aesthetic of the natural (*CP1,* 64–65).

In "Tract" (1916), Williams tries to make the poor conscious of just such an aesthetic. He must reteach them "how to perform a funeral" because they have been aping middle- and upper-class conventions rather than relying on their own "ground sense." The poem's rhetoric, however, does not reject artifice, but rather contrasts honest and dishonest artifice—a rite that acknowledges the facts of nature versus a rite that does not. Thus the redesigned hearse may have some decoration—the gilt wheels—but should also be "weathered—like a farm wagon," with the coffin exposed to the elements just as it will soon be exposed to weather of the grave: "He will have a heavier rain soon: / pebbles and dirt and what not. / Let there be no glass." The mourners must also be exposed: "Go with some show / of inconvenience; sit openly— / to the weather as to grief" (*CP1,* 72–74).

36. For some Shakespearean examples, see the speeches of Touchstone and the Duke in *As You Like It,* especially II, i, 1–17, and III, ii, 13–85. The best introduction to the conventions of pastoral is by Frank Kermode, *English Pastoral Poetry* (1952; rpr. New York, 1972), 11–44. He discusses the town and country debate on pages 37–42.

Such a debate between the natural and the artificial is a second traditional topic of pastoral—as Polixenes' famous reply to Perdita in *The Winter's Tale* shows.[37] Williams sides with Polixenes, for he refuses to draw a sharp line between nature and artifice, and he favors the kind of art that mends and changes nature while respecting her own laws. This "natural" aesthetic, of course, is highly idealistic, for it not only assumes that man can live in harmony with nature but also that nature is herself harmonious. One of Williams' wittiest poems, "On Gay Wallpaper" (1928), shows that we can't live completely "openly," as "Tract" might have us do; even our visions of a natural shelter involve an art that changes nature. The poem consequently celebrates the many ways in which we use that art. First punning on *ground* and *ruled* and pretending not to know whether he sees the real thing or merely our own picture of it, Williams then makes us conscious of the "ruling" moral idealism of all pastoral art:

> The green-blue ground
> is ruled with silver lines
> to say the sun is shining
>
> And on this moral sea
> of grass or dreams lie flowers
> or baskets of desires
> (*CP1*, 285)

Williams compares America's modern Arcadia, the endless bounty of its industry, with the repetitive riches of another kind of mass production, wallpaper design. Three roses, three stems, nine leaves, and a basket are

> Repeated to the ceiling
> to the windows
> where the day
>
> Blows in
> the scalloped curtains to
> the sound of rain
> (*CP1*, 285)

For all his gentle mocking of the wallpaper's simplicity, and, by

37.
> You see, sweet maid, we marry
> A gentler scion to the wildest stock,
> And make conceive a bark of baser kind
> By bud of nobler race. This is an art
> Which does mend nature—change it rather—but
> The art itself is nature.
> (IV, iv, 92–97)

See also Kermode, *English Pastoral Poetry*, 37–42. Kermode calls the "Art-Nature antithesis" "philosophically the basis of pastoral literature."

implication, the Precisionists' faith that industry *is* bounteous, Williams does not intend for us to contrast the wallpaper unfavorably with the scene out the window. Rather, artifice is treated as nature's equal: man-made curtains billow to the sound of rain, as if dancing to nature's music. And indoors, not outdoors, remains our home.

Sex is another favorite topic of pastoral. Williams' most intriguing exploration of the sexual drive present in urban culture is "The Attic Which Is Desire:" (1930), inspired in part by the attic study in which Williams did most of his writing in the 1930s and 1940s. The poem is as concerned with sexuality as the traditional passionate shepherd; as Wallace Stevens first noticed, it is filled with sexual innuendo: the triangular attic and its darkened windowpane are "transfixed" "exactly / down the center" by the intermittent flashing of an upright, phallic sign reading SODA outside (*CP1*, 325–26).[38] The "desire" of the poem, of course, is first and foremost a less romantic one, merely thirst inspired by the advertisement. ("Nature" does not wait outside of the attic nearly so "directly" as the modern world of mass-market commodities.) Although there is an ironic edge to the poem's association of desire and SODA—and, even more importantly, a hint of coercion in the word *transfix*—in general the poem seems very much entranced with the machinery of stimulating desire that it diagrams. In fact, the lean, rectangular shape of the poem on the page exactly reproduces the shape of the tall SODA sign, thus cunningly implying that the poem's ideas and physical detail may "transfix" and impregnate its unenlightened readers.

With "The Attic Which Is Desire:" Williams has once again gone somewhat beyond Sheeler's and Demuth's vision of Arcadia. To begin with, theirs is less erotic. Sheeler's America is as ascetic as a Shaker's, and the biomorphic profiles that Demuth occasionally gives his machines tend to portray the sexual energy of machinery ironically. Of the Precisionists, only Stieglitz explored territory similar to Williams', though he did so in quite a different way. His portraits of Georgia O'Keeffe, taken between 1917 and 1937 and first shown at his Anderson Galleries show in 1921, were, for their time, startlingly explicit. A series of closeup, sharply focused shots of O'Keeffe's hands, neck, face, and arms, this combination of eroticism and scientific precision revolutionized erotic photography,

38. Wallace Stevens, *Opus Posthumous* (New York, 1971), 256. Stevens' critique was originally published as a preface to Williams' *Collected Poems, 1921–1931* (New York, 1934). Marianne Moore and Stevens were Williams' best early readers.

which, as the many nudes published earlier in *Camera Work* will attest, still assumed that a sharp focus would make the body too tangible, thus destroying sexual interest. In 1933, three years after Williams published "The Attic" in *Blues*, Stieglitz made a set of portraits of O'Keeffe in and around automobiles. The most striking of these place her strong-fingered hands spread wide against the smooth curves of the car's fender and chrome; they effectively equate the powerful musculature of modern technology with that of the human body (see Illustration 3). The machine eros of both Williams and Stieglitz, of course, had been jointly influenced by New York Dada experiments in a similar vein, particularly Duchamp's *The Bride Stripped Bare by Her Bachelors, Even*, which they could have seen in Walter Arensberg's apartment, and Picabia's drawings and collages in the magazine *291*, such as his *Portrait d'une jeune fille americaine* as a spark plug. But the erotic machines of both Europeans (and Demuth) are satiric and fetishistic in a way that is entirely foreign to the comparable work of Stieglitz and Williams. For them, the bounty of modern consumer society, its cornucopia of flashing lights, glass, metal, and commercial products, could radiate health and sexual energy.[39]

The most important difference between Williams and the Precisionists is that Williams more frequently turns the gap between Precisionism's pastoral ideals and America's reality into the subject matter of his art. The poem "Horned Purple" in *Spring and All* (No. XIX) is a mock pastoral populated by "dirty satyrs," juvenile delinquents who are "vulgarity raised to the last power" (*CP1*, 221–22). Another poem in *Spring and All*, "To Elsie" (No. XVIII), tells a similar story. Elsie is both the Williams' servant and a girl emblematic of all the

39. An example of Demuth's biomorphic imagery is *Machinery* (1920), reproduced in Dijkstra, *Cubism, Stieglitz, and the Early Poetry of William Carlos Williams*, Plate XIX. Tashjian makes the excellent point in *William Carlos Williams and the American Scene*, 70–71, that Demuth's treatment of sexuality was often oblique and sardonic. He is surely wrong, however, to claim that when Demuth dedicated *Machinery* to Williams in 1920, he did so ironically, knowing that Williams deplored "faking the psychologic appearance of the machine, making perhaps a 'woman' of it" (p. 68). Tashjian quotes from an article Williams published in 1954 in *Art in America*, but Williams, marrying the gentler scion of Precisionism to the wildest stock of Dada, read his "Overture to a Dance of Locomotives" at the New York Independents Exhibition in 1917 and turned a Ford flivver into a woman in 1923 (*The Great American Novel*). Demuth's dedication was entirely apt. For Stieglitz's portraits, see Stieglitz, *Georgia O'Keeffe: A Portrait* (New York, 1978). The 1933 photographs are Plates 45–48. Doris Bry, in *Alfred Stieglitz*, notes that Stieglitz's 1921 show included "about fifty" prints of O'Keeffe "made between 1918 and 1920" (p. 17). For the best general discussion of New York Dada's machine eros, see Tashjian, *Skyscraper Primitives*. Picabia's *Portrait* appeared in *291*, V–VI (July–August, 1915).

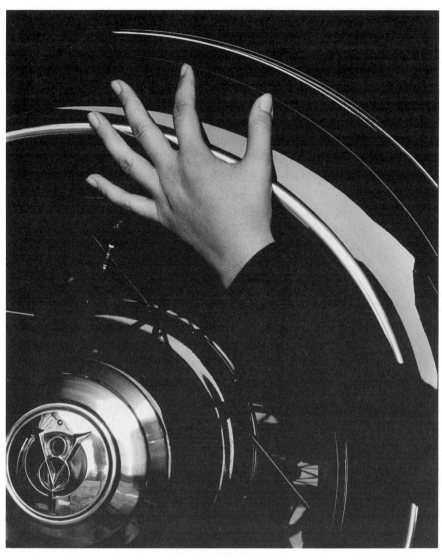

Alfred Stieglitz, *Georgia O'Keeffe—Hands, 1933*

Courtesy of Juan Hamilton and the Metropolitan Museum of Art,
Lent by Estate of Georgia O'Keeffe

women uprooted from country towns and precariously making a living in the cities. Lacking "peasant traditions," the moral models given by family, a stable community, and work, Elsie succumbs to advertising, "cheap jewelry," and "rich young men with fine eyes" and is apparently raped "under some hedge of choke-cherry / or viburnum." By the poem's end, her abuse becomes a representative example of the social dislocations caused by rapid industrialization: rather than teaching morality, the city is destroying it. Williams' bitter and frightened poem ends in despair, with America's motorized Arcadia careening out of control: "no one / to witness / and adjust, no one to drive the car" (*CP1*, 217–18).[40]

Yet although "To Elsie" at first seems to be a rejection of Precisionist pastoral, in fact the poem is something more complex, for its diagnosis of what is wrong with America is based upon Precisionist beliefs in what is right. Lacking a local tradition uniting work, morality, and the pursuit of happiness, Elsie has no chance. The Precisionists claimed that values could flourish in industrial America, if only her artists would be models for her citizens. Williams understood the frailty, idealism, and arrogance of their dream. But he did not renounce it. He believed that it provided the only possible hope for harnessing the accelerating forces of twentieth-century America for productive ends—the kinds of ends celebrated in poems like "Pastoral" or "Fine Work with Pitch and Copper" and called for in the work of the Precisionists and by cultural commentators such as John Dewey.

When the whole of Williams' urban and rural pastoral lyrics are compared, essential differences emerge. Williams' urban poems tend to consider social issues and the correct relation of artifice and nature. His nature lyrics, on the other hand, ground these humanistic issues in a larger, inhuman context; while they may celebrate nature's bounty, and even compare it with what man can produce, they most often portray what the poem "Spring and All" (1923) calls the "stark dignity" of life's entrance or exit, not its healthy (or decadent) middle. Like "Chicory and Daisies," these lyrics are concerned with the creation and destruction of a world. This too is a traditional topic of pastoral poetry—perhaps its most ambitious one.

Williams' most famous treatment of such a birth, of course, is the

40. See James Breslin's discussion of this poem in "William Carlos Williams and the Whitman Tradition," 177–79.

title poem of *Spring and All* (Poem I). Drawing together most of the features of Williams' other Precisionist pastoral lyrics—including their merging of still life and landscape, their use of personification, and their innovative celebration of both man-made and natural objects—"Spring and All" also reminds us of the Adamic or Messianic impulse within traditional pastoral poetry and alludes modestly but very explicitly to its sources in Genesis and the Messianic Fourth Eclogue of Vergil.

When "Spring and All" begins, Williams is driving "on the road to the contagious hospital" where victims of contagious diseases are treated (*CP1*, 183). From his car window, he has difficulty seeing outline or order in the landscape: *mottled, patches, waste,* and *scattering* are some of the words he uses. His problems culminate in the third stanza, where inexact adjectives, often afflicted with the suffixes *ish* or *y,* glut an entire line before a noun can be found. And even then the noun is imprecise:

> All along the road the reddish
> purplish, forked, upstanding, twiggy
> stuff . . .
> (*CP1*, 183)

Like the diseases in the hospital Williams is approaching, imprecision is a debilitating contagion of the mind.

As "one by one objects are defined" by spring, however, Williams' language is also reborn, and he can foresee the appearance of the wildcarrot, the only named species in the poem. His battle to see and to name has a "stark dignity" equal to spring's battle with winter, or a chicory's battle to create light from darkness. Like the plants, the poet's mind must "grip down," struggling to wrest a name from anonymity. The right name is a strong root; new poetry, and a new world, will grow from it as invincibly as the wildcarrot leaf uncurls. But the hidden *source* of names and new plants remains mysterious, identified only through an impersonal pronoun ("it quickens") (*CP1*, 183). As Thomas Whitaker has pointed out, the nouns and pronouns of the last stanzas of the poem are simultaneously precise and vague. The "all" created by nature may be named and enumerated, but "spring," the creative source itself, remains unknowable.[41]

Like many pastoral lyrics, "Spring and All" alludes to an Eden or a Golden Age, the loss of it, and its eventual return. In the Bible, of

41. Thomas R. Whitaker, *"Spring and All:* Teaching the Figures of the Dance," *William Carlos Williams Review,* X (Fall, 1984), 4.

course, such an event signifies the end of history, whereas in Vergil and other classical writers it inaugurates yet another historical cycle. Williams' poem well represents romanticism's distinctive revision of this archetypal plot. The large historical cycles between Iron and Golden Ages, or Old Adam and New Messiah, are internalized and speeded up: the rebirth experienced in "Spring and All," like spring itself, is continually lost, found, and lost again. Williams' poem ends poised on the verge of awakening, looking backward toward winter yet foreseeing spring:

> Now the grass, tomorrow
> the stiff curl of wildcarrot leaf
>
> One by one objects are defined—
> It quickens: clarity, outline of leaf
>
> But now the stark dignity of
> entrance—Still, the profound change
> has come upon them: rooted, they
> grip down and begin to awaken
> (CP1, 183)

"Burning the Christmas Greens" (1944) is an even richer dramatization of rebirth. With the possible exception of "The Descent," it is the most important lyric Williams wrote in the 1940s, and it demonstrates how he used the Precisionist techniques tested in his shorter lyrics to construct a medium-length poem. Like "Chicory and Daisies," it is a still life—but one that suddenly explodes into flames, matter instantly transformed into energy. And as in Williams' earlier still lifes, each detail is an Equivalent registered within: the flames are "red as blood wakes / on the ash" (CLP, 16). Between Williams' description of the moment of the burning of the greens, however, he intersperses short narrative sequences showing a family gathering and arranging the evergreen boughs, as well as a tender but stark meditation on the meaning of their midwinter rite. Williams had done something analogous at the end of "Queen-Anne's-Lace," when he exchanged the frozen moment of the still life for a leap forward in time ("empty, a single stem, / a cluster . . . / . . . / or nothing") (CP1, 162), and at the end of "Spring and All," which trembles on the edge of both winter and spring. "Christmas Greens," however, audaciously uses such a vibrating structure for an entire poem, rapidly shifting between a single, repeated spot of time centered on a still life and interpolated narrative sequences occurring before and after that moment.

The first narrative sequence in the poem (lines 12–34) is a flashback in which Williams tells of a family gathering the Christmas green during a "moment of the cold's / deepest plunge" and combining them with store-bought decorations. They build a make-believe forest on the fireplace mantel, using the hemlock sprays and some small white deer, perhaps made of china or porcelain. The narrator speaks for the whole group in third person plural, and details are kept generic, so that the family's rite could take place any midwinter, in any American home. After describing this ritual, Williams then jumps forward in time again to the moment of burning, when, "their time past," the decorations are cracked apart and stuffed on the top of a "half burnt out / log's smoldering eye, opening / red and closing under them" (CLP, 16–17). As the family waits for them to catch fire, Williams' meditation returns to the past a second time (lines 41– 55), not to describe gathering the greens but to meditate on the meaning of this midwinter ritual.

Williams stresses the pagan ritual behind the family's half-Christian, half-secular ceremony: greens forestall the cold by foretelling the arrival of spring. This section of the poem is in part a reworking of one of Williams' earlier (and best) pastoral poems, "To Waken an Old Lady" (1920). The "snow's / hard shell" and the birds' "plaintive, rallying cries" of "Burning the Christmas Greens" recall the setting of the earlier poem, but now the personification of the struggle of living creatures against winter is even more urgent. Williams turns what had been a birdsong tempering the winter wind into a man-made shelter: the boughs are "those sure abutments" and "a promise of peace, a fort / against the cold." The spiritual meanings that Williams is able to give these efforts are consequently more complex than in "To Waken an Old Lady"; gathering the greens symbolizes all human effort to reshape nature so that we may survive its harshness, from religious rituals to civilization's most advanced architecture.

Suddenly the greens burst into flame—and in the last five stanzas of the poem the mood shifts rapidly and becomes apocalyptic: "Transformed! / Violence leaped and appeared," and the branches are suddenly "Gone! / lost to mind // . . . / . . . in the contracting / tunnel of the grate" (CLP, 18). Yet as one world is destroyed, another appears; Williams transforms the ashes of the still-life greens into a view of our planet as it must have looked just after its creation:

> Black
> mountains, black and red—as

> yet uncolored—and ash white,
> an infant landscape of shimmering
> ash and flame
> (CLP, 18)

Williams is confident that his barren but brave new world may eventually be given human values, just as a newly created landscape is gradually colonized by plants. In fact, Williams' poem suggests that the twin worlds of the poem—ashes and evergreens, nature as desolate landscape and as a green world remade "to fill our need"—are doubles, twin images rapidly alternating between each other.

Williams does this brilliantly, by having the poem's last line, "the shining fauna of that fire," allude to a crucial earlier image, the white deer on the mantelpiece. By superimposing the two images, Williams creates a composite picture of the kind of creature that can live in the poem's double world. Such a creature, Williams tells us, must know that there is a time to fill our need for order and a time to expose ourselves to chaos—a time for gathering greens and a time for burning them. Man must repeatedly throw himself outdoors, out of the green world he constructs for himself, if his compulsion for shelter is to retain its integrity. This is why the poem constantly jumps back and forth in time: it is trying to teach us to live in both worlds. For Williams, his unnamed American family has this ability; they are both "lost" and "refreshed," symbolically bereft of home and excited by their discovery of a new world in which to live:

> breathless to be witnesses,
> as if we stood
> ourselves refreshed among
> the shining fauna of that fire.
> (CLP, 18)

The ending of "Burning the Christmas Greens" also alludes to "To Elsie" from Spring and All, both in its apocalyptic tone and in its repetition of crucial terms like witness and shining fauna. The earlier poem confronted chaos but despaired of ever being able to give it value; the poet remained alienated from his pastoral dream of perfection: "the imagination strains / after deer / going by fields of goldenrod" (CP1, 218). "Christmas Greens" is a revision, an answer to "To Elsie" and all the other mock pastorals in Spring and All, such as "Flight to the City." In it, Williams not only discovers "peasant traditions" that can substitute for the ones Elsie lost but also finds his own part to play in the ceremony. Significantly, those traditions are

largely unconscious, continually changing, and thoroughly hetero-
geneous—an American melting pot of pagan rites, Old World Chris-
tianity, and twentieth-century secular values. And at the center of
this pastoral vision, celebrating the end of one year and the birth of
another, stands the poet, truly the "happy genius" of his
household.[42]

"Burning the Christmas Greens" thus opens for us the kernel, the
heart of the heart of Williams' pastoral vision. Like earlier pastoral,
especially Vergil's, it has a pronounced Messianic strain, prophesying
the return of a Golden Age, of Adam to the Garden. But Williams'
pastoral (like that of the Precisionists) is also a distinctively Ameri-
can version of the myth, reworking the meaning of the new world
that is to be born. Although the return to harmony that Williams'
representative American family experiences is temporary and provi-
sional—next year they must symbolically repeat the rite of burning
all they have built—the joyous conclusion of the poem envisions an
ever-immanent rebirth of that Golden Age here and now, in the
United States. The poem ends not merely with a glimpse of a new
landscape but a Columbus-like discovery of an American Eden.

Williams' Precisionist lyrics are thus poems about prophetic vision
as well as the accurate recording of what is to be seen. Their concep-
tion of being "witnesses" to their age is hardly photographic or even
merely optic, at least as those words are usually (and narrowly) used.
Their pastoral vision has much in common with the *prospective* eye
celebrated by Emerson and Whitman, particularly the Emerson of
"Circles" and *Nature*. For this reason, references to vision play cru-
cial roles throughout "Christmas Greens." The moment the greens
catch fire is terrifying to watch: all "recognition" of what they were is
lost (l. 4), and the family's eyes momentarily "recoil" from the sight
(l. 59). Even more disturbingly, Nature's indifferent and destructive
power in the poem is represented as a malevolent "smoldering eye"
(l. 38) ready to destroy everything that mankind builds. The poem's
prophetic pastoral vision of a new world must *stare down* this chal-
lenging gaze, transform its holocaust into a vision of hope. One way
to read the drama of "Christmas Greens," therefore, is as a complex
gloss on the ending of Emerson's *Nature*: "As when the summer
comes from the south the snow-banks melt and the face of the earth
becomes green before it, so shall the advancing spirit create its orna-

ments along its path . . . it shall draw beautiful faces, warm hearts, wise discourse, and heroic acts, around its way, until evil is no more seen. The kingdom of man over nature, which cometh not with observation . . . he shall enter without more wonder than the blind man feels who is gradually restored to perfect sight."[43] Such an optative gaze is fundamentally the Precisionists' as well; the pastoral strain in their photographs, paintings, and essays is strongly mixed with prophecy, and their goal is not merely to depict America's modernity but to refashion an older vision of the Edenic potential of the New World so that it will be applicable to America's urban, industrial future.

The rich union of ideas from art and literature in many of Williams' Precisionist lyrics should not blind us to the struggles that came earlier in his career. When Williams first felt the poverty of his early Symbolist verse, he turned to the visual arts almost in desperation, certain that literary tradition had little to offer him and that the only really new and exciting artistic work being done in America was in the visual realm. So complex was his involvement in the arts that the two other most important formative influences on Williams from the visual arts—Cubism and Dada—have yet to be fully distinguished from each other and discussed. Encouraged by the avant-garde ideas he got from the arts, Williams often succumbed to temptation and divided all writers into those who championed the "new" and those who were merely "traditionalists of plagiarism" (CP1, 182). But a study of Williams' contact with the Precisionists shows that his poetry used the visual arts to renew, not renounce, literary tradition.

43. Stephen E. Whicher (ed.), Selections from Ralph Waldo Emerson (New York, 1957), 56.

TWO/THE POLYPHONY OF VOICES
Williams' Cubist Odes

> The new Little Review may print a short poem of mine. But the
> best work is still to be written. It will have edges—
> —William Carlos Williams to Marjorie Allen Sieffert

Williams studied Cubism concurrently with Precisionism,
and one of the most influential early descriptions of Cubism that
Williams read was an article by Marius de Zayas in the March, 1915,
issue of *291*, published in New York. Calling Cubist art "Simul-
tanism," de Zayas argued that it was concerned with "the simul-
taneous representation of the different figures of a form seen from
different points of view, as Picasso and Braque did some time ago." De
Zayas also defined a literary version of such an idea, though he was
skeptical that it would work on the page: "In literature the idea is
expressed by the polyphony of simultaneous voices which say differ-
ent things. Of course, printing is not an adequate medium, for suc-
cession in this medium is unavoidable and a phonograph is more
suitable."[1]

---

1. The de Zayas quotation is from *291*, I (March, 1915). Bram Dijkstra was the first critic to
attempt a comprehensive study of the influence of Cubist art and thought on Williams, in
Cubism, Stieglitz, and the Early Poetry of William Carlos Williams, especially 47–81. Mike
Weaver's *William Carlos Williams: The American Background* also added to our knowledge of this
subject, 37–42. But recently some of their conclusions about what Williams could have known
about Cubism have been modified in important ways by other scholars, including Perloff, *The
Poetics of Indeterminacy*; Sayre, *The Visual Text of William Carlos Williams*; Sayre, "Avant-Garde
Dispositions: Placing *Spring and All* in Context," *William Carlos Williams Review*, X (Fall, 1984),
13–24; Marling, *William Carlos Williams and the Painters*; Christopher MacGowan, *William
Carlos Williams' Early Poetry: The Visual Arts Background* (Ann Arbor, Mich., 1984); and
Patrick Moore, "Cubist Prosody: William Carlos Williams and the Conventions of Verse
Lineation," *Philological Quarterly*, LXV (Fall, 1986), 515–36. Perloff's, Sayre's, and Moore's are
the best discussions of Williams and Cubism, but Marling's book contains a very sensible
analysis of the dangers of applying too broadly the term *Cubist* to Williams' poetry on pp. 128–
33. Of the many general discussions of Cubism and its cultural context, the following are
especially recommended: Guillaume Apollinaire, *The Cubist Painters*, trans. Lionel Abel
(1949; rpr. New York, 1970); Arthur Jerome Eddy, *Cubism and Post-Impressionism* (Chicago,
1914); Roger Shattuck, *The Banquet Years: The Origins of the Avant-Garde in France, 1885 to*

De Zayas' definition was indebted to an article on Simultanism in poetry by Guillaume Apollinaire in the June 15, 1914, issue of *Les Soirées de Paris*, in which he defined a new species of "conversation poem" inspired by Cubist collages wherein "the poet at the center of life records its ambient lyricism." To do this, Apollinaire walked the streets and collected sense impressions and scraps of overheard conversation, merging them with his own first-person voice without transitions, connectives, quotation marks, or other devices to indicate who was speaking or where their voices left off and the poet's began. One poem, "Lundi Rue Christine," published in the December 15, 1913, issue of *Les Soirées*, mixed bits of conversation and narration more provocatively than any other poem of Apollinaire's from the period:

> I'm leaving on the 8:27
> Six mirrors in there all just staring at one
>   another
> In my opinion we're only at the beginning of this mess
> My dear Sir
> You stink you dirty crapper
> That lady's nose reminds me irresistibly of a
>   tapeworm
> Louise forgot her furs
> Well I haven't a fur to my name but I'm never in
>   the least bit cold
> The Dane perusing the train schedule puffs restlessly
>   at his cigarette
> The black cat crosses the bar-room floor[2]

Although Apollinaire called such agglomerations "conversation poems," they do not exhibit the unity or direction of a conversation in a drawing room. Rather, they reflect the isolated but simultaneous actions in the public places of modern cities, where many unrelated conversations and events may be juxtaposed by chance. To emphasize such connections, Apollinaire would sometimes stress the arbi-

---

World War I (1958; rpr. New York, 1968); Robert Rosenblum, *Cubism and Twentieth-Century Art* (New York, 1961); Rosalind Krauss, *Passages in Modern Sculpture* (New York, 1977), 39–67; Krauss, "Re-Presenting Picasso," *Art in America*, LXVIII (December, 1980), 90–96; Krauss, "In the Name of Picasso," *October*, XVI (Spring, 1981), 6–22; Marius de Zayas, "How, When, and Why Modern Art Came to New York," *Arts Magazine*, LIV (April, 1980), 96–126; Davidson, *Early American Modernist Painting*, 74–120; Wendy Steiner, *The Colors of Rhetoric: Problems in the Relation Between Modern Painting and Literature* (Chicago, 1982), 177–96; Marjorie Perloff, "The Invention of Collage," *Collage*, X–XI (1983), 5–47; Charles Altieri, "Picasso's Collages and the Force of Cubism," *Kenyon Review*, VI (Spring, 1984), 8–33.

   2. These excerpts from Apollinaire's article have been translated by Shattuck, in *The Banquet Years*, 286, and by Michael Benedikt in Benedikt (ed.), *The Poetry of Surrealism* (Boston, 1975), 25.

trary place and time in which the action recorded in his poems occurred, as in the title "Lundi Rue Christine" ("Monday Christine Street"). If Apollinaire's poems were inspired by Cubist collages, however, they nevertheless drew vigorously upon literary sources as well. For they are essentially a rethinking of the dramatic monologue form: as the whole text of "Lundi Rue Christine" makes clear, a single speaker remains dominant, "at the center of life," yet his voice also "records" the sights and sounds surrounding him and interrupts his own meditations on them.

When de Zayas wrote in *291* of a Cubist "polyphony" of voices, Williams ought to have placed it in the context of Apollinaire's conversation poems. *Les Soirées* was received regularly by Stieglitz and was used as a model for de Zayas's magazine *291*, which honored Apollinaire by reproducing his poem "Voyage" in its first issue, in March, 1915. *Les Soirées* was also discussed by the artists who frequented Stieglitz's gallery and his lunchtime sessions at the Prince George Hotel in which new developments in the New York and European avant-garde were examined. Regular attendants at those sessions included two of Williams' closest friends, Marsden Hartley and Alfred Kreymborg, but not, apparently, Williams himself, who visited Stieglitz's gallery many times but felt more comfortable with another patron of the avant-garde, Walter Arensberg, than with the more formal Stieglitz. Around 1915, however, Kreymborg became a central figure in the arguments about Cubism and new poetic forms at the artist's colony at Grantwood, New Jersey, that Williams said were a turning point in his career. It seems reasonable to assume that because of Williams' contacts with Stieglitz, de Zayas, and Kreymborg, he had at least heard of if not read Apollinaire's experiments in Cubist poetry and knew that Apollinaire's innovations included what de Zayas called "the polyphony of simultaneous voices." It was after the publication of the first issue of *291* and those discussions of Cubist poetry and painting at Grantwood in 1915 that Williams began experimenting with dramatic monologues that include many different voices, quite unlike the monologues in his earlier volume *The Tempers* (1913).[3]

3. My information in this paragraph is based on Williams, *The Autobiography of William Carlos Williams* (1951; rpr. New York, 1967), 134–42; Dijkstra, *Cubism, Stieglitz, and the Early Poetry of William Carlos Williams*, 3–46; and Mariani, *William Carlos Williams: A New World Naked*, 116–86. Dijkstra first identified de Zayas's piece in *291* as an important source for Williams' understanding of Cubist art and literature, but he did not mention that de Zayas' phrase "polyphony of simultaneous voices" alludes to Apollinaire's ideal of "conversation

Two other texts on Cubism known to Williams before he wrote *Spring and All* in 1923 are the two that laid the foundation for the understanding of Cubism that we have today, Albert Gleizes' *Du cubisme* (1912), written in collaboration with Jean Metzinger, and Apollinaire's *Meditations Esthetiques: Les Peintres cubistes* (1913). *Du cubisme* was translated into English in 1913, but Williams apparently came to know it from the author himself (or other Grantwood members), for Gleizes was briefly a member of the Grantwood group. Before coming to America, Gleizes had been at the center of Le Section d'Or, a circle of Cubist painters including Metzinger, Jacques Villon, Marcel Duchamp, and Fernand Leger that enthusiastically adopted the new pictorial language invented by Georges Braque and Pablo Picasso, exhibited at the Salon des Independents, held frequent meetings discussing theory, and carefully engineered publicity for their work by conducting interviews and publishing articles. Because both Braque and Picasso distrusted theorizing and remained aloof, Gleizes' group (along with Apollinaire) became the principal interpreters of Cubism for the general public. *Du cubisme* marks the culmination of their theorizing, and it is probable that the intellectual luggage of Le Section d'Or, if not *Du cubisme* itself, arrived in New York City and New Jersey with Gleizes. It may be odd to contemplate the leader of an exclusive Parisian avant-garde group leaving the city that was the center of European civilization and suddenly appearing, as if through a trapdoor, in a weekend artist's colony in rural New Jersey. But such are the underground passageways of art and literary history.

Gleizes' conception of Cubism has two main points. Placing Cubism firmly within the tradition of the French Modernism that began with Manet and the Impressionists, Gleizes argued, first, that Cubism was born of a distrust of the "whole" images given to us by the retina. Cubist art holds that these images, rather than being natural, are in fact largely conventional and artificial, being formed by past art: "The crowd long remains the slave of the painted image, and persists in seeing the world only through the adopted sign. That is why any new form seems monstrous, and why the most slavish imitations are admired." As a consequence, Cubist art chooses not to reproduce those images that we have been conditioned to accept as

---

poems," and he did not consider whether de Zayas and Apollinaire influenced more of Williams' work than *Kora in Hell* (Dijkstra, *Cubism, Stieglitz, and the Early Poetry of William Carlos Williams*, 67–76).

"realistic." It recognizes that "whole" objects and perspectival space are in themselves illusions, rational inventions or adopted sign systems inherited from art since the Renaissance. Although these inventions may be true to much of our visual experience, they are not true to all, particularly to those experiences that do not have a single-point perspective—the different views we have of an object over time, for example, or when we place it within conflicting sign-systems. "An object has not one absolute form, it has several," Gleizes maintained.[4]

Gleizes' second point was consequently that Cubism's task was to reproduce these different forms or perspectives simultaneously, as they might appear before the mind's eye. To do this, Cubism mimics the mind's power to abstract and synthesize its different impressions of the world into new "wholes," new sign systems. These new images or signs form a second, man-made nature, standing apart from the first but equal to it. "A painting carries within itself its raison d'etre. . . . Essentially independent, necessarily complete . . . it is an organism." Williams would have heard of both of these principles at Grantwood in 1915, and since his own education in Cubism had just begun, it seems reasonable to assume that the formulations of a Cubist artist and theorist newly arrived from Paris (whether heard only in conversation or also read) would have made a lasting impression.[5]

Williams came to know Apollinaire's *Les Peintres cubistes* more indirectly, but evidence of his knowledge of it is more secure. It was published in French in 1913, but Williams apparently read it first in translation in three issues of *The Little Review* (Spring, Autumn, and Winter, 1922) just as he was working on *Spring and All*. As Marjorie Perloff has pointed out, Williams was so excited by the essay that he immediately dashed off a letter to the magazine before it had even finished printing the Apollinaire article; it appeared in the "Letters" section along with the second installment. The letter repays study, for 1922 is the year in which *Spring and All* was written. Williams singles out Apollinaire ("I enjoyed thoroughly, absorbedly, Apollinaire's article") and salutes the issue as a whole: it is "a distinct success: it gives me the sense of being arrived, as of any efficient engine in motion, the sense of being on the tracks or resting on its

4. *Du cubisme* is excerpted in Robert L. Herbert, ed., *Modern Artists on Art* (Englewood Cliffs, N.J., 1964), 1–18.
5. *Ibid.*

wings firmly in the air if you prefer."[6] That last image, of a bird beating its wings against the air, occurs again near the conclusion of the prose of *Spring and All*, during a crucial passage in which Williams tries to express his art's relation to reality: "As birds' wings beat the solid air without which none could fly so words freed by the imagination affirm reality by their flight" (*I*, 150). Whether or not Williams consciously repeated the metaphor, his use of it for the conclusion of *Spring and All* is telling: it means that Williams found his own experiments creating "new forms, new names for experience" (*I*, 117) to have "arrived" at the same level of sophistication as the French theorists of Cubism.

The first installment of Apollinaire's essay in *The Little Review* contained Part I of *Les Peintres cubistes* in its entirety. Part I included a rather general, neo-Symbolist meditation on progress and purity in the arts and divided Cubist painters into several eccentric categories, none of which caught on. Williams, however, would have recognized several of Apollinaire's points as being eloquent, aphoristic restatements of Gleizes, whom Apollinaire modestly called "le premier theoricien du Cubisme."[7]

Like Gleizes, Apollinaire argued that the public's conception of reality has in fact been created by earlier artists and that "it is the social function of the great poets and the great painters to renew unceasingly the appearance which nature assumes in the eyes of men." He also claimed that the modern artist has renounced the imitation of familiar retinal images ("the reality of sight") in favor of his divine right to recreate nature according to his own inner vision of it: "Each divinity creates after his own images: so too, the painters." This artistic creation must thus contain within itself its own reason for being: "The picture must exist inevitably. The vision will be entire, complete." Such a vision must of necessity be a new sign system: "Today scholars no longer hold to the three dimensions of the euclidean geometries. The painters have been led quite naturally and, so to speak, by intuition, to preoccupy themselves with possible

---

6. For Apollinaire's articles, see *The Little Review*, VIII (Spring, 1922), 7–19; IX (Autumn, 1922), 41–59; and IX (Winter, 1922), 49–60. Apollinaire's translator for the excerpts in *The Little Review* was Mrs. Charles Knoblach, who was connected with the Société Anonyme. The now-standard, annotated translation of *The Cubist Painters* is by Lionel Abel. I quote from *The Little Review* translation throughout. Williams' letter in *The Little Review*, IX (Autumn, 1922), 59–60, is cited by Perloff in *The Poetics of Indeterminacy*, 109–54. Perloff does not consider the relevance of Apollinaire's concept of the "conversation poem" for Williams.
7. Cited by Abel, trans., *The Cubist Painters*, 61n.

new measures of space, which, in the language of modern studios has been designated briefly and altogether by the term the *fourth* dimension. . . . The fourth dimension . . . would show the immensity of space eternalized in every direction at a given moment. It is space itself, the dimension of the infinite: it is this which endows objects with their plasticity." Different views of an object are to be joined together on the Cubist bas-relief plane, "eternalized in every direction," giving images in art a newly discovered "plasticity" that would be equivalent to Einstein's newly announced four-dimensional relativity in physics.[8]

The second part of Apollinaire's article, entitled "New Painters" and published in the Autumn and Winter issues, includes specific discussion of Picasso, Braque, Gleizes, Duchamp, Gris, and others, accompanied by reproductions of a representative work by each. Of these short sketches, Apollinaire's enraptured and luminous appreciation of Picasso's art is by far the most important. Beginning by evoking Picasso's Blue and Rose periods, Apollinaire then considered the Cubist works. First, he gave a succinct description of Cubism's simultaneous perspectives, its use of "the fourth dimension": "Imitating the planes to represent volumes, Picasso gives to the divers elements which compose the objects an enumeration so complete, so sharp that they do not take the shape of the object." Cubist planes do not reproduce the illusion of three-dimensional volume but rather "enumerate" and make us self-conscious of the sign system by which the illusion of volume is created in Western art. Following Gleizes' assertion that such space is an adopted sign system, Apollinaire thus understood Cubism to be not merely an analysis of the "natural" truths of sight but of the cultural conventions or sign systems by which such illusions of three dimensions are created.[9]

Apollinaire then made a point nowhere mentioned by Gleizes, yet one that has since become essential to any understanding of Cubism's second, most important phase, now known as Synthetic Cubism and identified by its use of collage. He defined Braque's and Picasso's use of collage as *the* quintessential Cubist invention because it juxtaposes objects from the "real" world of sight with fragments of pictorial sign systems used to describe that world. Picasso "has not disdained to

---

8. *The Little Review*, VIII (Spring, 1922), 13. Through passages such as this one, Apollinaire's article also emerges as an important early source for Williams' later interest in the relation between a poet's "possible new measures" and Einsteinian relativity.
9. *Ibid.*, IX, 44.

confide actual objects to the light, a tu'penny song, a real postage stamp, a bit of oil cloth on which is printed the caning of a chair. The art of the painter would not add a single picturesque element to the verity of these objects." A paragraph later, Apollinaire defends the practice even more eloquently: "Surprise laughs savagely in the purity of the light, and it is legitimate that numbers, moulded letters should appear as picturesque elements, new in art, but long since impregnated with humanity." As Apollinaire well understood, such a juxtaposition of real objects and the signs meant to refer to them had revolutionary implications for the meaning of mimesis. "The real object or an illusion is no doubt called upon to play a more and more important role. It is the inner frame of the picture and marks the limits of its profundity, in the same way that the frame marks its exterior limits." Such a conception of Cubist collage was a good deal more accurate than Gleizes' rather romantic emphasis on Cubism's supposed organic unity.[10]

Roger Shattuck has done much to elucidate the meaning of Apollinaire's cryptic phrase "the inner frame of the picture," as well as his equation of real objects with illusionary ones. Shattuck states: "A sample of the real world erupts in the middle of a work of art and violates its separateness. The internal frame, being a gap or an intrusion, does not delimit one realm from the other but fuses art with reality. The newspaper clippings in cubist collages serve to link them to the surrounding world of events, and real fragments fill the poems of Max Jacob, Cendrars, and Reverdy." He continues: "This is no longer mere self-reflexiveness, art about art, but, rather, a disconcerting and amusing subversion of artistic immunity. We see through the internal frame (a fragment of reality) to ourselves seeing the work which now contains us. When the distinctions of art and reality have broken down, we are ourselves incorporated into the structure of a work of art. Its very *form* importunes us to enter an expanded community of creation which now includes artist and spectator, art and reality."[11]

Shattuck's paradox of the frame that unites art and reality is taken one step further by Robert Rosenblum, who argues that Cubist collages make life imitate art, not the other way around. Noting that Apollinaire's phrase "a bit of oilcloth on which is printed the caning of a chair" alludes to a particular collage of Picasso's, *Still Life with*

10. *Ibid.*, 44.
11. Shattuck, *The Banquet Years*, 330–31.

Chair Caning (1912), Rosenblum stresses that Picasso did not merely introduce real objects; he included a supposedly real object, an oilcloth scrap, covered with a pattern *imitating* something it was not, chair caning. "The oilcloth," Rosenblum writes,

> is demonstrably more "real" than the illusory Cubist still-life objects, for it is not a fiction created by the artist but an actual machine-made fragment from the external world. Yet, in its own terms, it is as false as the painted objects around it, for it purports to be only chair-caning but is only oilcloth. To enrich this irony, the most unreal Cubist objects seem to have a quality of true depth, especially the *trompe l'oeil* pipe stem. . . . Moreover, this destruction of the traditional mimetic relationship between art and reality becomes even more emphatic by the very choice of a material that in itself offers a deception. For here Picasso mocks the illusions painstakingly created by the artist's hand by rivaling them with the perhaps more skillful illusions impersonally stamped out by a machine. If reality is a relative matter, so, too, is the reality of this seemingly real chair caning, which is actually oilcloth.[12]

Thus although Cubist art retained the Symbolist belief that the work of art creates a second nature apart from the first, the Cubist's vision of the autonomy of the work of art is considerably more problematic and ironic. Instead of transcending the world, Cubist art turns it inside out, multiplying and merging objects and their representations *ad infinitum.* The real world is shown to be only a sign system that we take to be natural, whereas the best art is a sign system that teaches us that art and nature are cultural and historical constructs that (in Apollinaire's words) are "impregnated with humanity."

In *Spring and All* and in his prologue to *Kora in Hell,* Williams demonstrates a canny understanding of both Cubist theory and practice. He discusses the subject differently from Apollinaire or Gleizes, however, by interlacing their rhapsodic confidence with a caustic sense of humor and his native Yankee pugnacity.

Both *Kora in Hell* and *Spring and All* share with Cubism an urgent revolt against the past. Like Gleizes and Apollinaire, Williams defines tradition largely in terms of conventional or habitual ways of describing what is real. He boasts that he seeks "a break with banality, the continual hardening that habit enforces," implying that "naturally" whole images on the picture plane (or the retina) are merely borrowed "apparitions" to be shattered. "The attention has been held too rigid on one plane instead of following a more flexible, jagged resort. . . . The so-called natural or scientific array becomes

12. Rosenblum, *Cubism and Twentieth-Century Art,* 68–69.

fixed, the walking devil of modern life. He who even nicks the solidity of this apparition does a piece of work superior to that of Hercules when he cleaned the Augean stables" (I, 14). Williams also applies these general ideas specifically to literature. In Spring and All he uses the analogy of plagiarism to explain how tradition dictates to contemporary writers, robbing them of their own voice: the artist must free himself of "demoded" words and conventional associations "because meanings have become lost through laziness or changes in the form of existence which have let words empty" (I, 100). "Nothing is good save the new," Williams argued in his prologue to Kora in Hell (I, 23), and in Spring and All he imagines a comic apocalypse in which all forms of representation are destroyed so that artists may recreate the world anew.

Williams also stresses a second tenet of Cubism, that art creates a second reality to rival the first. Gleizes said that a painting was an "essentially independent, necessarily complete" organism, and Apollinaire that it must be "entire, complete." Williams, in turn, claims in Spring and All that art "must be real, not 'realism' but reality itself—; . . . It is not a matter of 'representation' . . . but of separate existence" (I, 117). He elaborates that "Nature is the hint to composition . . . because it possesses that quality of independent existence, of reality which we feel in ourselves. It is not opposed to art but apposed to it" and that "poetry has to do with the crystallization of the imagination—the perfection of new forms as additions to nature" (I, 121, 140). Williams also shows that he intuitively understood what Apollinaire meant by the "inner frame." Like Apollinaire, he defends the Cubist artist's right to include "familiar, simple things . . . touched by the hands during the day." But these "found objects" must then, in Williams' word, be "detached" from ordinary experience and placed within a composition (I, 110–11). At first glance, Williams appears merely to be describing a Gris painting, not Cubist collage techniques, because he refers to the Gris painting The Open Window (1921), which does not employ collage. But later references to Cubism in Spring and All make it clear that the detaching process that Williams has in mind also includes collage. Williams' principal analogy for detaching subject matter is verbal rather than visual; instead of speaking of found objects, he mentions "plagiarism" or quotation.

Williams' choice of the word plagiarism to describe one aspect of Cubist art is bound to seem puzzling to readers of Spring and All, for aside from being a word with distinctively negative connotations, it is also a word that Williams uses elsewhere in *Spring and All* to attack traditional art. He had castigated certain contemporary artists for advocating illusionistic "realism" in painting—"plagiarism after nature"—and in literature, "THE TRADITIONALISTS OF PLAGIARISM" (*I*, 111, 97). In both cases, such artists slavishly "employ that which has been made use of before" (*I*, 97). Yet elsewhere in *Spring and All* he advocates a "perfect plagiarism" in which "everything is and is new" while "only the imagination is undeceived" (*I*, 93). Williams' contradictory uses of *plagiarism* are an interpretive crux, for he uses *plagiarism* to praise new art and to damn traditional art without defining the various meanings it has for him, other than to imply that some forms of plagiarism are "perfect" and others are not.

If Apollinaire's definition of the inner frame of Cubist art is kept in mind, however, Williams' ambiguities may perhaps be clear. Apollinaire had said that "the real object or an illusion is . . . the inner frame." In *Spring and All*, Williams glosses Apollinaire's point. When "perfect plagiarism" occurs in painting and in poetry, it is perfect only if "the onlooker is not for a moment permitted to witness [the images] as an 'illusion.' One thing laps over on the other, the cloud laps over on the shutter, the bunch of grapes is part of the handle of the guitar, the mountain and sea are obviously not 'the mountain and sea,' but a picture of the mountain and the sea. All drawn with admirable simplicity and excellent design—all a unity—" (*I*, 111). Earlier in *Spring and All*, Williams had stated the same point more abstractly: "The terms 'veracity' 'actuality' 'real' 'natural' 'sincere' are being discussed at length, every word in the discussion being evolved from an identical discussion which took place the day before yesterday. Yes, the imagination, drunk with prohibitions, has destroyed and recreated everything afresh in the likeness of that which it was. Now indeed men look about in amazement at each other with a full realization of the meaning of 'art'" (*I*, 93). Following Gleizes and Apollinaire, Williams argues that Cubist art transforms the very nature of mimesis itself, so that concepts like "natural" or "likeness" are shown precisely for what they are—fictions that a particular culture has codified as "natural." Such a realization, Williams believes, represents a quantum jump, a new evolutionary stage in man's understanding of culture. We may *use* the same terms as we did yesterday, but now they require quotation marks: they are our own inventions, impregnated (for better or worse) with our prejudices.

Just as Apollinaire stressed that Cubist art parodies or "imitates" the process of imitation itself, so Williams argues that true art (as opposed to "art") must be a "perfect plagiarism" in which the techniques of imitation and representation are called into question as well as exploited.

The art of composition in *Spring and All* thus involves a twofold process. First, material that had not been used before in literature may be included, regardless of the breach of decorum that results. Such material must then be analyzed and reordered in the work so that several different, even conflicting views of it are presented at the same time and then fiercely held in balance. The artist must not pretend to present his subject without distortion but must reproduce it in such a way that we are forced to see that his representations of it are tentative, plural, and necessarily self-contradictory versions of the "real." Picture-frames can no longer offer us a neutral window to the world or a stable division between art and nature; what Cubism gives us instead are frames within frames, fictions set against fictions. *Reality* is a word that now must always bear quotation marks, or be spoken of in the plural.

Many of Williams' poems embody these Cubist principles. The admirer of Williams' work must admit, however, that although Williams' discussion of Cubist principles in *Spring and All* is often eloquent, it is also contradictory, defensive, and incomplete, both from the standpoint of Cubism itself and from that of Williams' own poems. Not only is his contradictory use of the word *plagiarism* bewildering, but he often has difficulty defining terms and paraphrasing abstract principles that had been sketched by Gleizes or Apollinaire but captured best only in painting, in the work of Demuth, Picasso, Gris. Hence there are the awkward starts, stops, restarts, run-ons, mixed metaphors, and contradictions that make the argument of *Spring and All* so energetically unparaphrasable: "Poetry does not tamper with the world but moves it—It affirms reality most powerfully and therefore, since reality . . . exists free from human action, as proven by science in the indestructibility of matter and of force, it creates a new object, a play, a dance which is not a mirror up to nature but—As birds' wings beat the solid air without which none could fly so words freed by the imagination affirm reality by their flight" (*I*, 149–50). Williams in *Spring and All* is also not very precise about whether Cubism's visual innovations could be translated from pictures into *literary* forms, or whether any writers had developed a Cubist style that he thought was successful.

Many of these inconsistencies are calculated, of course; they are part of *Spring and All*'s pedagogic method, which progresses in a Cubist mode, through contraries and contradictions rather than through linear argument. Williams' intense seriousness may often remind us of the Cubists' equal intensity, their belief that they could include newspaper clippings in their work because their art contained news about the complexities of modern life that could not be found elsewhere. In *Guitar, Sheet Music, and Wine Glass* (1912), one of Picasso's cropped headlines read, "La Bataille s'est engage" (see Illustration 4). *Spring and All* may also be read as a battle cry, as a series of bulletins from the front. Yet the Cubists were as interested in art's role as *jou* as well as its role as *un journal*. Above the headline about "La Bataille" in Picasso's painting, for example, are the words *Le Jou*. A Cubist painting by Juan Gris that was owned by Walter Arensberg and well known to Williams, *The Open Window: Place Ravignan*, includes just such a pun, and *Spring and All* provides us with all the evidence we need to prove that Williams well understood the Cubist's desire to provide *jou* and *jouissance* as well as up-to-the-moment cultural news. Thus every argument for avant-garde art in *Spring and All* is also confuted and parodied; every definition is shown to be inadequate. "It is a hard battle. I myself seek to enter the lists with these few notes jotted down in the midst of the action," Williams says at one point. But then he ambushes his argument's pretensions and parodies academic seriousness with a comically pedantic footnote: "In the midst of the action, under distracting circumstances—to remind myself (see p. 89, paragraph 2) of the truth" (*I*, 98). (That paragraph is a one-sentence celebration of *difference* in all its guises: "But today it is different.") Many of the inconsistencies in *Spring and All* hence are examples of what we would now call the book's deconstructive play: Williams understood that Cubism's *jou* could not be discussed too solemnly, despite the importance of the issues at stake. [13]

13. The ground-breaking analyses of the indeterminacies of *Spring and All* are J. Hillis Miller, "Williams' *Spring and All* and the Progress of Poetry," *Daedalus*, XCIX (1970), 415–29; and Perloff's chapter on it in *The Poetics of Indeterminacy*. See also three articles in a recent symposium on *Spring and All* in the *William Carlos Williams Review*, X (Fall, 1984): Thomas R. Whitaker, "*Spring and All*: Teaching Us the Figures of the Dance," 1–6; Lisa Steinman, "Once More, with Feeling: Teaching *Spring and All*," 7–12; and Henry Sayre, "Avant-Garde Dispositions: Placing *Spring and All* in Context," 13–24.

Pablo Picasso, *Guitar, Sheet Music, and Wine Glass*
The Marion Koogler McNay Art Museum, Bequest of Marion Koogler McNay

The indeterminacies of *Spring and All* may be read for the uncon-scious as well as conscious intentions that they reflect, however. The contradictions, gaps, and deferrals in the text, however calculated, in part also result from Williams' own anxieties about being worthy to enter what he called the "lists" of the heroes of the avant-garde (*I*, 98). De Zayas, Gleizes, Apollinaire and the Grantwood group were all crucial formative influences on Williams' Cubist aesthetic, but they are nowhere mentioned in his most important avant-garde manifesto. And if he talks with ease about the revolutionary implica-tions of Cubism for painting, he endlessly defers any very particular analysis of the prospects for *literary* Cubism. Indeed, Williams' most explicit comment on the possibilities of literary Cubism came not in *Spring and All* but many years later, in his autobiography. Remember-ing the Grantwood discussions but neglecting to name names, he said: "We'd have arguments over cubism which would fill up an afternoon. There was a comparable whipping up of interest in the structure of the poem. It seemed daring to omit capitals at the head of each poetic line. Rhyme went by the board" (*A*, 136). Williams emphasizes the independence and inventiveness of the Grantwood artists here, but he lets slip that he was indeed familiar with at least some of the experimental Cubist poetry that Apollinaire had pub-lished in *Les Soirées*, for Apollinaire's free, Cubist verse was then notable for the very things that Williams cites as being characteristic of literary Cubism—the absence of rhyme and the experimentation with new kinds of typography. Williams does not further define his phrase "the structure of the poem"; in fact, the above passage in the autobiography unfortunately implies that he thought of structure and typography as being almost the same thing. Yet because Apollinaire's conversation poems in *Les Soirées* are also important for their experi-ments with the structure and the conception of the dramatic mono-logue—particularly in their use of what de Zayas called a "polyphony of voices"—Williams may have had those changes in mind when he spoke of a Cubist "structure." Indeed, several poems discussed later in this chapter experiment with the dramatic monologue in ways similar enough to Apollinaire's to support this hypothesis. Despite the apparent importance for Williams of Apollinaire's poems and essay, however, Williams never mentions him in *Spring and All*, *Contact*, or his later autobiography. He is similarly silent on how the techniques he associated with Cubism could be adapted to literature. He never specifies what the literary equivalent of the found objects in

Cubism painting might be, for example, nor does his prose in *Spring and All* show any overt interest in "polyphony" as de Zayas defined it or Apollinaire used it. Perhaps Williams was afraid that if he brought up a connection between Gleizes or Apollinaire and himself, his experimental poetry would thereafter be treated as a belated, provincial version of theirs. Or perhaps he felt that acknowledging a "tradition" of Cubist theory would immediately render it academic and sterile.

Both Williams' seriousness and his self-mockery are more strident than his French competitors'; there is a dark edge of frustration and bitterness around the sparkling fragments that make up *Spring and All* that cannot be found in the Apollonian confidence of Gleizes and Apollinaire. Williams' theoretical discussion of Cubism is thus as full of repressions as it is of revelations. Williams instinctively chose to do his most radical thinking about Cubism in his poetry, trusting his ability to work in the lyric more than in discursive prose. As he somewhat wryly admitted during one particularly chaotic moment of theorizing in *Spring and All*, "Whatever of dull you find among my work, put it down to criticism, not to poetry" (*I*, 111). It is the poems that must embody this brave new world; the job of the prose is merely to announce it. Williams' true bid to join the "lists" of the avant-garde is in part based on the Cubist poems that he wrote before, during, and after *Spring and All*.

Williams' Cubist poems have numerous identifying features. Their forms are marked by fragmentation and juxtaposition. Many of the sentences in these poems are grammatical fragments (often signaled by dashes), and these fragments tend to cluster in groups without a set left-hand margin and with plenty of white space around the lines. The poems also speak in many voices, but sometimes one voice comes to dominate, usually that of the character who figures centrally in the poem's narrative. Some revel in employing a verbal version of Cubist quotation, juxtaposing "real" but also highly artificial "found" language with words that are the poet's own. When they do this their intent is precisely the same as that of a Synthetic Cubist collage, to question boundaries that have been drawn between "reality" and "art." Finally, like all Cubist art, these poems delight in the power of artifice, the mind's rage to order. As Williams developed this style after *Spring and All*, however, his Cubist poems began to explore how such creative acts counter the constant presence of death and disintegration. In doing so, his Cubist style became more autumnal, less springlike.

As with Precisionism, Williams' exploration of the possibility of creating a literary Cubist style also involved a rethinking of the relevance of a traditional lyric form. In this case, the form was not the pastoral poem but the ode—particularly the greater, or sublime, ode. Williams' interest in the literary uses of polyphony made the ode a natural form to turn to, for it is originally choral in form, emphasizing contrasting voices and often an irregular meter. Williams' exploration of the possibilities of such a form began gradually and developed fairly slowly; his first experiments with Cubist devices were undertaken in the dramatic monologue, and it was only with the odes of the 1930s and 1940s that he began explicitly to call the reader's attention to these poems' literary as well as art historical heritage.

Not all of Williams' experiments with literary Cubism employed lyric forms, of course; beginning with *The Great American Novel* and *In the American Grain* (both of which employ polyphony and fragmentation), and continuing with the prose sections of *The Descent of Winter* and *A Novelette*, Williams explored the possibilities of applying Cubist techniques to narrative as well. There is not enough room here to consider these fascinating texts, unfortunately, though all of them (particularly *The Great American Novel*) deserve more critical attention than they have yet received. Ultimately, Williams would attempt to unite his different Cubist modes (along with many others) in his most ambitious collage text of all—the epic *Paterson*.

Williams' first efforts to write poetry with a Cubist polyphony of voices began soon after he read Marius de Zayas' article linking polyphony and Cubism in *291* in March, 1915. At first, with "March" (1916) and "January Morning" (1917), Williams experimented with polyphony tentatively, as if he still felt dependent upon the dramatic monologue that he had used for so many of the poems he was assembling for publication in *Al Que Quiere!* in 1917. But with "Overture to a Dance of Locomotives" (1917), Williams confidently concluded the poem as Apollinaire might have done, by having the voices of people in a train station (in Williams' case, the newly opened Penn Station in New York City) interrupt the meditations of the poem's speaker.[14]

14. This audacious Cubist expansion of the dramatic monologue form may explain why "Overture" was not included in *Al Que Quiere!*, even though it was completed in time to be read at the Independents' Exhibition of the Society of American Artists in New York in April,

In "January Morning," Williams' use of many voices is restrained, a matter of changes of inflection rather than of obviously different characters; the poem remains essentially a dramatic monologue unified by its voice but broken up into very short, fashionably Imagist sections. The poem is about a ferry trip Williams took home to New Jersey after apparently staying up all night on duty in a New York City hospital. The fifteen short sections of the poem, composed of things he saw and imagined on his way home, tend to separate into independent details and different moods, thus pulling against the centripedal forces that a monologue should maintain. The shortness of the stanzas and the incompleteness of the sentences further this fragmenting effect; the most common transition from one sentence fragment to the next is simply a dash and an *and:* "—and the worn, / blue car rails (like the sky!) / gleaming among the cobbles!" (*CP1*, 101). In addition, Williams uses the first person in only four out of seventeen sections and gives us few clues as to who is speaking and what action is taking place. All these aspects of the poem begin to displace the first-person speaker from the center of this monologue, unlike what happens in a classic monologue by Robert Browning or even any of those in *Al Que Quiere!*

This displacement may have been one reason why Williams subtitled the poem "Suite." The name primarily refers to the collection of impressions that make up the poem but may perhaps also be taken to refer to the "suite" of tones in his voice. There is first the sober, reflective voice of the opening section, in which Williams stands the genre of the exotic travel narrative on its head by focusing on the local and the familiar. "I have discovered," the poet reports portentiously, that

> the domes of the Church of
> the Paulist Fathers in Weehawken
> against a smoky dawn—the heart stirred—
> are beautiful as Saint Peters
> approached after years of anticipation
>
> (*CP1*, 100)

1917. Williams may have felt that the plain-spoken monologues of *Al Que Quiere!* were already radical enough, remembering that when he read "Overture" and "Portrait of a Woman in Bed" at the exhibition some of his audience had walked out on him. Williams did include "Portrait" along with the other dramatic monologues in *Al Que Quiere!* but saved "Overture" for his next volume, *Sour Grapes* (1921). For background on Williams' participation in the exhibition's festivities, see Williams' *Autobiography*, 136 (where Williams confuses the show with the Armory Show of four years earlier); Dijkstra, *Cubism, Stieglitz, and the Early Poetry of William Carlos Williams*, 35n; and Mariani, *William Carlos Williams: A New World Naked*, 106. De Zayas' quotation on Cubist polyphony is in *291*, I (March, 1915). On the opening of Penn Station in February, 1913, see Davidson, *Early American Modernist Painting*, 58.

Then there is the exclamatory voice that takes over the poem after the *I* disappears in Section II; it seems to be the voice not of a veteran traveler but of one experiencing the trip for the first time. It excitedly announces the details described in Sections II through VII with merely a dash and an *and* for each:

> —and from basement entries
> neatly coiffed, middle aged gentlemen
> with orderly moustaches and
> well-brushed coats
> (*CPI*, 101)

In the middle of Section VIII, the poem modulates again, as Williams leaves the city behind to board the ferry. Being on the open water increases his excitement, and instead of merely naming objects exuberantly, as he did before, in Sections VIII and IX he addresses them directly and uses extravagant figures of speech as if to portray the excitement of being on the open water. The ferry, christened the *Arden,* is changed by Williams into a dream ship piloted by Shakespeare's Touchstone, while the river's brown waves become adorned with "circlets of silver" and the sky is turned into a magical seagull with "delicate pink feet / and a snowy breast for you [the sea] to / hold to your lips delicately!" (*CPI*, 102).

In Section XI the more sober narrator of Section I returns, speaking as authoritatively as he did in Section I, and on the same topic, too: "Who knows the Palisades as I do / knows the river breaks east from them / above the city" (*CPI*, 102–103). The emphasis here is on the importance of repeated, familiar experience, not the exclamatory revelations of the earlier sections. In Section XII, Williams' mood continues to calm; he describes the long yellow rushes on the approaching New Jersey shore as if they lay still, "in contemplation." The excitement of the city streets and the open water ebbs as the ferry ride nears its end.

Sections XIII and XIV deal with death, and for the first time Williams' voice is tired, caustic, ironic: "Work hard all your young days / and they'll find you too, some morning / staring up under / your chiffonier at its warped / basswood bottom" (*CPI*, 103–104). This memory, perhaps recalling a corpse Williams attended that morning, appears without apparent reason—little that he sees in the landscape would seem to remind him of death. It may be that Williams' slowly fading exuberance prompts it. But the slightly somber mood of these lines contrasts markedly with the unrestrained joy of the earlier sections, or with the joy that returns in the codalike last section of the poem as Williams tells the story of his all-nighter to his mother:

> Well, you know how
> the young girls run giggling
> on Park Avenue [in Rutherford] after dark
> when they ought to be home in bed?
> Well,
> that's the way it is with me somehow.
>
> (CP1, 103–104)

Cynic, giggling girl, young doctor, experienced old-timer who like Henry Thoreau or Whitman knows the joys of traveling close to home—all these characters seem to have bought passage with Williams on the ferry. The poem's strength is that it makes his monologue dramatic and varied. But Williams would only have to vary and to juxtapose these voices more assertively and he would begin moving away from the form of the dramatic monologue altogether.

That is just what happens in the middle of "Overture to a Dance of Locomotives." Williams began by writing a monologue in a single mood, but he ended the poem with suite of contending voices. The slow meditation with which "Overture" opens is not unlike Sections XII or XIII in "January Morning." Here is the third stanza:

> Covertly the hands of a great clock
> go round and round! Were they to
> move quickly and at once the whole
> secret would be out and the shuffling
> of all ants be done forever.
>
> (CP1, 146)

The crowds streaming through the darkened corridors of Penn Station suggest Hades. This impression is strengthened by references elsewhere to "descending stairways" and "earthcolored walls of bare limestone" (CP1, 146). But if these details suggest a lugubrious and bitter portrait of life in an Unreal City like that in Eliot's *The Waste Land*, other details in the same stanzas contradict.[15] Williams' de-

15. Compare *The Waste Land*, I, 60–68:
> Unreal City,
> Under the brown fog of a winter dawn,
> A crowd flowed over London Bridge, so many,
> I had not thought death had undone so many.
> Sighs, short and infrequent, were exhaled.
> And each man fixed his eyes before his feet.
> Flowed up the hill and down King William Street,

scription of the light in the cavernous main hallway of the station, for example, implies that it is womblike: the light is "soft" and "rocks / to and fro, under the domed ceiling" (CP1, 146). Trains then steam into the poem, filling it with their own raw power and dissipating any impression of a wasteland. The marmoreal tetrameter stanzas of the poem's melancholic monologue are shattered by dashes, frequent stanza breaks, eruptive rhythms, and new voices:

> two—twofour—twoeight!
> Porters in red hats run on narrow platforms.
> This way ma'am!
>   —important not to take
> the wrong train!
>   —Lights from the concrete
> ceiling hang crooked but—
>   Poised horizontal
> on glittering parallels the dingy cylinders
> packed with a warm glow—inviting entry—
> pull against the hour. But brakes can
> hold a fixed posture till—
>   The whistle!

(CP1, 146)

Williams ends his poem by comparing the train's androgynous sexual energy to the industrial power that is rebuilding America. The train's passenger cars are phallic, cylinders "packed with a warm glow," but they also seem feminine, "inviting entry." And both the train and the modern technology that it represents are participating in an unending "dance" of movement as "rivers are tunneled," "trestles / cross oozy swampland," and "rails forever parallel / return on themselves infinitely." "Overture to a Dance of Locomotives" begins with a single point of view but then rapidly, even discordantly increases the number of perspectives through which it views its subject. The repetitive motions that seemed so lifeless to the poet at the start of the poem ("inevitable postures infinitely / repeated" is one of his descriptions of the crowd) become by the end movement full of meaning, a dance in which trains, passengers, and the entire city seem to be moving in time, on time.

Williams' poem should not be read as if its depiction of trains belongs to the ironic Modernist tradition of Eliot's *The Waste Land* and *Burnt Norton*, Hart Crane's "The Tunnel" from *The Bridge*, and

---

To where Saint Mary Woolnoth kept the hours
With a dead sound on the final stroke of nine.

Sour Grapes was published in 1921, while Eliot was working on *The Waste Land*. Did Eliot read newly published books by Pound's American friends?

Allen Tate's "The Subway." Although when the poem opens Williams sees the crowd as a dehumanized mob, by the middle of the poem the scene is portrayed more sympathetically, especially when we overhear a porter helping a woman find her train. For Williams, other more celebratory views of the urban world were possible, ones that did not gain their powers by interpreting modern life cynically or ironically. Williams thus uses ventriloquist techniques in "Overture" to a much different end than Eliot was soon to do in *The Waste Land*. Whereas all the voices in Eliot's poem except those chanting religious phrases are viewed ironically, Williams' voices are all examples of the city's productive "dance" of energy. "Overture" and a later poem from *Spring and All*, "Rapid Transit," are the only American poems of the period that do not turn a subway or an underground train journey into a trip through hell. One obvious source of inspiration for "Overture" was Apollinaire, who often treated modern technology as miraculous and who also used a Cubist polyphony of voices to describe the experience of waiting for a train in "Lundi Rue Christine." As for Williams' American mentors, they are, first, Whitman, whose poems "Crossing Brooklyn Ferry," "To a Locomotive in Winter," "Song of the Broad-Axe," and "Passage to India" saw American technology as yet another example of her spiritual and technological progress; and, second, Stieglitz and the Precisionists, who proposed a working industrial model for the ideal modern community. "Overture to a Dance of Locomotives" may not be a fully unified work of art, but it gains interest precisely because of that fact; if the dominant mode at the start of the poem is irony, by the end Williams uses the essentially optimistic urban aesthetic of Whitman, Precisionism, and Apollinaire's Cubism to exorcise it.

After including "Overture to a Dance of Locomotives" in *Sour Grapes* (1921), Williams became intrigued with the possibilities posed by the fragmented ending of that poem. In his next volume, *Spring and All* (1923), he published several Cubist poems, including two that directly pick up where his 1917 train poem left off—"Rapid Transit" (Poem XXV) and "The Rose" (Poem VII). These two works are much more self-consciously Cubist than "Overture," perhaps reflecting the influence of Apollinaire's *Les Peintres cubistes*. They not only collage different voices but also include the paradoxical play between artifice and nature that Apollinaire stressed was essential to Cubism's new aesthetic.

In "Rapid Transit," Williams' use of quotation is a good deal more

complex than in "Overture." It is perhaps partly inspired by Mat-
thew Josephson's article in *Broom* in praise of American advertising,
"The Great American Billboard," which appeared in the November,
1922, issue while Williams was working on *Spring and All.* Williams
quotes the kind of information we might read in a newspaper's inves-
tigative article ("Somebody dies every four minutes / in New York
State"); an excerpt from what sounds like a cliché-ridden promo-
tional brochure describing the places one may visit on New York
City's transit system ("Acres and acres of green grass / wonderful
shade trees, rippling brooks // Take the Pelham Bay Park Branch / of
the Lexington Ave. (East Side) / Line"); a scrap of a pop tune one
might hum while driving ("Ho for the open country"); an argument
between a writer and one of his offended readers ("To hell with you
and your poetry / —You will rot and be blown / through the solar
system"); and the kind of tip one could read in the public-service
announcements displayed on buses and subway cars or mailed to
drivers ("Careful Crossing Campaign / Cross Crossings Cautiously")
(*CP1*, 231–32). Such language introduces the same paradoxes into
Williams' composition that the Cubist painters did in theirs. "Real"
objects or "nonliterary" and merely referential language are often
more stilted and artificial than the controlled, self-conscious artifice
of art. The poem's title is thus rightly chosen. As readers, we get on
board the poem for a rapid, exhilarating shuttle back and forth
between the different ways in which we use and misuse language
every day.

Williams' most famous Cubist poem in *Spring and All,* "The Rose,"
stresses above everything else the artist's responsibility to engender a
second, man-made order that may rival nature's own. The work is
full of playful conflations of the real and the artificial, especially as
they are revealed by the word *edge,* one of the key words in the poem.
Edge comes to mean the physical edge of the rose petals, the edge of
the poetic line as it ends on the page, the boundary between the
physical rose and the roses constructed by the artist in painting and
poetry, and, finally, the interface between traditional and new uses of
the rose in art. Williams can achieve these simultaneous meanings
for the word partly because he employs fragmentary, ambiguous syn-
tax, as in the following lines, where the series of adjectives in the
second stanza refers both to an actual flower petal and to love, to an
artist's own work paying homage to the rose in metal, majolica, and
other media both traditional and contemporary. Each of these con-

structed worlds is autonomous, as Williams said that all Cubist art must be. He therefore describes these artificial worlds as artificial roses placed at the edge of Nature's rose, adjacent to it physically and equal to it in importance:

> It is at the edge of the
> petal that love waits
>
> Crisp, worked to defeat
> laboredness—fragile
> plucked, moist, half-raised
> cold, precise, touching
> (CP1, 195)

Williams' description of this imaginary Cubist still life assumes that a real rose petal has been included in the work (an impossibility, of course, at least for long, but easily conjured up in literature). He thus shows how well he understood Apollinaire's point about the inner frame of the Cubist collage: such a work pretends to juxtapose objects from the real world with man's own reconstructions of them.

Later in "The Rose" Williams seems to reject his previous attempts to describe the rose in order to improvise two more. He doesn't finish one, but the second is a conceit that, carefully elaborated, ends the poem:

> The place between the petal's
> edge and the
>
> From the petal's edge a line starts
> that being of steel
> infinitely fine, infinitely
> rigid penetrates
> the Milky Way
> without contact—lifting
> from it—neither hanging
> nor pushing—
> The fragility of the flower
> unbruised
> penetrates space
> (CP1, 195–96)

These last three stanzas of the poem have all the trademarks of literary Cubism: juxtaposed sentence fragments, including the "scrap" at the start of the quotation; a mixture of the intimate and the monumental; and a heady faith that man's reason (represented here by the steel line) has the right to penetrate, abstract, and reconstruct nature. In part, the poem dramatizes Gleizes' point that the "real" is a construct, a set of "adopted" signs made to seem natural. A rose by any other name would smell as sweet, but it is only through our names and our conventions for using roses that we can know the rose at all or give its scent meaning. These lines also give an emphatic new reading to Apollinaire's dictum that Cubist art must include materials new to art but long since "impregnated with humanity." For Williams implies that all "nature" (not just a single rose) is fundamentally engendered by the mind—by that phallic, rigid "line" that penetrates and recreates all space in the poem and in the world.

These two Cubist poems from *Spring and All* represent an interesting crossroads in Williams' development of a Cubist poetics. After he had decided that he could include many different voices within some of his dramatic monologues, he then had to decide whether to open up the form all the way, as he does in "Rapid Transit," juxtaposing as many voices as possible without letting a single one dominate, or just partially, including many voices but keeping them subordinate to one. "The Rose" in fact represents a compromise. In it, we are given different descriptions of its subject—indeed, it is as if at several points the poem includes its cancelled drafts in the final composition—but the figure of the poet-narrator remains dominant. He stands at the center of his composition, improvising order and commenting upon its importance. The Cubist poems that Williams wrote after *Spring and All* strike different balances; some are as open and as thoroughly heterogeneous as "Rapid Transit"—particularly the poem "April" in the sequence "Della Primavera Trasportata al Morale" (1930), which extends the collage principles of "Rapid Transit" to create one of Williams' longest poems of the period—while others use quotation but always subordinate it to a central voice, such as "The Waitress" (1928), "Sunday" (1931), "Perpetuum Mobile: The City" (1936), "To All Gentleness," "Choral: The Pink Church," and "Russia" (all written in the 1940s). Of these Cubist poems, "The Cod Head" (1932), "The Sea-Elephant" (1930), "Two Pendants" (1949), and "The Desert Music" (1951) are among the most impressive, both for the variety of their voices and for their complex dramatic structure.

"The Cod Head" (1932) appears to be a sort of literary still life created from memories of a summer trip Williams took with his wife in 1931 to the seacoast provinces of Canada. Like some Cubist still

lifes (and very unlike "The Rose"), "The Cod Head" at first appears
to be all fragmentation and no order. Here is the first stanza:

> miscellaneous weed,
> strands, stems, debris—
> firmament
>
> to fishes
>
> (CPI, 357)

Later on the syntax becomes even more splintered, confusing sky and
sea and night and day; it is as if Williams' dashes and line breaks, like
the relentless surf, were pulverizing all they encounter:

> oars whip
> ships churn to bubbles—
> at night wildly
>
> agitate phospores-
> cent midges—but by day
> flaccid
>
> moons in whose
> discs sometimes a red cross
> lives—
>
> (CPI, 357–58)

A later comment on the poem that Williams made is so lucid that,
after one has read the above lines, it may seem that he is speaking of a
different work. He even explains the meaning of the "red cross
discs": "Cod was the only thing being caught at that place [Labrador]
and [I] had seen many of the assistant fishermen cutting up the fish
preparatory to laying the flesh out on prepared boards to be sun-
dried. * You might, in the same poem[,] have wondered about the
"red cross." But there is actually a plainly marked red cross, just like
the ordinary "plus" mark in arithmetic[,] figured on the back of the
large jelly-fish or stingeree [stingever], seen so commonly in the
waters of Labrador. . . . * I saw hundreds of the heads thrown back
into the sea."[16] Admittedly, the "red cross" and the "flaccid moons"
in the poem are probably unintelligible to a reader without Williams'
gloss. But this is the only time when Williams' Cubist fragmentation
in this poem has been perhaps too severe. A supple organizing princi-
ple soon emerges upon rereading, and it turns out that it is the same
one that Williams had used to order other less aggressively frag-

16. Williams to Kenneth Burke, 1945, quoted in Emily Mitchell Wallace, *A Bibliography of William Carlos Williams* (Middletown, Conn., 1968), 34.

mented poems: he follows the imagined movement of the eye as it takes in the scene.

In this case, Williams imagines the journey a visionary eye might take as it views the water's surface, descends "four fathom" to the ocean's floor, then rises again, all the while without its vision being clouded. After repeatedly struggling to find the best way of organizing his poem,[17] Williams decided to mark the stages of his imaginary journey by sounding the fathoms as the poem moved along:

> moons in whose
> discs sometimes a red cross
> lives—four
>
> fathom—the bottom skids
> a mottle of green
> sands backward—
>
> amorphous waver-
> ing rocks—three fathom
> the vitreous
>
> body through which—
> small scudding fish deep
> down—and
>
> now a lulling lift
> and fall—
> red stars—a severed cod-
>
> head between two
> green stones—lifting
> falling
> (CP1, 358)

After opening the poem with a description of the many ways in which the surface of the water may be agitated (oars, propellers, flotsam, jellyfish), Williams dives down four fathoms, then moves up

---

17. Wallace's *Bibliography* cites three earlier versions, in *Contempo*, April 1, 1932; in *Contact* (new series), May, 1932; and a chapbook published by Harvest Press, San Francisco, "probably summer, 1932" (p. 33). Compare *Contact's* version of "The Cod Head":

> moons in whose
> discs sometimes a red cross
> lives—darkly
>
> the bottom skids
> a mottle of green sands
> backward—
>
> amorphous waver-
> ing rocks—a vitreous
> body through
>
> which the oartips—
> small scudding fish deep
> down. . . .

again amid a school of skittish fish at "three fathom," then breaches, floats, and rests, contemplating the lulling (rather than "agitated") lift and fall of the waves. Williams's calculated contrasts between surface and depth and agitation and calm are less discernible in the earlier versions of the poem, principally because he had not yet hit upon the strategy of calling out the fathoms. Despite the broken miscellany of detail, then, a subtle but convincing order has been achieved; Williams is right to call it a "firmament." Moreover, the time he took in cutting, arranging, and revising his sentence fragments is indicative of the central aesthetic of his Cubist poems, as different as they may appear on the surface: care and craft, order and arrangement, are paramount.

Cubist collages were notorious for introducing actual souvenirs of the artist's everyday life into the composition—newsprint, rope, wallpaper, oilcloth, a calling card from a Miss Stein and a Miss Toklas. Other artists who followed Picasso and Braque, especially the Americans Joseph Stella and Arthur Dove and the German Kurt Schwitters (all of whom exhibited in New York City in the 1920s), widened the range of found objects that could be included in still lifes. Dove, a member of Stieglitz's circle, added magazine advertisements, needlepoint, pieces of bamboo fishing rod, and natural objects such as pressed flowers. Schwitters collected scraps of wood, metal, and paper that were not relics of his own life so much as they were the anonymous refuse of urban civilization. "The Cod Head" also includes references to living things and debris, and Williams thinks of all these materials as souvenirs of his Canadian trip. Despite the personal references, though, Williams' own presence in the poem remains austere and impersonal, in the best Cubist manner; we feel the strength of his personality through his arrangement of the objects, not through any commentary or storytelling. By the end of "The Cod Head," Williams has not only redefined the decorum for the proper material in poetry but has also reaffirmed the power of the sharp eye and the shaping mind.[18]

18. Williams knew of Dove's work, for he exhibited regularly in Stieglitz's succession of galleries; for one example of a Dove still life incorporating organic material, see his collage *Long Island*, in Dijkstra, *Cubism, Stieglitz, and the Early Poetry of William Carlos Williams*, Plate XV. With the cases of Stella and Schwitters, the problem of how well Williams knew their work is more vexing. Stella did have a one-man show at the gallery of the Société Anonyme, at 19 East 47th Street, in January, 1923, as announced in *The Little Review*, IX (Autumn, 1922). That same issue of the *Review*, as well as continuing the Apollinaire essay, illustrated several of Stella's still lifes made from scraps of paper, including *The Bookman* and *Study for Skyscraper* (between pp. 32 and 33). Schwitters had exhibitions in New York City of his collages under the

Yet if we continue to contemplate the debris with which the poem is constructed, another thought emerges. "The Cod Head" is as much about chaos as it is about precision and order. The constant motion, the unclear referents, the hallucinatory instability of the lines (which both break apart and run on into each other), the emphasis on decaying debris (especially the "red stars" caused by the blood of the severed cod heads floating on the water)—all these details make the poem's firmament a violent and death-filled one. Williams surely wants us to recall that the French words for still life are *nature morte*. There is even a hint that a human body lies decomposing among the debris. The phrase "vitreous body" may refer to the glassy, opaque seawater at three fathoms down; but as Williams of course knew it is also the medical term for the gelatinous body of matter in the eyeball between the retina and the lens. If we accept that second meaning for the phrase, it implies that the fish in the third stanza from the poem's end may be feeding on a corpse's eyes. The sea changes in "The Cod Head" are thus not only rich and strange, they are Darwinian.[19]

When Wallace Stevens wrote the preface to Williams' *Collected Poems, 1921–1931,* he was correct in calling "The Cod Head" "anti-

---

auspices of the Société Anonyme in 1920 (his first American show), 1921 (along with other *Der Sturm* artists), 1928, 1930, and 1931; in 1926 he was included in the Brooklyn Museum's International Exhibition of Modern Art, which was also shown, in part, at the Anderson Galleries in Manhattan later that same year. See Werner Schmalenbach, *Kurt Schwitters* (New York, 1967), 369.

19. Williams pushes the logic of fragmentation further in "The Cod Head" than he does in any other Cubist lyric, including "The Locust Tree," a poem whose use of splintered syntax is probably more well-known because of J. Hillis Miller's fine reading. See Miller, *Poets of Reality* (Cambridge, Mass., 1965), 303–306.

Another perhaps equally severe example of fragmentation and abstraction in Williams' work is "To Have Done Nothing" (Poem VI) in *Spring and All*. It is a witty compliment to and critique of Gertrude Stein's severely intellectual adaptations of Cubist ideas. Treating sentence elements in the most rarefied and self-conscious way, as self-referential objects to be broken apart and reassembled in patterns entirely removed from "common" usage, Stein's syntactic experiments represent a correct but narrow verbal parallel, perhaps, to the visual effects of Analytic Cubism. Williams understood Stein's intent very well, and in fact gave us the first rational explanation of her work, his essay "The Work of Gertrude Stein" (1930). "To Have Done Nothing" may be taken as a demonstration of Stein's Cubist theories in action: the poem exploits the paradox that "nothing," when described in language, becomes "something," a verbal object. The phrase "to have done nothing" is "made up of / nothing / and the diphthong // ae // together with / the first person / singular / indicative // of the auxiliary/verb / to have." But both "Locust Tree" and, in particular, the Stein poem are removed from the mainstream of Williams' work, even from that of his Cubist compositions, by their high degree of linguistic abstraction. "The Cod Head" and Williams' other Cubist still-life poems live in a larger, less hermetic and intellectually "pure" world, and show Williams' instinctive ties to the more eclectic wit of Gris, Demuth, and Picasso.

poetic," for its use of debris violated the decorum of the lyric in much the same way that Picasso's collages did of the still life. Williams was infuriated by Stevens' term, but despite the unfortunate negative connotations of "anti-poetic," Stevens meant to praise Williams when he said that he "is more of a realist than is commonly true in the case of a poet." Stevens added that Williams was still a "romantic" despite his realism because his work was essentially "the result of the conjunction of the real and the unreal, the sentimental and the anti-poetic, the constant interaction of two opposites." If we translate this passage from Stevens' Latin to Williams' *lingua franca*, we have something very like Williams' own statement in *Spring and All* defending the artist's use of "everyday" material: "Things with which he is familiar, simple things—at the same time to detach them from ordinary experience to the imagination" where they may be joined "with admirable simplicity and excellent design" (*I*, 110–11). Williams obviously thought that his words were more accurate than Stevens' descriptions of "anti-poetic" and "sentimental." But Stevens was awed by the accuracy of Williams' eye and praised his ability to wrestle with miscellany until it became a firmament, an order. Indeed, as Stevens guessed, the real drama of "The Cod Head" is a battle between nature's endless shapes and the mind's rage to order.[20] Unlike Williams' celebration of man's impregnation and dominance of nature in "The Rose," in "The Cod Head" his Cubist effort of synthesis struggles to keep pace with nature's decomposing power. The poem is a most unstill still life.

In "The Sea-Elephant" the sea represents unlimited fecundity, not universal decomposition; it is impetuous and playful, not disorienting and foreboding. But "The Sea-Elephant" is also a poem that greatly varies its voices and employs clipped sentence fragments marked by dashes. Together, these two poems on sea subjects show the striking range of tone, rhythm, and texture that Williams' Cubist poems achieve.

The poem begins with a description of a circus audience at Barnum & Bailey's Circus in Madison Square Garden in New York City (*CP1*, 527), watching an elephant seal perform. The poet assumes several guises: a sideshow hawker exhibiting an exotic natural phenomenon ("Ladies and Gentlemen! / the greatest / sea-monster

20. Stevens had praised Williams much more ambiguously in 1918, saying that although he liked Williams' *Al Que Quiere!* he also found it too much a "miscellany." See the prologue to *Kora in Hell*, in which Williams excerpts Stevens' letter (*I*, 15).

ever exhibited / alive"); a sensible woman offended by the spectacle of the crowd and the imprisoned seal ("[In // a practical voice] They / ought / to put it back where / it came from"); a translator for the animal who speaks an ur-language filled with vowel-sounds and is hungry to gulp down or describe the entire world ("Blouaugh! [feed // me] . . . / . . . / I / am love. I am / from the sea—"); and the poet himself, who occasionally interrupts this lively chorus as a narrator might, describing the scene and reacting to it. The poet is both tender and mocking: "O wallow / of flesh where / are // there fish enough for / that / appetite stupidity / cannot lessen?" Yet like the woman in the audience, he pities the monster, noting its "troubled eyes—torn / from the sea" (CP1, 341–43). That pity also extends toward the people in the audience, and himself. If the beast in the sea is love with all its primordial creative power, the beast captured and put on display must be a metaphor for love in its fallen, mundane form. Going to the circus to ogle freaks, beasts, and high-wire contortionists from the safety of the stands, the people in the crowd, suddenly, are forced to see themselves in the acts they watch. Each person sees that his own unnatural posturing in work and marriage is a show just as grotesque and comic as the one he came to gawk at. The elephant seal thus admonishes the crowd, reversing who is in the ring and in the stands:

> Blouaugh!
> Swing—ride
> walk
> on wires—toss balls
> stoop and
> contort yourselves—
> But I
> am love. I am
> from the sea—[21]

As well as being an image of love, the huge, omnivorous sea beast also reminds Williams of the unlimited bounty, "a kind of heaven," that is spring. His description of the monster echoes several earlier passages in his poetry, especially the description of the coral island rising out of the sea in the poem dated "9/30" in *The Descent of*

21. (CP1, 342–43). Williams also alludes, perhaps too elliptically, to the folklore traditionally associated with the beast, the stories about how sailors once saw a sea cow from a distance and thought they had sighted a mermaid. These legends are all the more ludicrous now that the cow can be seen closeup: "Strange head / told by sailors / rising / bearded to the surface." For another poem in which Williams compares love (and trees) to a beast "fresh-risen" from the sea, see "Rain" (1929).

Winter (1927) and his many depictions of spring's birth in *Spring and All.* And it foreshadows several details in Williams' best elegy, "To Ford Madox Ford in Heaven" (1940). Williams first compares the sea elephant to spring as he watches it feed. With no more warning than a stanza break, he suddenly veers from his description of the beast feeding to these lines: "Sick / of April's smallness / the little / leaves—" (*CP1*, 341). He then does not finish the thought but returns to the beast itself, mimicking its great throaty voice. At the poem's end, though, the analogy between spring and the seal surfaces again, in the form of two metaphors and a literary allusion.

Williams compares the seal's breaching the ocean surface to the birth of an island and the arrival of spring; the entire wealth of the ocean, even the world, seems to gush forth from the beast's head and glisten in the sun. It is a kind of aquatic Genesis:

> —comes
> to the surface
> the water
>
> boiling
> about the head the cows
> scattering
> fish dripping from
>
> the bounty
> of . . . and Spring
> they say
> Spring is icummen in—

Williams rarely made overt literary allusions in his lyrics written between 1915 and 1940, but in this case the allusion was probably irresistible, for his poem, like the medieval one that it quotes, "Sumer is icummen in," is in the tradition of the *reverdie* lyric, a pastoral poem celebrating the arrival of spring by invoking animal voices and praising the newly awakened sexual energy of animals and men. "Lhude sing, cuccu!" is a traditional refrain for such poems.[22] For them, April is the *loudest* month.

If we wonder what literary tradition most appropriately fits "The Sea-Elephant" and other Cubist poems with many voices, however, the *reverdie* obviously will not do. Such a poem is essentially a short song in praise of spring, and although that may be one way to describe "The Sea-Elephant," it will hardly suffice for the other aspects

22. Williams knew Thomas Nashe's *reverdie* lyric "Spring," for example, the first poem in Francis Palgrave's anthology *The Golden Treasury of English Verse.* Its refrain is "Cuckoo, jug-jug, pu-we, to-witta-woo!" See *CP1*, 495.

of the poem, or for poems like "Overture to a Dance of Locomotives" or "The Waitress." Nor is the dramatic monologue an adequate name for these kinds of poems, for their polyphony contrasts strikingly with works in that genre such as "The Ogre" (1915) or "Impromptu: The Suckers" (1927) that Williams continued to write even as he was experimenting with expanding the monologue form. "The Sea-Elephant," however, does give us a clue. It is essentially an address to a deity, a fantastical god of spring in the shape of a bearded elephant seal, and the traditional lyric form for such an address to a god is the ode, particularly the greater, or sublime, ode as practiced by Pindar, John Dryden, Thomas Gray, and others. Other, more technical qualities of the sublime ode also seem to be shared, at least in part, by the poems "January Morning," "Overture," and "The Desert Music," as well as "The Sea-Elephant." We usually think of the longer ode as being visionary or sublime because although it often deals with a particular event (an athletic victory, St. Cecilia's birthday), it may also freely range over various settings, time periods, moods, and topics. It is traditionally exclamatory in tone, invoking and addressing its subjects as well as describing them. And reflecting its origins in Greek choral drama (the word *ode* derives from the Greek verb for "to sing"), the sublime ode contrasts voices and moods, conventionally called the strophe, antistrophe, and epode. Sung before an audience, these contrasts apparently were sometimes emphasized visually, as the chorus swayed to one direction, then in another, then stood erect. In the lyric, these "sublime" effects are reproduced verbally by making sharp changes in tone and subject matter during the course of the ode.[23]

We need not seek to define the sublime ode more precisely, or to enumerate the many differences between the form as used by Pindar and his successors, in order to admit that there are general, useful correspondences between the genre and Williams' Cubist "choral" poems. Unlike other recent adapters of the form, such as Frank O'Hara, Williams does not mimic Pindar's complicated and irregular stanza forms. But in retaining other features of the sublime ode, particularly its effusive style, contrasting voices, and elevated subject matter, Williams has kept its essential characteristics. The lyrics

23. Essential background reading for students of the ode include George N. Shuster, *The English Ode from Milton to Keats* (New York, 1940); Carol Maddison, *Apollo and the Nine: A History of the Ode* (Baltimore, 1960), especially 4–38; Lillian B. Lawler, *The Dance of the Ancient Greek Theatre* (Iowa City, 1964); and John D. Jump, *The Ode* (London, 1974).

using sentence fragments and polyphony to celebrate creation and order may most appropriately be called Williams' Cubist odes.

The most pertinent reason for studying the literary as well as the artistic traditions that the Cubist poems employ is that Williams did so himself. As he began to write *Paterson* in the 1930s and 1940s, he started to apply the techniques learned from short, collage-like Cubist lyrics such as "Overture to a Dance of Locomotives" and "Rapid Transit" to longer and longer poems. As he did so he gradually began to openly acknowledge the literary tradition to which they all belonged, rather than the avant-garde art movement that had inspired many of the surface features of their style. In the 1940s, Williams named two of his Cubist odes in such a way that their literary heritage was inescapable, even if the poems themselves seemed unconventional. The titles "Choral: The Pink Church" and "To All Gentleness" emphasize that the poems aspire to be sublime odes that use a chorus of voices to address or praise a noble subject. In fact, "The Pink Church" was set to music by Celia Zukofsky, a composer and the wife of Williams' friend Louis Zukofsky.[24]

Despite the ambitions of Williams' Cubist odes of the 1940s, for the most part they aspire too much and achieve too little. Compared with the wit and grace of "The Sea-Elephant," they are poorly organized, bombastic, and excessively self-conscious. "The Pink Church" is an especially dreadful poem, one of the most embarrassing things that Williams ever did. He strives for a cultivated, "sublime" voice—"O Dewey! (John) / O James! (William) / O Whitehead! / teach well" (*CLP*, 161)—but far from giving the effect of a casual familiarity with great men, the reversal of first and last names in this list sounds more as if it were being read off alphabetized card catalog entries by a neophyte student. Williams is never less sagacious than when trying to play the sage.

The best Cubist ode of the 1940s, "Two Pendants: For the Ears," had less contrived circumstances for its creation; it was inspired as Williams struggled to cope with his emotions as his mother died. Including excerpts from a nightmare about a doctor unable to prevent death, conversations with his wife and his mother as she drifted in and out of lucidity, memories of things seen and heard in Rutherford, reflections on his own art, and a moving choral phrase, "Elena

---

24. For a thorough discussion of "Choral: The Pink Church" and its circumstances of composition, see Donald W. Markos, "William Carlos Williams: Embodying the Universal," *William Carlos Williams Review,* XIII (Fall, 1987), 21–32.

is dying / goodbye" (*CLP*, 221), spoken as if by a child saying farewell, "Two Pendants" proved to be a rehearsal for Williams' most ambitious Cubist ode, "The Desert Music." Both poems employ many voices and heterogeneous materials, and have a complex tone shifting from tragedy to comedy and back within the space of a line beat. And both are meditations on resurrection: "Two Pendants" repeatedly refers to Easter, and "The Desert Music" is an ode to recovery and survival in this life.

How "The Desert Music" (1951) avoids the mistakes of the odes of the early and middle 1940s while retaining much of their ambition is worth some study. Unlike in the poem "Rapid Transit," in "The Desert Music" Williams is not satisfied with juxtaposing fragments of what he sees, hears, and thinks; he wants to include yet another voice in the poem that stands apart from the action and comments abstractly upon its significance. In "The Sea-Elephant," this commentary had been handled subtly, by speaking through the voice of the seal or by including short asides of the poet's. By the 1940s Williams was trying to show that he, too, could compete with Pound, Eliot, and the others in learning; the discursive narrator of those poems discourses and judges. Unlike the speaker in those odes, though, the narrator in "The Desert Music" is not a static figure. His desires to be an authoritative commentator are continually undercut by the poem's action, which draws him in again and threatens his distant, superior stance. Thus the role of commentator in "The Desert Music" is *dramatic* rather than simply theoretic, and the pretentiousness that so mars a few earlier odes is continually deflated. Williams expands the role played by the speaker in the odes of the 1920s and 1930s without succumbing to the excesses that tempted him in works like "The Pink Church." "The Desert Music" represents a culmination for Williams' Cubist odes in yet another way as well: it is a daring combination of the violence and terror at the heart of a poem such as "The Cod Head" with the sense of bounty and *jouissance* of poems such as "The Rose" and "The Sea-Elephant."

"The Desert Music" presents us with the poet's two roles of actor and commentator from the very start.[25] Williams had been touring El

25. All readers of this late ode are indebted to James Guimond, *The Art of William Carlos Williams*, 221–23, and to Sherman Paul's book-length study of the poem, *The Music of Survival* (Urbana, Ill., 1968). I depart from Guimond and Paul principally in emphasizing the dramatic evolution of the speaker's character, the importance of the speaker's being blocked by the rag-covered body at the beginning of the poem, and the way in which the work culminates Williams' experimentation with the Cubist ode form.

Paso, Texas, and Juarez, Mexico, with his wife Flossie and friends, including his old compatriot in the avant-garde, Robert McAlmon. Walking back to the United States from Mexico, on a bridge crossing the Rio Grande, Williams notices what appears to be a rag-covered vagrant sleeping huddled up next to the girders. As Williams describes what happens, he emphasizes both the dramatic action and his own role as narrator and interpreter. First and second person are employed:

> The others waited while you inspected it
>
> . . . .
>
> What a place to sleep!
> on the International Boundary. Where else,
> interjurisdictional, not to be disturbed?
> How shall we get said what must be said?
> Only the poem.
> (PB, 108)

With memories of his own recent brushes with death in 1948 and 1950 still fresh, Williams feels compelled here to turn away from this image of death and to discourse on the imagination's ability to heal and reanimate. "But a dance! to dance / two and two with him," he says nervously, using the infinitive. Williams' language, however, remains haunted by the image of the man's motionless, prone form: "NOT, prostrate, to copy nature." "The Desert Music" thus begins with a fear that death can vanquish art's dance ("—the dance begins: to end about a form / propped motionless—on the bridge"), and by the end of the first section of the poem Williams is unable to cross the bridge because of the specter of the body. He says in frustration, "Heave it into the river. / A good thing" (PB, 110). Williams tries to play the distant commentator because the events of the poem press him too closely. Moreover, after we read the ending of the poem we realize that its apparent "present" action is actually a long series of memories of the trip's events that are helping the poet forget the traumatic event described in the poem's opening lines until he can prepare himself to pass the deathlike body and cross the bridge at the end of the poem.

The first flashback features Williams and Flossie on their way to El Paso by train, and then an extended series of scenes involve drinks and a dinner with friends in the old market section of El Paso and across the border in Juarez. These scenes are constructed in a manner that will be familiar to readers of Williams' earlier odes, but their events are rendered more spaciously, with many of the words that were spoken and the sights that were seen. Williams has a novelist's skill in the vignette as he moves freely among many episodes from the day, revealing his humor and seriousness, generosity and fear. We move deftly in and out of his mind:

> What makes Texans so tall?
> We saw a woman this morning in a mink cape
> six feet if she was an inch. What a woman!
> Probably a Broadway figure.
>
> —tell you what else we saw: about a million
> sparrows screaming their heads off
> in the trees of that small park where
> the buses stop, sanctuary,
> I suppose,
> from the wind driving the sand in that way
> about the city   .
>
>   Texas rain they call it
> —and those two alligators in the fountain   .
> There were four
>   I saw only two
>   They were looking
> right at you all the time   .
> Penny please! Give me penny please, mister.
>   Don't give them anything.
>   . instinctively
> one has already drawn one's naked
> wrist away from those obscene fingers
> (PB, 111–12)

These scenes are also interrupted with fragments of Williams' own meditations on the role of art, continuing the speculations that had erupted when Williams spotted the form on the bridge. He repeats the paradox that the artist must imitate nature, not copy her; that is, he must tap nature's boundless creative energy, not reproduce her forms. Thus (as in *Paterson*, Book One, published five years before), Williams lays himself down next to the stream of life to record its polyphony as it cascades from the present to the future:

> I lay myself down:
> The Old Market's a good place to begin:
> Let's cut in here—
>   tequila's only
> a nickle slug in these side streets
> (PB, 110–11)

Williams' meditations on art in the middle of "The Desert Music," however, have little of his earlier confidence that art can be a healing "dance"; in fact, they ask whether the "music" of the present will always be worth lying down next to and recording. What if all the poet hears is "lying" and ugly music?

Watching an overweight striptease dancer in a Juarez bar, for example, Williams becomes fascinated by her cynical realism—by the way she seems to judge the place harshly even as she goes through the motions that are required of her. Williams tries to turn her into a Kora figure, an "Andromeda of those rocks, / . . . / in her mockery of virtue / she becomes unaccountably virtuous" (PB, 116). He even insists that she can still dance to another music, a purer one in her head. But then he quickly loses his ability to believe in such a transformation:

> Let's get out of this.
>   In the street it hit
> me in the face as we started to walk again. Or
> am I merely playing the poet? Do I merely invent
> it out of whole cloth?
> (PB, 116)

Both the cliché about "whole cloth" and the self-conscious cynicism in this passage are a new, frightening element in the poem; Williams has begun to interrupt his own role as commentator to question his fitness for the job. This is a marked change from the beginning of the poem, where he felt doubts about his ability to make the deathlike form dance but repressed them.

Williams's new cynicism is matched by a heightening of the "lying" music of everyday life that the poet is forced to hear. The scene in the poem that follows the striptease includes a strained discussion over drinks and dinner in a Mexican restaurant with several Texans whom the Williamses are meeting for the first time. They talk about the role of the poet in the modern world, but the words that Williams records (including one of his cynical witticisms, which he keeps to himself) are a comic reversal of all the high themes about renewal that Williams announced at the start of the poem: Orpheus has become a *tourista*, and his rite of dismemberment and rebirth is applied to quartered hearts of lettuce and being scatterbrained:

> Old fashioneds all around?
>   So this is William
> Carlos Williams, the poet   .
>   Floss and I had half consumed
> our quartered hearts of lettuce before
> we noticed the others hadn't touched theirs   .

You seem quite normal. Can you tell me? Why
does one want to write a poem?
        Because it's there to be written.
Oh. A matter of inspiration then?
        Of necessity.
Oh. But what sets it off?
        I am that he whose brains
        are scattered
          aimlessly

        —and so,
the hour done, the quail eaten, we were on
our way back to El Paso.
        Good night. Good
night and thank you   .   No. Thank you. We're
going to walk   .
(PB, 117–18)

Later, as the Williamses are nearing the bridge over the Rio
Grande, the Mexican scenes that made the poet so cynical suddenly
seem as distant as the urchins standing in the shallow water of the
river below begging the Americans to throw them some coins. "The
music has reawakened," Williams says, meaning not the music of
mundane sights and sounds that he has been close to all day but an
inner music for the mind's ear. Williams' old idealistic and transcen-
dental faith in the power of art to create a separate world has re-
turned. He remembers the sound of Pablo Casals' cello, and hears it
under the calling of the street children:

        the music! the
        music! as when Casals struck
        and held a deep cello tone
        and I am speechless   .
        (PB, 119)

Like the striptease dancer, Williams listens to an inner music while
still paying attention to the noise of everyday. This understated
tribute to the dancer's ability to instruct him is more believable than
the rather self-conscious attempts to analyze her that Williams made
when he first saw her.

In front of Williams on the bridge, however, lies the shapeless and
deathlike figure of the vagrant; it must still be passed. When the
poem returns to his meeting with the vagrant this time, he shows
little of the defensive idealism of his earlier meditations. He stares at
the form closely and then releases a volley of analogies to describe

what he sees. These tropes do not deny the fact of death but link it inseparably with life:

> There it sat
> in the projecting angle of the bridge flange
> as I stood aghast and looked at it—
> in the half-light: shapeless or rather returned
> to its original shape, armless, legless,
> headless, packed like the pit of a fruit into
> that obscure corner—or
> a fish to swim against the stream—or
> a child in the womb prepared to imitate life,
> warding its life against
> a birth of awful promise.
>
> (PB, 119–20)

Williams' confrontation with the inert mass here does not end in a grim joke, as it did earlier when he wanted to heave it off the bridge. Rather, Williams transforms the shape from being deathlike to being the source of all life, an active verb rather than an inert noun. The "dance" takes place in the present tense rather than in the infinitive (as it did earlier), and the once dormant "egg-like" form is fertilized, gestated, and born:

> The music
> guards it, a mucus, a film that surrounds it,
> a benumbing ink that stains the
> sea of our minds—to hold us off—shed
> of a shape close as it can get to no shape,
> a music, a protecting music   .
>
> I *am* a poet! I
> am. I am. I am a poet, I reaffirmed, ashamed
>
> Now the music volleys through as in
> a lonely moment I hear it. Now it is all
> about me. The dance! The verb detaches itself
> seeking to become articulate   .
>
> (PB, 120)

Williams' own inner music protects him when he faces the world even as the striptease dancer's music did. It restores to him the faith that he can reanimate all that is chaotic and inert. The conclusion of "The Desert Music" also recalls both the opening pages of *Paterson*, Book One, and Madame Curie's discovery of radiation in Book Four. Williams rediscovers in the shapeless bum's body on the bridge all the mythic creative power of Paterson the Giant lying with his ear to the water's music.

Like the wanderer on the bridge, "The Desert Music" is a poem of great power hiding beneath what appears to be a poem of great shapelessness. Its intentionally discordant tone changes, contradictions, and heterogeneous matter and forms—its mixing of a bum's rags and a Mexican restaurant's quartered hearts of lettuce among meditations on the meaning of art—imitate the different strains that Williams heard that day as he traveled back and forth across the border separating mundane and sublime, beautiful and lying music. Sometimes the cacophony of Texas and Mexico invades his voice and threatens to take it over; at other times, Williams remains distant from the scene abstractedly meditating upon its meaning until present events pull him back down to earth and overturn the interpretations he has just constructed. The only sustained epiphany occurs at the end of the poem, yet there too Williams' voice modulates from the defiant joy of "I am a poet!" to the understated humility with which the poem concludes:

> And I could not help thinking
> of the wonders of the brain that
> hears that music and of our
> skill sometimes to record it.
>
> (PB, 120)

Building upon Williams' earlier experimentation with the ode form, yet including a greater diversity of collage materials and a much more dramatic and intimate role for the central speaker to play, "The Desert Music" is also a critique of Williams' early Cubist odes and a redefinition of what such an ode might be. All of Williams' Cubist odes pay homage to what Apollinaire called the mind's right to "impregnate" nature, to create new forms. Beginning with "The Cod Head," however, Williams' later Cubist odes make that act of impregnation a death-defying feat, a poignant counter to a death's-head, nature's continual acts of decomposition. "The Desert Music" thus brings together both the celebratory music and sexual exuberance of earlier Cubist poems like "The Sea-Elephant" with the darker disturbances of a work such as "The Cod Head." In doing so, Williams emphasizes a grimmer element in Cubism that his favorite Cubist painters—the Spaniards Picasso and Gris—certainly understood (see Illustration 5), but one that had been slighted in Gleizes' and Apollinaire's more Apollonian accounts of the movement's intentions. Richly weaving together artistic and literary traditions, Williams' last great Cubist ode celebrates poetry at its most thoroughly "interjurisdictional" (PB, 108).

Pablo Picasso, *Still Life with Steer's Skull*

THREE/THE IMPROVISATIONS
Williams, Dada, and the Theory of Automatic Writing

Believe me, that's the way writing often starts, a disaster or a
catastrophe of some sort. . . . [B]y writing I rescue myself
under all sorts of conditions, whatever it may be that has upset
me or some trouble that I've got myself into [*laughs*] through
my excessive energy, let's say, if there is any at times, then I can
write and it relieves the feeling of distress. I think quite
literally, speaking as Freud might think [*laughs*], that writing has
meant that to me all the way through.

—William Carlos Williams, 1950

From the very beginning, Dada's influence on Williams'
work contrasted sharply with that of Precisionism and Cubism. Al-
though Dada exploited Cubism's techniques of calculated fragmenta-
tion and quotation (and Futurism's celebration of rapid movement),
its inherent nihilism and irrationalism made it rebel against those
parental movements. Williams' poems and prose that were influ-
enced by Dada consequently contradict the aesthetic principles of
his Cubist and Precisionist writing and require us to learn other ways
of reading.[1]

1. The topic of Williams' relation to the Dada movement was first treated by Dijkstra in
Cubism, Stieglitz, and the Early Poetry of William Carlos Williams, quickly followed by Weaver,
William Carlos Williams: The American Background and Tashjian, *Skyscraper Primitives*. Recent
critics have made important contributions to the discussion, however, most notably Homer,
Alfred Stieglitz and the Avant-Garde; Marling, *William Carlos Williams and the Painters*, which is
particularly good on Walter Arensberg's influence on Williams, 36–54; Sayre, *The Visual Text
of William Carlos Williams*; Sayre, "Ready-mades and Other Measures: The Poetics of Marcel
Duchamp and William Carlos Williams," *Journal of Modern Literature*, VIII (1980), 3–22;
Sayre, "Avant-Garde Dispositions: Placing *Spring and All* in Context"; and Perloff, *The Poetics
of Indeterminacy*, 109–54. I build upon the work of all of these critics, but differ from them
chiefly in my emphasis on the importance of automatic writing and the disparity between
Cubist and Dadaist collage techniques. Tashjian's *Skyscraper Primitives* remains the best general
history of the New York Dada movement. But it may also be supplemented by Marius de Zayas'
memoir, "How, When, and Why Modern Art Came to New York," with introduction and
notes by Francis M. Naumann, *Arts Magazine*, LIV (April, 1980), 96–126; Francis M. Nau-

Williams called his Dadaist works "decompositions" rather than compositions, emphasizing their rejection of aesthetic unity and the ideals of artistic decorum and intellectual progress.[2] All Dada art is characterized by its disgust and satire and by its belief that modern consciousness is an artificially induced psychosis that may be cured only by a return to the mind's most primitive and unconscious powers, to what André Breton called its "automatic" ones. More than any other American artist, Williams undertook a systematic exploration of both of these aspects of Dada. He explored Dada's dream of releasing new mental powers through his own versions of Dadaist "automatic writing" in the highly experimental prose Improvisations that he wrote between 1917 and 1929, from *Kora in Hell* (published 1920) to *A Novelette* (published 1932). As this chapter and the next will show, Williams' work and his discussions of the principles involved in automatic writing not only measure up to but *predate* the more well known experiments by Breton, the founder of Surrealism. Williams well understood the bitterness and despair at the heart of Dada as well as its sense of humor. The Dadaist lyrics and prose passages in *Spring and All* contrast markedly with the Cubist sense of *jouissance* that may be found in that volume; instead of metaphysical wit, we find rage, the Dadaists' cry, *rien rien rien*. If Williams' Precisionist and Cubist visions produce pastorals, his Dadaist writing creates mock pastorals, despairing satires of the decadent modern culture that invented the mechanized destruction of lives and the mechanized production and selling of consumer goods with equal fervor.

Although the European Dada movements in Zurich, Paris, Berlin,

---

mann, "The Big Show: The First Exhibition of the Society of Independent Artists," Part I, *Artforum*, XVII (February, 1979), 34–39, and Part II, *Artforum*, XVII (April, 1979), 49–53; Naumann, "The New York Dada Movement: Better Late Than Never," *Arts Magazine*, LIV (February, 1980), 143–49; Naumann, "Walter Conrad Arensberg: Poet, Patron, and Participant in the New York Avant-Garde, 1915–1920," *Philadelphia Museum of Art Bulletin*, LXXVI (Spring, 1980), 2–32; David E. Shi, "Matthew Josephson and *Broom*: Cultural Nationalism in the Jazz Age," *Southern Review*, XIX (July, 1983), 573–95; and a special issue on New York Dada in the journal *Dada/Surrealism*, XIV (1985). The following sources were especially important for me in placing New York Dada in the context of the European Dada movement: Robert Motherwell (ed.), *The Dada Painters and Poets: An Anthology* (New York, 1951); Willy Verkauf, *Dada: Monograph of a Movement* (London, 1961); Michel Sanouillet, *Dada à Paris* (Paris, 1965); William S. Rubin, *Dada, Surrealism, and Their Heritage* (New York, 1968); William C. Seitz, *The Art of Assemblage* (New York, 1968); Lucy R. Lippard, ed., *Dadas on Art* (Englewood Cliffs, N.J., 1971); Joseph Masheck, ed., *Marcel Duchamp in Perspective* (Englewood Cliffs, N.J., 1975); Dawn Ades, ed., *Dada and Surrealism Reviewed* (London, 1978); and Ileana B. Leavens, *From "291" to Zurich: The Birth of Dada* (Ann Arbor, Mich., 1983).

2. See *Contact*, I (1920), 10, and *Contact*, V (1923), 2.

and Cologne had more members and publicity than the American Dada group, New York Dada was equally precocious. Even before the highly publicized activities at the Cabaret Voltaire in Zurich in 1916, a loosely organized collection of New York avant-garde artists offended the New York critics with their antics and their suspiciously foreign names—Benjamin de Casseres, Jean Crotti, Marius de Zayas, Marcel Duchamp, Francis Picabia. Dadaists before Dada had a name, these artists were informally connected with Stieglitz's gallery at 291 Fifth Avenue and his magazine, *Camera Work*. Eventually they released a volley of short-lived but lively little magazines of their own, including de Zayas' *291*, Picabia's *391*, Man Ray's *Ridgefield Gazook* and *TNT*, and Man Ray's and Duchamp's *The Blind Man*, *Rongwrong*, and *New York Dada*. They also found support from patron Walter Arensberg and (later) from more established little magazines such as Margaret Anderson's and Jane Heap's *The Little Review* and Harold Loeb's *Broom*, which published a series of articles on Dada by Matthew Josephson in 1922, as well as from Marsden Hartley, who devoted a chapter to them in his *Adventures in the Arts* (1921). There were other Dada figures, too, not really artists so much as professional social eccentrics—figures such as the Baroness Elsa von Freytag-Loringhoven, a modern Eumenides in a flapper's dress and bobbed hair who gained entry to *The Little Review* and then ranted so tediously about William Carlos Williams playing Hamlet to her Ophelia that the editors resorted to printing the second installment of her diatribe in miniscule type at the back of the issue; and characters like Arthur Cravan, an erstwhile boxer who once tried to turn a lecture into a striptease, scandalizing many of those present until Duchamp had the presence of mind to declare the debacle a Dadaist event.[3]

The fusillades of the New York and European Dadaists were inspired by a reaction against the institutions that had blundered into World War I. Dada was always most eloquent when most nihilistic. It convulsively rejected the European rationalistic tradition of Descartes, Locke, Kant, Hegel, and others that gave priority to memory and analytic logic; its members felt that this tradition was ultimately

3. For the most thorough account of the Cravan episode, see Naumann, "The Big Show," Part I, 34–39. See *The Little Review*, VII (January/March, 1921), 48–60, and VIII (Autumn, 1921), 108–11, for the Baroness' "commentary" on *Kora in Hell*. Jane Heap defended *The Little Review*'s interest in the Baroness in the Spring, 1922, issue, stating, "The Baroness is the first American dada" (VIII, 46).

responsible for inventing the weapons and the rhetoric with which wars were fought. As Duchamp recalled, "The Dada movement was an anti-movement which corresponded to a need born of the first World War." Tristan Tzara, in his Dada Manifesto of 1918, defined this ambitious negativism much more stridently. He called it "Dadaist Disgust" and aimed it at philosophers, politicians, generals, capitalists, and all supporters of middle-class values:

> Let each man proclaim: there is a great negative work of destruction to be accomplished. We must sweep and clean. Affirm the cleanliness of the individual after the state of madness, aggressive complete madness of a world abandoned to the hands of bandits, who rend one another and destroy the centuries. Without aim or design, without organization: indominable madness, decomposition. . . . I proclaim bitter struggle with all the weapons of DADAIST DISGUST. . . .
> abolition of logic . . . abolition of memory . . . abolition of prophets: Dada . . . to spit out disagreeable or amorous ideas like a luminous waterfall. . . . Freedom: Dada Dada Dada, a roaring of tense colors, and interlacing of opposites and of all contradictions, grotesques, inconsistencies: LIFE.[4]

Such rhetorical violence was an intentional parody of the violence of the war; its verbal bombshells and laughing gas were aimed at the minds that created such things in real life. If the high technology of modern civilization might be trained against cathedrals (as it was during World War I), then a Dadaist would learn to make his satire and his disgust as deadly as the new weapons perfected for the war. With the fragment beginning "Without aim or design" in the above passage, it is hard to know whether Tzara is speaking ironically of the madness of the war effort or is describing the tactics that the Dadaists would use to counter that war effort. He is really doing both. Dada art was to look as blasted, broken, and cluttered as the buildings and landscapes of France after an assault.

We cannot be certain that Williams ever saw Tzara's manifesto, although as we shall see there are remarkable parallels between its conceptions and its choice of words and those that Williams associated with Dada. What is certain is that Williams saw a collective broadside of the Parisian Dada group published in *The Little Review* in 1921. That broadside seems to have altered Williams' sense of what the Dada movement stood for. Earlier, in his prologue to *Kora in Hell* (written in 1918), Williams associated Dada with a love of irrever-

---

4. Lucy R. Lippard, ed., *Surrealists on Art* (Englewood Cliffs, N.J., 1970), 115; Lippard, *Dadas on Art*, 20. For the French text, see Tristan Tzara, *Oeuvres Complètes*, ed. Henri Behar (5 vols.; Paris, 1975), I, 367.

ence and novelty; his vision of its goals and techniques is more lighthearted than it is later in the 1920s. He retold amusing anecdotes of Duchamp scandalizing the art critics and the public (though he got some of his facts wrong),[5] and approvingly quoted a statement of Arensberg's that stressed Duchamp's love of novelty, not Tzara's bitter nihilism. Arensberg stated "that the only way man differed from every other creature was in his ability to improvise novelty and, since the pictorial artist was under discussion, anything in paint that is truly new, truly a fresh creation, is good art." Williams also quotes a remark of Duchamp's about destroying cathedrals, but he brings to the topic none of the rage of Tzara. He is rather a connoisseur of chaos: "Thus, according to Duchamp . . . a stained-glass window that had fallen out and lay more or less together on the ground was of far greater interest than the thing conventionally composed *in situ.*" Occasionally, it is true, the prologue to *Kora in Hell* has intimations of the violence at the heart of European Dada, as when Williams writes of his Improvisations that "by the brokenness of his composition the poet makes himself master of a certain weapon which he could possess himself of in no other way. The speed of the emotions is sometimes such that thrashing about in a thin exaltation or despair many matters are touched but not held, more often broken by the contact." Dada's calculating parody of the violence of World War I is well captured here: the "brokenness" of a composition may become a weapon against the culture's dangerous clichés and what Williams elsewhere calls the "continual hardening which habit enforces" (*I,* 8, 16, 28). And the Improvisations in *Kora* proper are frequently punctuated with exclamations of disgust and derision. But by and large such an apocalyptic tone remains muted in the prologue to *Kora,* and the exclamations in *Kora* can hardly match those of *Spring and All.*

The Paris Dada manifesto that Williams saw in 1921 probably had much to do with this change. That manifesto was entitled "Dada Soulève Tout" ("Dada Excites Everything") and was published in Paris in January, 1921, and reprinted in French in the January/March, 1921, issue of *The Little Review,* which Williams read regularly (see Illustration 6).[6] Its cosigners included the New York

5. Williams unaccountably switches Duchamp's urinal to a pickax, perhaps misremembering Duchamp's readymade sculpture employing a snowshovel, *In Advance of The Broken Arm* (*I,* 10).

6. The piece has been translated by Lippard and reprinted in Lippard's *Dadas on Art,* 162–63.

Les signataires de ce manifeste habitent la France, l'Amérique, l'Espagne, l'Allemagne, l'Italie, la Suisse, la Belgique, etc., mais n'ont aucune nationalité.

DADA SOULÈVE TOUT

DADA connaît tout. DADA crache tout.

MAIS........

DADA VOUS A-T-IL JAMAIS PARLÉ :

de l'Italie
des accordéons
des pantalons de femmes
de la patrie
des sardines
de Fiume
de l'Art (vous exagérez cher ami)
de la douceur
de d'Annunzio
quelle horreur
de l'héroïsme
des moustaches
de la luxure
de coucher avec Verlaine
de l'idéal (il est gentil)
du Massachusetts
du passé
des odeurs
des salades
du génie. du génie. du génie
de la journée de 8 heures
et des violettes de Parme

NON = oui
NON = oui
NON = oui

JAMAIS JAMAIS JAMAIS

DADA ne parle pas. DADA n'a pas d'idée fixe. DADA n'attrape pas les mouches

LE MINISTÈRE EST RENVERSÉ. PAR QUI ? PAR DADA

Le futuriste est mort. De quoi ? De DADA
Une jeune fille se suicide. A cause de quoi ? De DADA
On téléphone aux esprits. Qui est-ce l'inventeur ? DADA
On vous marche sur les pieds. C'est DADA
Si vous avez des idées sérieuses sur la vie,
Si vous faites des découvertes artistiques
et si tout à coup votre tête se met à craquer de rire,
si vous trouvez toutes vos idées inutiles et ridicules, sachez que

oui = NON

C'EST DADA QUI COMMENCE A VOUS PARLER

le cubisme construit une cathédrale en pâté de foie artistique — Que fait DADA ?

l'expressionnisme empoisonne les sardines artistiques — Que fait DADA ?

le simultanéisme en est encore à sa première communion artistique — Que fait DADA ?

le futurisme veut monter dans un lyrisme + ascenseur artistique — Que fait DADA ?

l'unanimisme embrasse le toutisme et pêche à la ligne artistique — Que fait DADA ?

le néo-classicisme découvre les bienfaits de l'Art artistique — Que fait DADA ?

le paroxysme fait le trust de tous les fromages artistiques — Que fait DADA ?

l'ultraïsme recommande le mélange de ces 7 choses artistiques — Que fait DADA ?

le créationisme le vorticisme l'imagisme proposent aussi quelques recettes artistiques — Que fait DADA ?

Que fait DADA ?

DADA

50 francs de récompense à celui qui trouve le moyen de nous expliquer DADA

Dada passe tout par un nouveau filet.
Dada est l'amertume qui ouvre son rire sur tout ce qui a été fait consacré oublier dans notre langage dans notre cerveau dans nos habitudes. Il vous dit : Voilà l'Humanité et les belles sottises qui l'ont rendue heureuse jusqu'à cet âge avancé

☞ DADA EXISTE DEPUIS TOUJOURS
☞ LA SAINTE VIERGE DÉJÀ FUT DADAÏSTE

DADA N'A JAMAIS RAISON

Citoyens, camarades, mesdames, messieurs
Méfiez-vous des contrefaçons !

Les imitateurs de DADA veulent vous présenter DADA sous une forme artistique qu'il n'a jamais eue

CITOYENS,
On vous présente aujourd'hui sous une forme pornographique, un esprit vulgaire et baroque qui n'est pas l'IDIOTIE PURE réclamée par DADA

MAIS LE DOGMATISME ET L'IMBÉCILITÉ PRÉTENTIEUSE !

Paris 12 Janvier 1921

Pour toute information
S'adresser "AU SANS PAREIL"
37, Avenue Kléber.   Tél. PASSY 25-22

E. Varèse, Tr. Tzara, Ph. Soupault, Soubeyran, J. Rigaut, G. Ribemont-Dessaignes, M. Ray, F. Picabia, B. Péret, C. Fournaire, R. Huelsenbeck, J. Evola, M. Ernst, P. Eluard, Sus. Duchamp, M. Duchamp, Cruti, G. Cantarelli, Mary, Buffet, Geb. Buffet, A. Breton, Baargeld, Arp, W. C. Arensberg, L. Aragon.

*Issued at the contra-Marinetti demonstration in Paris recently.

"Dada Soulève Tout" manifesto, reprinted in *Little Review*, VII, No. 4 (January- March, 1921)

Dadaists Man Ray, Picabia (who by then had left New York for Paris), Duchamp, and Arensberg, as well as Tzara, Philippe Soupault, and Breton. The manifesto was more violent and bitter than Duchamp's and Picabia's art or the elegantly coarse New York Dada magazines such as *291, Rongwrong,* or *New York Dada.* Williams could have learned essentially all he needed to know about the Parisian movement from this one manifesto.

In the intervening three years since Tzara's 1918 manifesto had been published, the transitive verbs most important to Parisian Dada had not changed. In "Dada Soulève Tout," a Dadaist must *crache* (spit out) and mock everything that his society has taught him: "Dada is the bitterness which opens its laugh on that which has been *made consecrated forgotten* in our language in our brain in our habits." The manifesto employs many different font types placed in several directions on the page, as if a newspaper had been cut up and rearranged. In 1918 Tzara had said that Dada works should not look like "arrangements" but should be "decomposition[s]," appearing to "spit out disagreeable or amorous ideas like a luminous waterfall."[7] "Dada Soulève Tout" is just such a work; it seems to have digested the kinds of texts one sees when living in cities—signs, ads, posters, newspapers—and then thrown them back in the reader's face, despairing and angry news about the state of the world.

The April, 1921, issue of *New York Dada* also parodied newspaper layout. But it was elegant rather than violent; its third page mixed a mock society column featuring Marsden Hartley's exploits with the following public service announcement printed upside down:

VENTILATION

On the question of proper ven-
tilation opinions radically differ.
It seems impossible to please all.
It is our aim, however, to cater to
the wishes of the majority. The
conductor of this vehicle will
gladly be governed accordingly.
Your cooperation will be appre-
ciated.

DADATAXI, Limited

Unlike such shenanigans—or Hartley's assessment in *Adventures in the Arts* that Dada was a delightful "dissipation," a "pastime"— "Dada Soulève Tout" dramatizes Dada's anger and violence as well as its sense of humor. It therefore emerges as a particularly important

7. *Ibid.*, 163, 19–20.

source for *Spring and All*—as important for its conception of Dada as Apollinaire's articles in the same magazine a year later were for its conception of Cubism.[8]

The unforgettable opening pages of *Spring and All*, in contrast with the prologue to *Kora in Hell*, have much of the apocalyptic anger of European Dada. There, "the continual hardening which habit enforces" that Williams deplored in *Kora in Hell* has become "a constant barrier between the reader and his consciousness of immediate contact with the world." Slowly obstructing sight like a cataract hardening over the eye, this barrier is composed of the burden of the past: "The whole world is between [the mind and 'contact' with the world]: Yesterday, tomorrow, Europe, Asia, Africa." The result is that all true creativity is lost: "All things [are] removed and impossible, [including masterworks such as] the tower of the church at Seville, the Parthenon" (*I*, 28, 88). Accordingly, Williams advocates his own holocaust, one as satiric and violent as any in either German or French Dada. The trope of warfare was muted in *Kora in Hell*, but no reader of *Spring and All* can miss being caught in the cross-fire of Williams' rhetoric. He bitterly parodies the language the American press used when the United States entered "the war to end all wars" and astutely connects the self-righteous idealism surrounding our entry into the war with the passage of the Prohibition amendment in 1920:

> Imagine the monster project of the moment: Tomorrow we the people of the United States are going to Europe armed to kill every man, woman and child in the area west of the Carpathian Mountains (also east) sparing none. . . . Kill! kill! the English, the Irish, the French, the Germans, the Italians and the rest: friends or enemies, it makes no difference, kill them all. The bridge is to be blown up when all Russia is upon it. And why?
>
> Because we love them—all. That is the secret: a new sort of murder. We make *leberwurst* of them. Bratwurst. . . .
>
> The imagination, intoxicated by prohibitions, rises to drunken heights to destroy the world. Let it rage, let it kill. (*I*, 90–91)

---

8. My reading of Hartley's appendix on Dada is partially indebted to Naumann's article "The New York Dada Movement"; see p. 147 for these Hartley quotations. While working on *Spring and All*, Williams may also have read issues of Francis Picabia's magazine *391*, then published out of Paris, Rome, and Zurich; an article on Dada in the New York *Evening Journal* of January 29, 1921; an article by the art critic Sheldon Cheney in the May, 1922, issue of the *Century Magazine* entitled "Why Dada?" (pp. 22–29); and Tristan Tzara's "Memoirs of Dadaism" in *Vanity Fair*, July, 1922, pp. 70, 92, 94. Unlike Hartley, Tzara and Cheney praised the "malice and irony" of German Dada and argued that America needed Dada "to destroy our whole mechanized system, which has blindly clamped the acquisitive supply-and-demand principles of business down over the realms of art and spiritual life." We do not have firm evidence that Williams saw such sources. However, *Vanity Fair* does figure prominently in an early episode of *The Great American Novel*. See *Imaginations*, 161.

Like other Dadaists, Williams hoped that his nihilism would not only open people's eyes to hypocrisy but also give him the freedom he needed to invent new forms to replace the useless old ones. Tzara had spoken of "cleanliness," the relief a sick body feels after it has vomited out poison: "Affirm the cleanliness of the individual after the state of madness." Duchamp argued that seeking "novelty" was imperative and that his nihilism was a carefully chosen first step. For him, Dada was "a way to get out of a state of mind—to avoid being influenced by one's immediate environment, or by the past: to get away from cliches—to get free. . . . Dada was very serviceable as a purgative. . . . I recall certain conversations with Picabia along these lines."[9] For similar reasons, Williams' description of an apocalypse in Spring and All softens and becomes comic after only a few pages. He imitates the upside-down typography of New York Dada and imagines a different kind of drunkenness, one in which a city celebrates the coming rebirth of all the virtues thought to have perished in the war: "Only a day is left, one miserable day, before the world comes into its own. Let us hurry! Why bother for this man or that? In the offices of the great newspapers a mad joy reigns as they prepare the final extras. Rushing about, men bump each other into the whirring presses. How funny it seems. All thought of misery has left us. Why should we care? Children laughingly fling themselves under the wheels of the street cars, airplanes crash gaily to the earth. Someone has written a poem" (I, 92).

A little further on in this section in Spring and All the broken stained-glass window, the Dadaist emblem of nihilism in Kora in Hell, is revised. We see Death looking gigantically down from a monument to the past, a cathedral tower, upon a young artist who was driven to kill himself because he was so oppressed by the specter of past masterpieces. But Williams, although angry, remains confident: "Peaceful, dead young man, the money they have put into the stones [of the cathedral] has been spent to teach men of life's austerity. You died and teach us the same lesson. You seem a cathedral, celebrant of the spring which shivers for me among the long black trees" (I, 92). As every reader of Spring and All knows, the miracle of rebirth does occur. The broken cathedrals of the past are cleared away, and Spring arrives bearing new poems, an immediate contact with the world, and the chance to build new masterpieces on par with "the tower at

9. Lippard (ed.), Dadas on Art, 19, 141.

Seville" and "the Parthenon." But that rebirth could not have oc-
curred without the Dadaist apocalypse that preceded it and cleared
the way.

Together, *Kora in Hell* and *Spring and All* allow us to distinguish
between two distinct but intertwined strains of Dadaism in Williams'
work. Williams' prose Improvisations reflect especially eloquently
the excitement and idealism of Dada, its belief that when the corrupt
conventions of social and artistic life were swept aside new forms of
freshness and innocence would be released. His Dadaist lyrics, es-
pecially the collage poems of *Spring and All*, emphasize Dada's other
side, its black humor.

In this chapter I will discuss Williams' theories about writing Im-
provisations as they evolved between 1918 and 1929 and will place
his experiments within the general context of New York and Parisian
Dadaist experiments in automatic writing. Especially useful for com-
parative purposes will be the early automatic writing of André
Breton, which was written almost contemporaneously with *Kora in
Hell*. While Breton's work was not a "source" for Williams, compar-
ing the two can help define what kind of writing automatic writing is,
the role that it plays for the avant-garde artist, and the distinctive
nature of Williams' achievement in the mode. I will close this chap-
ter with a reading of *Kora in Hell*, the volume that contains the best
Improvisations that Williams wrote. My interpretation will recog-
nize Williams' ties to the Dadaists but will also place his Improvisa-
tions within the larger and more American context of the poetry of
Whitman. Williams had long been keeping notebooks with Whit-
manesque impressions, "quick spontaneous poems" (*IWWP*, 5), and
one way to think of *Kora* is that it is an expansion of the methods and
goals of those early (now largely lost) notebooks.[10] Thus the rather
vague Dadaist talk about spontaneity that Williams heard was
changed by the rigorous meaning that Whitman gave the word. If
Wassily Kandinsky's and the Dadaists' interest in spontaneity pro-
vided the initial impulse for Williams' free writing from *Kora* onward,
they also helped Williams tap more deeply than he yet had the riches
of a local American tradition celebrating unpredictability and un-
selfconsciousness.

Williams' work also reflects the darker side of Dada, its despair and

10. One of those notebooks has been republished, edited by Emily Mitchell Wallace: "The
Little Red Notebook of William Carlos Williams (1914)," *William Carlos Williams Review*, IX
(1983), 1–34.

disgust, which will be the topic of Chapter Four. Although such a strain surfaces in Williams' writing as early as 1916, with "March," the first of what I will call Williams' Dadaist "black wind" lyrics, and is present now and again in *Kora in Hell,* it becomes especially promi- nent in Williams' work of the 1920s, after Williams read "Dada Soulève Tout" in *The Little Review* in 1921. This side of Dada de- spairingly sees the unconscious as not being free from the corruption of the modern world but thoroughly immersed in it, grossly depen- dent upon its materialist values and its sham novelties. From Parisian Dada, Picabia, Duchamp, and Demuth, Williams learned to read contemporary events for the frightening truths they revealed about how easily manipulatable the collective unconscious is in modern commercial culture. Instead of searching for new sources of spon- taneity, as he does in his Improvisations, Williams in his Dadaist collages uncovers hidden agents of coercion—the hidden persuaders of commercial society, particularly mass media and advertising. In a devastating series of poems in *Spring and All,* Williams developed this other strain of Dadaism to full effect, keeping the New York Dadaists' deadpan humor but also merging it with anger and irony as savage as anything in European Dada.

The standard account of how Williams came to undertake the year of daily experimental writing that became *Kora in Hell: Improvisations* (1920; written 1917–1918) is that he got the idea from Kandinsky, by reading excerpts of his *Concerning the Spiritual in Art* (1911) in Pound's and Wyndham Lewis' *Blast* in 1914 and possibly also Stieglitz's *Camera Work* in 1912. Kandinsky had written that one of the artist's responsibilities was to create "a largely unconscious, spon- taneous expression of inner character." This he called an "Im- provisation." It is likely that Williams heard Kandinsky's idea ex- plained further by Hartley, who had met Kandinsky in Munich and later had conversations about art with Williams in his Manhattan studio. Kandinsky's book was also much talked about in the group of artists and writers close to Stieglitz and Walter Arensberg.[11]

11. See *Imaginations,* 26, where Williams quotes Kandinsky in his prologue to *Kora;* he had seen those passages in Pound's and Wyndham Lewis' magazine *Blast,* I (June, 1914), 119. Williams may also have associated the word *improvisation* with Picabia: in the catalog to his 1913 show at Stieglitz's gallery, 291, Picabia wrote, "I improvise my pictures as a musician improvises music." See Jan Thompson, "Picabia and His Influence on American Art, 1913– 1917," *Art Journal,* XXXIX (Fall, 1979), 15.
    Critics who discuss Kandinsky's importance for Williams include Dijkstra, *Cubism, Stieglitz, and the Early Poetry of William Carlos Williams,* 70; Weaver, *William Carlos Williams,* 37–39;

But what meaning might Williams have given to Kandinsky's terms *unconscious* and *spontaneous expression?* We have no proof that he read more of Kandinsky's book than the excerpts in little magazines, and those short passages were hardly self-explanatory. The American and European little magazines, especially *Camera Work, 291, 391, The Blind Man, Broom, The Little Review,* and *Littérature,* were full of other discussion about the unconscious, however, and these sources, all associated with Dada, ought to be at least as important as the writings of Kandinsky for the student of Williams. Beyond that, when Williams read or heard discussion of the unconscious he placed it within the context of work by Whitman, especially Whitman's ideal of "spontaneous me." (Williams had reread *Leaves of Grass* closely in 1913.)[12] Together, these various sources allow us to reconstruct more fully the meaning that the word *Improvisation* had for Williams.

Before Duchamp and Picabia arrived from Europe and de Zayas began publishing *291,* several articles on irrationalism and the unconscious were published in *Camera Work* by the eccentric intellectual dilettante Benjamin de Casseres. De Casseres was not Dada so much as proto-Dada (the earliest of his articles on the unconscious was published in October, 1911), but his interest and the violent excesses of his rhetoric are probably best understood within the context of the upcoming New York Dada movement. In his October, 1911, article, de Casseres claimed that the true artist was purely "a tool in the hands of the Unconscious" who should seek to attain "the realm of the gorgeous, monstrous hallucinations." Two years later, in another piece for *Camera Work,* he gave such hallucinations oracular authority: "chance, danger, and the irrational constitute the new Trinity." De Casseres' pronouncements reflected the mounting interest of American and European intellectuals in Freud's publications, but although he appropriated Freud's sense of the unconscious,

---

Reed Whittemore, *William Carlos Williams: Poet From Jersey* (Boston, 1975), 123; Sherman Paul, "A Sketchbook of the Artist in his Thirty-Fourth Year: William Carlos Williams' *Kora in Hell: Improvisations,*" in Melvin J. Friedman and John B. Vickery (eds.), *The Shaken Realist: Essays in Modern Literature in Honor of Frederick J. Hoffman* (Baton Rouge, 1970), 27; and Marling, *William Carlos Williams and the Painters,* 68–70, 92–93. The translated excerpts from Kandinsky's book that Williams may have seen are in *Camera Work,* XXXVIII (April, 1912), 34, and *Blast,* I (June, 1914), 119.

12. See Breslin, "William Carlos Williams and the Whitman Tradition," 153. For a discussion of the popular meaning that the ideal of "spontaneity" had in early twentieth-century America—far different from the meaning that the New York avant-garde was to give it—see Lears, *No Place of Grace,* 141–81, especially 144–60.

de Casseres used it in an obviously nontechnical way. His vision of the artist as seer owes more to Rimbaud than it does to Freud. After 1913, his mystical irrationality became increasingly apoplectic, and Stieglitz, always the rational practitioner, broke with him. But de Casseres' demand that the artist record the words of his new oracle the Unconscious remained one of the stated goals of the "experimental laboratory" for the arts run by Stieglitz. [13]

The first and second issues of de Zayas' magazine 291, published in March and April, 1915, picked up where de Casseres had left off. They offered their readers several attempts to reproduce irrational mental states, including a piece by Alfred Stieglitz recording three of his dreams and an attempt to reproduce stream of consciousness by Agnes Meyer. Entitled "One Hour's Sleep—Three Dreams," Stieglitz's journal is a fascinating document, not only because it reflects his private doubts about his worth as an artist but also because it reveals certain methods that he thought were appropriate for recording dreams. In the first dream, Stieglitz imagines himself being buried, with an anonymous woman crying over him; in the second, he and another woman have undertaken a quest for spiritual truth, but she quickly succumbs to the need for food and leaves Stieglitz to journey on alone. The third dream is the longest and most interesting. Its principal figures are once again Stieglitz and "the Woman," an ambiguous figure at once threatening and inspiring. The plot could describe an Edvard Munch painting: a raving woman kisses Stieglitz, then cries, "Why are you not HE? . . . it is HE I want, not you. And yet I kissed you." Stieglitz stands impotent with fear, then at last is able to admit that she is right. But "as I said that the Woman took a knife from the folds of her dress and rushed at me. She struck the heart. . . . She turned around. Upon the immaculate white wall she saw written in Blood Red Letters: 'He killed himself. He understood the kisses.'—There was a scream. I awoke." Despite their highly charged content, Stieglitz's narratives are intentionally set down as if they were entries in an experimenter's logbooks: they are written in the past tense, in a terse and objective style lacking inflammatory adjectives or any analysis of the dream's meaning. The

13. For this last phrase, see a short article by Paul B. Haviland in 291 I (March, 1915), in which he asserts that the gallery 291 is "nothing but a laboratory, a place for experiments." For further discussion of de Casseres, see Tashjian, Skyscraper Primitives, 22–23. De Casseres' quotations may be found in Camera Work, XXXVI (October, 1911), 17, and Camera Work, special number (June, 1913), 22.

material is presented as straightforwardly as possible; no effort is made to adjust the data to social or aesthetic norms.[14]

Meyer's piece, entitled "Mental Reactions," is the earliest attempt by an American writer to employ the stream-of-consciousness technique that James Joyce had just made famous in *A Portrait of the Artist*, serialized in *The Egoist*. Like Joyce, Meyer mixes sense perception and a wandering interior monologue; details like "Parfumerie de Nice" or the sound of a clock striking join musings such as this one: "Odd. He gives me all he has to give. I think about myself. Are the passions of others ever real to us."[15] Compared with *A Portrait of the Artist*, "Mental Reactions" is timid and stilted, but it and Stieglitz's piece represent two kinds of writing, the one dispassionately recording the facts of the dream, the other combining random sense perceptions and thoughts, that de Zayas' magazine recommended for those artists who sought to transcribe the workings of the unconscious. For *291*, *the unconscious* was a loosely defined term; it meant both the strict unconscious of the dream and also the unselfconscious stream of thoughts and perceptions when awake. Both would be important to Williams' *Kora in Hell*.

The conclusions that Williams drew from what he knew of Kandinsky's and Dada's ideal of spontaneity parallel, in startling ways, those that the Dadaist André Breton himself drew, even though Williams did not know of Breton's activities in detail until his visit to Europe in 1924, when his own study of Dada had largely been completed. Indeed, Williams' experiments with spontaneous or automatic writing precede Breton's. Williams wrote *Kora in Hell* and its explanatory prologue in 1917–1918, whereas Breton wrote his first automatic prose, *Les Champs magnétiques*, in collaboration with Philippe Soupault in 1919 and did not compose a major theoretical statement on the subject until his Surrealist manifesto in 1924. Of all the members of their respective Dadaist groups in New York and Paris (with the possible exception of Tristan Tzara), Williams and Breton sought to develop Dada's ideal of automatism with the most rigor and inventiveness. A comparison of their work has much to teach us about the theory and practice of automatic writing.

One of Dada's working principles had been what Tzara called an

---

14. Alfred Stieglitz, "One Hour's Sleep—Three Dreams," *291*, (March, 1915).
15. Agnes Meyer, "Mental Reactions," *291*, (March, 1915).

"absolute and unquestionable faith in every god that is the immediate product of spontaneity." Breton, in announcing his Surrealist platform in 1924, took the need to rediscover such a saving faith as one of the tenets of his movement: "The mind which plunges into surrealism relives with glowing excitement the best of its childhood. . . . From childhood memories, and from a few others, there emanates a sentiment of being unintegrated, and then later of *having gone astray*, which I hold to be the most fertile that exists."[16] Earlier, Williams reached similar conclusions. The opening of his prologue to *Kora in Hell* contains a portrait of a figure—Williams' own mother—who is portrayed as never having left that childlike state the Dadaists idealized. This portrait of her is intentionally stylized and incomplete. In *Yes, Mrs. Williams*, Williams would render her much more complexly, but in *Kora in Hell* his goal is not to make a fully rounded portrait but to turn her into an example of the special state of mind that his Improvisations attempted to produce. Needing a Muse for his book, Williams invented one.

Like a child, or William Faulkner's Benjy Compson, Williams' mother is said to have "always been incapable of learning from benefit or disaster. If a man cheat her she will remember that man with a violence that I have seldom seen equaled, but so far as that could have an influence on her judgment of the next man or woman, she might be living in Eden. And indeed she is, an impoverished, ravished Eden but one indestructible as the imagination itself." Williams also recalls when his mother lived in Rome: "Never did my mother go out but she was in fear of being lost. By turning to the left when she should have turned right, actually she did once manage to go so far astray that it was nearly an hour before she extricated herself from the strangeness of every new vista and found a landmark." Williams gives his mother here the genius of selective forgetfulness. She exactly remembers what Locke called primary sensations but is unable to abstract, compare, and arrange those memories into generalizations, or what Locke called secondary sensations. She literally comes upon each thing as if for the first time. In Williams' words: "seeing the thing itself without forethought or afterthought, but with great intensity of perception, my mother loses her bearings or

16. Tzara's quotation is from his "Dada Manifesto 1918," in Lippard (ed.), *Dadas on Art*, 20. For Breton's remark, see the excerpts from *The First Surrealist Manifesto*, trans. Lucy R. Lippard, in Lippard (ed.), *Surrealists on Art*, 25; and André Breton, *Les Manifestes du Surrealisme* (Paris, 1955), 36.

associates with some disreputable person or translates a dark mood."
The goal of Williams' Improvisations, similarly, is to teach Williams
to "lose his bearings" and see "without forethought or afterthought"
(*I*, 6–8).

In spite of agreeing on the importance of tapping the unconscious,
Williams and Breton differ significantly when it comes to defining
what unconscious thought will be like. For Breton, it is Freudian
dreamwork, a trancelike state. His classic definition of Surrealism,
coined for the 1924 manifesto, ran as follows: "*surrealism, n.* Psy-
chic automatism in its pure state, by which one proposes to express—
verbally, by means of the written word, or in any other manner—the
actual functioning of thought, in the absence of any control exer-
cised by reason, exempt from any aesthetic or moral concern."[17]
Breton's automatic writing is thus hallucinatory narcissism: the
writer must shut himself off from both the norms of rational discourse
and (in its most extreme form, as in *Les Champs magnétiques*) the
stimuli of the outside world. Not accidentally, the first chapter of *Les
Champs magnétiques* is entitled "Les Glace sans tain" ("The Un-
silvered Mirror"). The title expresses what Breton and Soupault
believed to be the correct relationship between the writer and his
thought: an unsilvered mirror is a window revealing the spectator's
inner state of mind rather than his facial features. A later sentence
from that same chapter echoes this idea: "The window hollowed out
in our flesh opens onto our heart."[18] Breton's synonym for automatic
writing, "psychic dictation," is well chosen. It implies a single voice
whose authority within the ideally closed realm of automatic writing
is as dictatorial and "automatic" as the dream state itself.

For Williams, automatic writing was neither so pure nor so vision-
ary. Williams' mother was fascinated with the occult and held se-
ances in Williams' home when he was growing up. She frequently
became possessed and spoke "automatically." Williams, however,
was terrified of these scenes and resolved never to give his mind up to
such trancelike states.[19] Yet because of his contact with the New
York avant-garde, he came to recognize the therapeutic use of tem-
porarily relaxing conscious control over his thoughts and his writing.

17. Lippard (ed.), *Surrealists on Art*, 20; Breton, *Les Manifestes*, 24.
18. "La fenêtre creusée dans notre chair s'ouvre sur notre coeur." André Breton and
Philippe Soupault, *Les Champs magnétiques* (1919; rpr., Paris, 1971), 33. The translation of this
and all subsequent passages from the book is my own, done in collaboration with Jeffrey Cox.
19. Mariani, *William Carlos Williams: A New World Naked*, 17–18.

In his Improvisations, he transcribes not so much unconscious states—he recorded very few dreams—but rather a turbulent stream of conscious ones. The Improvisations mix sense impressions, memories, hallucinations, irony, and even discursive reasoning. If Breton and Soupault in *Les Champs magnétiques* look solely inward seeking purity, Williams in *Kora in Hell*, like his mother in Rome, looks outward as well as inward and finds the utmost heterogeneity. Williams thus chose the name for his experimental prose as carefully as had Breton: *Improvisation* implies a great medley of voices, styles, and what Whitman in "Song of the Open Road" called "duplicate" selves. Also, such prose could be written under a variety of degrees of conscious control. It was the most open and democratic of forms.

Williams and Breton were in full agreement on another point of theory, however. Automatic writing was visionary therapy, not "art." Breton's work was an outgrowth of the technique that he had learned in medical school of treating mentally disturbed patients by having them give a spontaneous and uninterrupted monologue. His mentors Pierre Janet and Sigmund Freud had strongly recommended such therapy, and Breton practiced it on shell-shocked soldiers when he was attached to a French army psychiatric clinic during World War I.[20] Williams of course also went to medical school, but the program at the University of Pennsylvania was much more conservative; he did not take a course in psychology.[21] Yet Williams intuitively realized that his Improvisations were therapeutic, a way to purge himself of learned clichés and private anxieties. Two of his best pieces of automatic writing, *Kora in Hell* and *A Novelette*, were written during influenza epidemics when his medical services were in constant demand; he compensated for feverish overwork by feverish writing. And in 1917 and 1918, the years in which he was moved to write Improvisations for the first time, he had the added pressures of his father's slow dying of cancer, his being suspected of pro-German sympathies, his brother Ed's rise to public recognition as an architect, his rivalries with competing doctors in town, and his estrangement from his wife, Flossie, who was angry with him for chasing other women.[22] Writing to a troubled author in 1935, Dr. Williams knew what cure to prescribe; he had previously recommended such

20. For an account of Janet's and Freud's influence on Breton as a young medical student, see Anna Balakian, *André Breton: Magus of Surrealism* (New York, 1971), 27–44.

21. Mariani, *William Carlos Williams: A New World Naked*, 779.

22. See Williams' *Autobiography*, 158–59; Whittemore, *William Carlos Williams: Poet From Jersey*, 156–57 and 334–39; and Mariani, *William Carlos Williams: A New World Naked*, 116–86.

writing for himself and ironically had even done some of it on the only paper handy at the time, his own medical prescription blanks: "Write for Chrisake, write, write drivel, write crap but write lots and lots, as fast as you can, string it out. Open the hatch and put a firecracker into it. Something will come out."[23]

For both Williams and Breton, automatic writing was valuable to the degree that it did not claim to be art. Its importance as therapy effectively liberated it from the aesthetic and moral responsibilities traditionally assumed by art. Its justification came instead from the fact that it appeared to transcribe the mind's preconscious thoughts, which Williams and Breton felt were older and more authoritative than any aesthetic or moral standard created by society. Moreover, they believed that there was a necessary connection between violating learned literary conventions and returning to the spontaneous creative source from which those conventions had first sprung. In a telling passage from his long Improvisation "Rome" (1924), Williams succinctly merges his disdain for imitating traditional, "classical" form with his faith that automatic writing could actually recapture the energy of thought in motion. Automatic writing is

> *Not* a mere arrangement—laid
> side by side—but as if
> things strove with each other in
> the work—*No* significance . . .
> but as they are *left*
> by the motion to *show* the
> force: are the force . . .
>   the result of too much modelling
> is not radiance but plaster . . .
>   the thing lost is clarity or
> motion itself—better is a complete
> confusion as in an improvisation—
> which is too an attempt to separate
> the motion from the stultifying
> *unity* of the thing.[24]

Automatic writing teaches an artist to distrust all that he has learned about the value of study, discipline, revision, conscious choice, and

23. Quoted by Whittemore, *William Carlos Williams: Poet From Jersey*, 334.
24. "Rome" has been edited and published, along with an essay on Williams' theory of the Improvisation by Gerald L. Bruns, by Steven Ross Loevy in *Iowa Review*, IX (Summer, 1978), 1–78. The excerpt quoted is from pp. 57 and 59. Bruns's article, entitled *"De Improvisatione,"* is on pp. 66–78, and is reprinted in his *Inventions: Writing, Textuality, and Understanding in Literary History* (New Haven, Conn., 1982), 145–59. In the 1940s Williams collaborated on an "improvised" novel, "Man Orchid," with two other writers, Fred Miller and Lydia Carlin, just as Breton and Soupault had worked together on *Les Champs magnétiques* in 1919. (I do not

"unity"—in short, all the traditional skills that masters teach and apprentices learn. As Breton wrote, "Surrealism . . . asserts our complete *nonconformism*"; he believed its processes were "exempt" from society's aesthetic conventions and moral codes.[25]

Williams' and Breton's theory of automatic writing is thus based upon two premises. First, there is an essential distinction between artistic forms and the minds that create them; the two are not synonymous and in fact are often at odds. Artistic forms do not provide a permanent norm defining beauty and creativity but rather are transient and quickly antiquated reflections of them. Second, inspiration may be recaptured only by systematically violating the rules of previously created forms; unless they are displaced, they will permanently block new manifestations of creative genius. As Gerald L. Bruns has written, automatic writing is made to disrupt the expectations of both its author and its readers. It is calculatedly "ungeneric," for "it confounds the signals that we normally use to complete a text we have not finished reading; it dismantles the virtual or heuristic whole that we need to construct in order to guide ourselves and make orderly progress through the parts of what we read."[26] It is of course debatable whether such contrived unpredictability will actually allow an artist to transcribe unconscious thoughts rather than merely to traduce learned conventions. Michael Riffaterre has argued that no writer or reader can verify that the result is truly "spontaneous," only that it *seems* to be so to the degree that it violates our standards for what a planned and coherent text looks like. For this reason automatic writing ironically remains dependent upon the conventions that it violates.[27]

know whether Williams knew of the circumstances of the composition of *Les Champs magnéti-ques*; the parallel may be merely a coincidence. Williams did meet Soupault in Paris in 1924, however—see Mariani, *William Carlos Williams: A New World Naked*, 286—and he translated Soupault's novel, *Les Dernières Nuits de Paris*, in 1929.) "Man Orchid" is reprinted in the *Massachusetts Review*, XIV (Winter, 1973), 76–117, along with an introduction by Paul Mariani, 67–75; the author of each chapter is indicated. For more information on the circumstances in which both "Rome" and "Man Orchid" were written, see Mariani, *William Carlos Williams: A New World Naked*, 227–29, 514–16.

25. Lippard (ed.), *Surrealists on Art*, 26.
26. Bruns, *"De Improvisatione,"* 69.
27. See Michael Riffaterre, "Semantic Incompatibilities in Automatic Writing," in Mary Ann Caws (ed.), *About French Poetry From Dada to 'Tel Quel'* (Detroit, 1974), 223–41. Discussing Breton's automatic text *Poisson soluble* (1924), Riffaterre argues that what separates an automatic text from a normal one is "the automatic text's departure from logic, temporality, and referentiality, that is to say, from the rules of verisimilitude. Although there is nothing ungrammatical about the syntax [in Breton], the words make sense only within the limits of relatively short groups, and there are semantic incompatibilities between those groups. Or else the semantic consecution of the sentences does not present any problem, but their overall

The most perceptive recent critic to discuss automatic or spon-
taneous discourse is Stephen Fredman, who notes the special, sub-
versive function that such a tradition—which he calls "poet's
prose"—has had in American literature, beginning with Emerson
and Whitman (and Emily Dickinson's letters) and continuing in this
century with certain prose by Pound, Williams, and contemporary
poets such as John Ashbery, Robert Creeley, and David Antin. For
Fredman the identifying characteristic of such experimental prose is
what he dubs the "generative sentence."

> The generative sentence abandons the normative aspect of completeness,
> often represented by hypotactic syntax, and instead follows the paratactic
> organization of speech into an image of the sentence as a whole. The gener-
> ative sentence proceeds by the method of *discovery:* forms and ideas are held to
> be at large in the world (or inside the self) waiting to be discovered. This
> notion ultimately traces back to the American predilection for typological
> interpretation, the tendency to see God at work in the world and nature as
> revelatory of his presence. The opposite attitude is that forms and ideas are
> willed and artificial organizers of inchoate experience which valiantly main-
> tain a completeness that is wholly sufficient unto itself (see Poe's "The Philos-
> ophy of Composition").[28]

As we shall see, paratactic syntax (as well as riddling, contradictions,
non sequitur, and taunting) drives Williams' Improvisations, and if
Williams seems motivated by what is fundamentally a transcendental

---

meaning is threatened or checked by smaller nonsensical groups. . . . Departures from these
[various conventions of 'verisimilitude'] are therefore interpreted as the elimination of this
control by subconscious impulses. This is precisely what creates the appearance of automatism
(regardless of whether this appearance is obtained naturally or by artifice). I shall it the
automatism effect. The presence of this effect in a text places the text in a genre by itself" (223–
24). Riffaterre's is a fine discussion, particularly because he discriminates between the "effect"
of automatism (which *can* be proven and discussed) and the actual presence of automatism
(which cannot be proven, even by the writer himself). I think, however, that semantic
incompatibilities as Riffaterre defines them can be found to a greater or lesser degree in any text
that revises the generic conventions of its predecessors, however modestly. I see no way of
discriminating as sharply as Riffaterre does between incompatibilities created by revising
generic expectations and incompatibilities generated by conflicting semantic patterns in a
single sentence. Both are in fact "semantic" as well as generic. Automatic writing may be
considered a special genre because it takes its normative principle to be a tactic that is abnormal
and comparatively rare in other texts, where they are assumed to be present because of the
conscious intention of the author.

    28. Stephen Fredman, *Poet's Prose: The Crisis in American Verse* (New York, 1983), 33. See
also Inez Hedges, *Languages of Revolt: Dada and Surrealist Literature and Film* (Durham, N.C.,
1983), especially 66–69 and 93–96. Also helpful for understanding automatic texts, I believe,
is Mikhail Bakhtin's principle of "dialogic heteroglossia," particularly as outlined in Michael
Holquist (ed.), *The Dialogic Imagination: Four Essays,* trans. Caryl Emerson (Austin, 1982).
Although Bakhtin's ideas were developed in reference to the novel, I have found them very
suggestive for my own reading of automatic texts such as Williams'—particularly Williams'
emphasis on dialogue. Unlike Riffaterre, Bakhtin would probably argue that automatic writing
is not a genre unto itself but simply a heightening of the "dialogic" principle that he claims is
essential to the novel.

urge to escape from all inherited generic forms, historical confines, and the mind's own repressions, he is also as *skeptical* as Riffaterre (or, say, as Nathaniel Hawthorne) about whether such an escape is possible. Begun and pursued as a form of liberating iconoclasm, Williams' *Kora in Hell* taught its author as he assembled it for publication to see the inevitable and tragic failures of his enterprise as well as its successes.

Aside from sharing many points of theory, Williams and Breton independently developed remarkably similar working principles. Their shared requirements for automatic writing, broadly speaking, involved three things: the scheduling of writing time, the rule barring revision, and the tactics used during writing to make the result as purely unconventional and unpredictable as possible.

Automatic writing was apparently best done at regular intervals. Unexpected examples of it certainly occurred; Breton himself narrated one in which words came to him while he was waking up.[29] But Williams and Breton normally scheduled it as rigorously as if they were keeping a journal. At the start of their work on *Les Champs magnétiques*, for example, Breton and Soupault resolved to write a chapter each for nine or ten hours straight, compare the results, then begin again the next day; they stopped when they had a book-length manuscript after nine days. *Poisson soluble* (1924), Breton's second major piece of automatic prose, was composed during a similarly intense burst.[30] Williams was a working physician without as much free time on his hands, and so he tells of arbitrarily deciding to sit down during a free moment once a day for a year and write for as long as his inspiration lasted: "I decided that I would write something every day, without missing one day, for a year. I'd write nothing planned but take up a pencil, put the paper before me, and write anything that came into my head. Be it nine in the evening or three in the morning, returning from some delivery on Guinea Hill, I'd write it down" (A, 158). In the prologue to *Kora in Hell*, Williams aptly calls this process an exercise for the muscles of the imagination that will slowly train them to make larger leaps: "The virtue of it all is in an opening of the doors, though some of the rooms of course will

29. See Lippard (ed.), *Surrealists on Art*, 17–18n.
30. See the preface to Breton and Soupault, *Les Champs magnétiques*, by Philippe Audoin, 14; and Balakian on *Poisson soluble*, in *André Breton*, 64. *Poisson soluble* has been translated by Richard Seaver and Helen R. Lane, in *André Breton, Manifestos of Surrealism* (Ann Arbor, Mich., 1969), 49–109.

be empty, a break with banality, the continual hardening which habit enforces. . . . An acrobat seldom learns really a new trick, but he must exercise continually to keep his joints free" (*I*, 28).

Williams' later Improvisations were written under a similarly rigorous schedule. "Rome" was begun in daily installments on a borrowed typewriter during the spring of 1924 while Williams was in Italy during a yearlong vacation from medical practice.[31] Two years later, with *The Descent of Winter*, Williams' texts began openly to display rather than disguise this routine; each entry was dated so that we know that the entire piece was composed with more or less daily additions from September 27 to December 18, 1927. And the last piece of straightforwardly experimental prose that Williams published, *A Novelette*, mentions in the second chapter that "this is the second paragraph of the second chapter of some writing on the influenza epidemic in the region of New York City, January 11, 1929" (*I*, 276). If Williams never entirely concealed the place and time in which his automatic writing took place, however, Breton did; he acknowledged dates only in external comments on his work. Breton thus sought to emphasize the oracular, timeless nature of automatic writing; Williams, the fact that it might be begun at any time and might use *any* material (not just a dream vision) to start it off—a thing seen, a memory, a thought.

Another feature of both American and French automatic writing is the commandment "thou shalt not revise." In his 1924 manifesto, Breton described the temptation to revise and the reasons why that temptation should be resisted: "any effort to retouch or correct" would represent second or third thoughts, reason's intervention, whereas automatic writing was supposed to be "*spoken thought*"—first thoughts.[32] Williams had come to the same conclusion earlier. In the prologue to *Kora in Hell*, he mentioned that the only control he exercised over the materials was through rearrangement, not revision: "I have placed the following Improvisations in groups [of three], somewhat after the A.B.A. formula [in music], that one may support the other, clarifying or enforcing perhaps the other's intention" (*I*, 28). In the *Autobiography*, he elaborated: "Not a word was to be changed. . . . I did tear up some of the stuff" (*A*, 158). By 1929, with *A Novelette*, Williams' theorizing on this matter had become

31. See Loevy, Introduction to "Rome," 1–9.
32. Lippard (ed.), *Surrealists on Art*, 18.

aphoristic: "The compositions that are smoothed, consecutive are disjointed. Dis-jointed. They bear no relation to anything in the world or in the mind." He argued that it is "better to learn to write and to make a smooth [that is, unrevised] page no matter what the incoherence of the day, no matter what erasures must be sacrificed to improve a lying appearance[,] to keep ordered the disorder of the pageless actual" (*I*, 274–75). In other words, when a writer makes a composition, he revises in order to make the material more balanced, consecutive, and coherent. But such words miss capturing what is random and disordered and unpredictable in a scene or a thought—the natural "disorder of the pageless actual." That disjointedness is precisely what Williams' free writing is designed to render. A disordered and uneven Improvisation, even one that loses its inspiration in the middle and has to swerve and start over, is an orderly reflection of its true subject matter, the mind as its movements succeed, falter, or fail. It is imperative that the artist not succumb to conventional definitions of coherence if he is to discover "recesses of the understanding still untouched" (*I*, 304).

Williams' comment on his Improvisations does not deny that there are kinds of "understanding" in art that stress consecutiveness and balance. He is not arguing that *all* subjects are equally disordered or that all his art follows the working principles of an Improvisation. Indeed, in the essays that he wrote for *Contact* between 1920 and 1923, he explicitly associated "disjointedness" with "dadaesque" compositions and contrasted them with more rigorously controlled inventions in which revision and deliberation were required.[33] Williams' theorizing on his Improvisations is meant to be applied solely to those forms, not to his writing practices as a whole.

Williams and Breton also developed similar techniques for ensuring that their automatic writing remained unconventional and ungeneric. To do this, they had to invent tactics for subverting the writer's instinctual attempts to improvise coherence even as he wrote. One way was to write as quickly as possible. In his 1924

33. See *Contact*, V (June, 1923), 2. By the time of *A Novelette* (1929), Williams associated the theory and practice of disjointedness with the Surrealists as well as the Dadaists, as was natural since Breton, Tzara, and Picabia had all become Surrealists. But Williams added a characteristic qualification to his praise of Surrealism in *A Novelette*, designed to separate *his* American inventions from theirs: "Language is in its January. How shall I say it? The surrealists are French. It appears to them to knock off every accretion from the stones of composition. . . . Did the academicians but know it, it is the surrealists who have invented the living defense of literature. . . . But it is French. It is *their* invention: one. That language is in constant revolution, constantly being covered, merded, stolen, slimed. Theirs" (*I*, 280–81).

manifesto on Surrealism, Breton recalled that in Freudian therapy a patient was to describe his feelings "as rapidly as possible" to prevent "any intervention on the part of the critical faculties." Later, Breton offered a typically complicated system for clocking the speeds at which automatic writing could be written: "v" to "v′′′′."[34] For his part, Williams in *Kora in Hell* hoped to write "without forethought or afterthought but with great intensity of perception" (*I*, 8). In later Improvisations, he amplified this idea both in theory and practice. When a 1929 influenza epidemic forced him to work swiftly and efficiently, he became convinced that stress and speed would have a salutary effect on his Improvisations if he could only hold the pace long enough. He wrote: "It is because the stresses of life have sharpened the sight. Life is keener, more pressed for place—as in an epidemic. The extraneous is everything that is not seen in detail. There is no time not to notice. . . . [S]tress pares off the inanity by force of speed and a sharpness, a closeness of observation, of attention comes through" (*I*, 273). Williams thought so highly of his driving ability and quick reflexes that he even tried to write while driving from one patient to another during the epidemic: "A short novel. Write going. Look to steer" (*I*, 278). Indeed, most of *A Novelette* seems, literally, to be written on the run, so that the poet not only resolves not to order his work but also realizes that he could not even if he wanted to. Much comedy results: Williams shows us that even when he tries to record his theories of disorder on paper, his subject matter, the disorder of the world, continually interrupts him. "I blunder not at all. But the difficulty is immense, not to be solved by quietness, but by greater fracture. In the haste, stillness: It is fused. . . . Try as I will the thing comes only when I have one stocking on, the telephone is ringing, my mind is full of difficulties and you have asked me a question. In a flash it comes and is gone. Words on a par with trees. A humane matter that will sweep through the confusions of the world as the thought of the new world swept Europe—and ended in the Great Pox—perhaps" (*I*, 294).

Even though both Williams and Breton sought to write without premeditation, Williams' application of the technique of speed writing was more aggressive and unrefined than Breton's. Breton knew that both the long run-on sentence and the multiple metaphor were

---

34. Lippard (ed.), *Surrealists on Art*, 18; André Breton, "En Marge de *Les Champs magnetiques*," *Change*, VII (1970), 9–11.

essential to Dadaist and Surrealist writing because they were two ways to lose control of a sentence's direction—to imply more possible connections between a sentence's parts than a writer could foresee while writing. Here is a sample from Soupault's first day of work on "Le Glace sans tain": "Our skeleton becomes transparent like a tree through the successive dawns of the flesh, where a child's desires sleep with their fists closed."[35] The standard connectives *like, through, where,* and *with* are used to transform a series of nouns, including *tree, dawn, flesh, desire,* and *fists,* into a single multiple image whose beauty and essential mystery do not diminish with rereading. The sentence parts are joined irrationally by multiplying and misusing connectives and employing metaphors that contradict each other. A leafless tree and a skeleton may be comparable, for example, but it is hard at first to think of them as transparent until the image of *dawn* is given to us (presumably, the rising sun shines through the tree). But how can a rising sun be said to shine through a skeleton? *Dawn* solves one problem, but complicates the other, and then complicates everything further by being allied to *flesh:* how can flesh have successive dawns? The sentence's last clause multiplies such contradictory clues even further, for aside from the relatively easy problem of how a child's desires can sleep or possess fists (closed in anger? in sleep?), there is the major question of which part of the rest of the sentence the clause modifies. Do the child's desires sleep permanently in the skeleton and the tree, or solely when the dawns of the flesh make them transparent? And why does the dawn occasion sleeping rather than waking up? The sentence's meanings multiply and contradict, running on ahead of any organizing efforts that reason can muster.

Williams uses multiple metaphors and run-ons to ambush rational reading habits too. Several of the sentences in the best Improvisations in *Kora in Hell* have a fairly regular, conventional syntactic structure that makes them (like Breton's sentences) at first *sound* reasonable. But this small bit of syntactic order stands in quite comic contrast to the headlong irrationality of the sentence's multiple meanings. Part of Improvisation X.3, for example, has the classic structure of a riddle: "What do a + b have in common? X." But the actual sentence goes like this: "Turn back till I tell you a puzzle: What

35. "Notre squelette transparait comme un arbre à travers les aurores successives de la chair où les désirs d'enfant dorment à poings fermés" (Breton and Soupault, *Les Champs,* 31).

is it in the stilled face of an old menderman and winter not far off and a darky parts his wool, and wenches wear of a Sunday? It's a sparrow with a crumb in his beak dodging wheels and clouds crossing two ways" (*I*, 50). This is a Dadaist riddle: the answers raise more questions than the original query did.

Other Improvisations that Williams wrote experiment with open syntax; they read like perpetual motion run-on machines. No run-on sentence of Breton's comes close to having the brutal, aggrandizing energy of the slew of single-sentence paragraphs that Williams wrote during and after his European trip in 1924 and published, appropriately enough, in two later little magazines with close ties to Dada and Surrealism—*1924*, a successor to *291* and *391*, and *transition*, the magazine Eugene Jolas brought out in the middle 1920s to promote the French Surrealists and other visionary or "Orphic" writers. The following is an excerpt from an Improvisation entitled "THEESSENTIALROAR":

> It is the roar first brilliantly overdone THEN the plug in the pipe that carries them home with a ROAR and a cigarette and a belly full of sweet sugar and the roar of the film or to sit at the busy hour in the polished window of Union Club at the northeast Corner of fifty-first street across the street from St. Patrick's (so to speak) neat gray cathedral and feel the roar pleasantly pricking the face but they're all face as the Indian said to Ben Franklin who also knew French women like the New York Journal which knows that unless it roars it does not do the trick and that's the trick that you have to have the money for like Weissmuller when he slaps the water with his hands, quick the way they talk and THAT's what makes them WIN, it just HAPPENS but when a baby drops a ball of twine and it rollllllls unwinding about their feet neatly semicolon placed in rows while the cigar train is sucked at by the throat of the tube and it rolls without WITHOUT any roar at all along among the feet of everybody smiles because it DOES something to everybody it SURPRISES them all.[36]

Here is speed writing for the age of mechanized transportation: it roars along like a subway train, passing by subjects as rapidly as an express train passes through stations. But the sentence also gives the impression of numerous activities occurring simultaneously—trains whoosh into stations, the Olympian Weissmuller swims laps, Benjamin Franklin and an Indian converse, a child plays with twine, the editors of the New York *Journal* think up ways to capture the public's attention. Moreover, this typist's prose poem enthusiastically ex-

---

36. Along with two previously unpublished Improvisations, the six that appeared in *1924* and *transition* have been republished in *Antaeus*, XXX/XXXI (Summer/Autumn, 1978), 26–33. The republication of Williams' Improvisations in *Iowa Review, Massachusetts Review,* and *Antaeus* shows that the interest of young writers in Williams' automatic writing is very strong.

ploits the unique advantages of the typewriter for speed writing: repeated letters may mimic action, capitalized rows of letters (EASILY DONE by pressing the correct key) increase the decibel level, and, most important of all, the greater speed of typing over handwriting allows Williams' automatic writing to be more properly automatic. Breton's run-on sentences seem handcrafted and reflective by comparison, their tempo closer to that of the previous century.

Williams' and Breton's use of irrational syntax also included having whole sentences (as well as sentence parts) contradict each other. Breton and Soupault were fond of beginning sentences in *Les Champs magnétiques* with a phrase like "il n'y a plus que" ("There is nothing but"), thereby erasing beforehand all the assertions that were to come. Breton argued that the "forms of Surrealist language adapt themselves best to dialogue" because dialogue may use argument and contradiction: "Here, two thoughts confront each other; while one is being delivered, the other is busy with it. . . . In *Les Champs magnétiques* . . . this is the way [the] . . . *Barrières* [chapter] must be conceived of—pages wherein Soupault and I show ourselves to be impartial interlocutors."[37] Thoughts and voices also confront each other in the first chapter of *Les Champs magnétiques*, "Le Glace," but the disagreements are kept courteous and the argument is summarized, not dramatized: "Don't speak to us about everyone agreeing; it's not the time to argue about toothpaste and we have just finished veiling the teeth of our cogwheel that calculates so well."[38] The decorum governing these "dialogues" in Breton's automatic writing reflects his belief that such writing must be "dictation" by the unconscious in its "pure" state.

Williams similarly conceived of automatic writing as being composed of several voices, but unlike Breton he thought that the voices might interrupt each other, even breaking sentences apart in the process: "The stream of things having composed itself into wiry strands that move in one fixed direction, the poet in desperation turns at right angles and cuts across current with startling results to his hang-dog mood" (*I*, 17). Such "cutting across current" sometimes meant a shift in tone in midsentence in *Kora in Hell*: "Here's

---

37. Breton, *Manifestos of Surrealism*, 34–35; Breton, *Les Manifestes*, 32–33.
38. "Ne nous parlez pas de consentement universel; l'heure n'est plus aux raisonnements d'eau de Botot et nous avons fini par voiler notre roue dentée qui calculait si bien" (Breton and Soupault, *Les Champs*, 32).

the way! and—you're hip bogged." "Why go further? One might conceivably rectify the rhythm, study all out and arrive at the perfection of a tiger lily or a china doorknob. One might lift all out of the ruck, be a worthy successor to—the man in the moon" (*I*, 32).

The principle of contradiction may also shape an entire Improvisation. The model for this is given in the very first group of Improvisations: I.3 is explicitly constructed as an argument. A first voice leads off with, "Talk as you will, say: 'No woman wants to bother with children in this country'; speak of your Amsterdam and the whitest aprons and brightest doorknobs in Christendom." A second voice then emphasizes the virtues of desire and mystery rather than duty and order: "And I'll answer you: Gleaming doorknobs and scrubbed entries have heard the songs of housemaids at sun-up and—housemaids are wishes. Whose? Ha! The dark canals are whistling, whistling for who will cross to the other side" (*I*, 31–32). Despite the use of first- and second-person voice, this is less an argument between Williams and external social conventions than it is an internal debate between separate selves—the kind of argument from which another twentieth-century poet, William Butler Yeats, reminded us that poetry is made. For Williams, "psychic dictation" recorded sharply divisive voices, not the gently modulated courtesies of Breton's "impartial interlocutors."

After *Kora in Hell* was published in 1920, Williams' Improvisations over the next decade, interesting as they are, become increasingly self-conscious. Beginning with the on-the-spot theorizing in *Spring and All* and culminating with the extended aesthetic discussions in *A Novelette*, improvised discursive argument moves into the foreground of his experimental writing at the expense of its playful and visionary qualities. It is as if the prologue to and the commentaries on *Kora in Hell* (which Williams wrote after the Improvisations themselves had been completed) were to merge with, and gradually push to one side, the paragraphs of spontaneous fantasy that make up *Kora in Hell* proper. Admittedly, one result of this change is that the theoretical basis for Williams' experiments becomes clearer as time goes on. But it is perhaps fair to wish that there were more passages in *A Novelette* like the witty pair of chapters that concludes that work and fewer reformulations of ideas about Shakespeare, spontaneity, and the difference between prose and poetry that had been explored more originally and provocatively in *Spring and All*. The richness, audacity, and suppleness of *Kora in Hell* coarsened in later Improvisations as theorizing took over and did not return to Williams' automat-ic writing until he reproduced its techniques and ideas in abbreviated form for the violent Book Three of *Paterson*. Using Williams' own standards for what an Improvisation should be like, we must admit that *Kora in Hell* contains his best ones. Williams himself seems to have felt this. Even though he thought that the later Improvisations were "more sophisticated," he also admitted that *Kora in Hell* "is the one book which I have enjoyed referring to more than any of the others. It reveals myself to me" (*IWWP*, 49, 26). A discussion of *Kora in Hell* will thus conclude this chapter, because of the richness with which it embodies Dadaist techniques and because it shows how Dada's ideal of spontaneity led Williams back to Whitman—to an American tradition of spontaneity and experimentation that ante-dated Dada.

The October, 1917, issue of *The Little Review* published the three prose paragraphs that now make up Section I of *Kora in Hell*. There is no way to know whether Williams actually wrote these pieces first, but since he published them while he was still in the midst of his yearlong experiment in automatic writing, it is safe to say that they were among the earliest.[39] Along with the prologue to *Kora in Hell*, these three Improvisations can teach the skills necessary to read the rest. The paragraph of italicized commentary by Williams on Section I.3 is also exemplary, for it contrasts with the Improvisation that it interprets in much the same way that the later commentaries do.

    Kora in Hell begins with a threat and a promise. The opening paragraph contrasts the mass-produced and predictable art of mass

---

39. In Improvisation XII.I, Williams writes, "The browned trees are singing for my thirty-fourth birthday," September 17, 1917. But since Williams admits in the prologue (*I*, 28) that he later rearranged the Improvisations according to a loose A.B.A. musical formula, we have no way of knowing whether Williams had actually written twelve sets of Improvisations by September 17. The published criticism of *Kora in Hell* has set a high standard for work on such a difficult text. I have learned most from Paul, "A Sketchbook of the Artist in His Thirty-Fourth Year," 21–44; Joseph N. Riddel, "The Wanderer and the Dance: William Carlos Williams' Early Poetics," in Friedman and Vickery (eds.), *The Shaken Realist*, 45–71; Breslin, "William Carlos Williams and the Whitman Tradition," 151–79; Breslin, *William Carlos Williams: An American Artist*, 55–61; Joseph Evans Slate, "Kora in 'Opacity': William Carlos Williams' Improvisations," *Journal of Modern Literature*, I (May, 1971), 463–76; Ron Loewinsohn, " 'Fools Have Big Wombs': William Carlos Williams' *Kora in Hell*," *Essays in Literature*, IV (Spring, 1977), 221–38; Marling, *William Carlos Williams and the Painters*, 136–56; Roy Miki, *The Pre-Poetics of William Carlos Williams: "Kora in Hell"* (Ann Arbor, Mich., 1983); and Kerry Driscoll, "Mother Tongue, Mother Muse: *Yes, Mrs. Williams,*" *William Carlos Williams Review*, XI (Fall, 1985), 61–83, which contains an extended discussion of the relation between *Kora* and the late text *Yes, Mrs. Williams*.

culture ("Fools have big wombs") with work that is unconventional and therefore threatening. Williams compares the latter to "penny-royal," an herb once used to produce abortions, thus giving a wry example of what avant-garde artists want to do to popularly successful art: "Fools have big wombs. For the rest?—here is penny-royal if one knows to use it. But time is only another liar, so go along the wall a little further: if blackberries prove bitter there'll be mushrooms, fairy-ring mushrooms, in the grass, sweetest of all fungi."[40] The long last sentence of this paragraph describes the genuinely new beings that Williams the poet-obstetrician hopes to bring into the world and the reasons why he thinks his free-writing experiment may discover them. The artist must skirt the blockading wall of contemporary popular culture and its notion of fame and history: "Time is only another liar, so go along the wall a little further." The new discoveries that Williams hopes he will make may at first seem bitter, like unripe blackberries. But other, sweeter finds are promised: "If blackberries prove bitter, there'll be mushrooms." The image of the poet here is of a hiker or scavenger who explores "a little further" than others are willing to go; he knows how to follow a crooked path, to dodge, burrow, skirt, or overleap. He is the master of the surprising detour, the strategic digression. He ignores social and aesthetic conventions that might restrict him and tastes and tests all things as resolutely as the poet of "Smell!," a poem also published in 1917.

> Oh strong-ridged and deeply hollowed
> nose of mine! what will you not be smelling?
> What tactless asses we are, you and I, boney nose
> always indiscriminate, always unashamed
> . . . .
> Must you taste everything? Must you know everything?
> (CP1, 92)

It is no accident, moreover, that Williams in his first improvisation stresses that he may find mushrooms by the wall. For mushrooms, like *Kora in Hell* itself, decompose dead forms and have "fairy-rings" that suggest hidden supernatural powers unknown to wall builders.[41]

40. Improvisation I.1. Hereinafter the Improvisations will be cited by their number in the text. The text of *Kora in Hell* is reprinted in full, including Williams' original 1918 prologue and a new prologue written for the City Lights edition in 1957, in *Imaginations*, ed. Webster Schott (New York, 1970), 1–82.
41. Williams had Prospero's address to "Ye elves of hills, brooks, standing lakes, and groves" (*The Tempest*, V, i, 33–57) in mind. He conflates Prospero's references to mushrumps and sour ringlets:

> Ye elves of hills, brooks, standing lakes, and groves,

In the second Improvisation, I.2, Williams starts with bitter and plain material, an account he had recently read or heard of a hobo whose corpse had been discovered in a nearby cemetery. This is an example of the many kinds of material that Williams would use to base his Improvisations on. The free-writing techniques of each may be similar, but the material he uses to get started may vary from the completely subjective—memories of a dream or daytime fantasies— to raw, random facts that Williams recalled from that day's work: "For what it's worth: Jacob Louslinger . . . found lying in the weeds 'up there by the cemetery.'" He also includes a scrap of a conversation in which respectable citizens from the town, perhaps a policeman or the county mortician, discuss the dead man's last days— "Looks to me as if he'd been bumming around the meadows for a couple of weeks.'"

As Williams records this evidence, however, he also embellishes and transforms the impoverished facts, seemingly of so little "worth"; his description of Louslinger moves away from being metonymic and ironic and begins to explode with metaphors: "white haired, stinking . . . cave bellied, mucous faced—deathling." That last noun, a grotesque variation of "changeling,"[42] accurately captures the motive for metaphor in *Kora in Hell*: through metaphor, Williams will turn the bitter into the sweet, tapping the powers of transformation suggested by those fairy-ring chanterelles in Improvisation I.1. In the very next detail, we see these powers at work: the bum's boots suggest flowers blossoming, not shoes falling apart. The painful evidence of Louslinger's wandering has been twisted into a flower whose natural home—rather than place of exile—is the meadow in which he died.

Suddenly, separated by parentheses, a new voice interrupts the Improvisation: "Shoes twisted into incredible lilies: out at the toes, heels, tops, sides, soles. . . . (Rot dead marigolds—an acre at a

---

And ye that on the sands with printless foot
Do chase the ebbing Neptune, and do fly him
When he comes back; you demi-puppets that
By moonshine do the green sour ringlets make,
Whereof the ewe not bites; and you whose pastime
Is to make midnight mushrumps, that rejoice
To hear the solemn curfew
(33–40)

42. The word *changeling* is prominent in *A Midsummer Night's Dream*, II, i, 118–45. This text as well as *The Tempest* is essential for understanding *Kora in Hell*.

time! Gold, are you?) Ha, clouds will touch world's edge and the great pink mallow stand singly in the wet, topping reeds and—a closet full of clothes and good shoes and my-thirty-year's-master's-daughter's two cows for me to care for and a winter room with a fire in it—. I would rather feed pigs in Moonachie and chew calamus root and break crab's claws at an open fire: age's lust loose!" This new voice complains about another meadow flower, the profuse and coarsely constructed marigold. This sudden change of voice is the first example in *Kora* of how Williams will "cut across current," as he puts it in his prologue; in the midst of affirming the beauty of the lily, he swerves to attack its opposite and, by implication, the kind of people represented by the marigold's commonness and false gold. We cannot be sure yet who those people might be, but we can be certain they will be as different from Louslinger as the marigold is from the lily. The next sentence carries the principle of contradiction further. No longer is the new, contentious voice separated from the old voice by parentheses and a period. Rather, it erupts in midsentence, breaking the syntax in half with a dash. The sentence begins by celebrating the strength and singularity of Louslinger's vagabond life, but then the *opposite* kind of life is suddenly praised.

Who is this new speaker? Perhaps a hired hand on a farm, a lower-class man like Louslinger, but with a job, thirty years' worth of roots, and a love of the hearth. This new speaker, however, speaks in the first person, as the first one did. This fact is of central importance. Williams makes it clear that he is not setting up a simple opposition between himself or the outcast Louslinger, and society or the conventional farmhand. In *Kora in Hell,* Williams sees the struggle between convention and freedom as primarily an internal, psychological one. The method of the Improvisation is thus that of a dramatic debate without resolution, with Williams miming as many voices as he can without reconciling the dispute. Such debate also dominates *Kora in Hell* as a whole: there is no sustained dramatic action, in which the poet, say, sheds one or more selves and recreates himself by the end. Rather, his many different selves continue in conflict, and the poet merely learns to try to transcribe the argument. The motto for this contentiousness is succinctly stated in Williams' next Improvisation, I.3: "Talk as you will. . . . And I'll answer you."

Such volatility is nowhere better illustrated than in Williams' third Improvisation, in which conformity is represented by a well-kept Amsterdam interior, not a New Jersey farm. Williams probably picked Amsterdam because half of his mother's family came from that city. For him the city exemplified man's worship of order, neatness, and finish to the exclusion of everything else. In this Improvisation, the contending voices are not so much those of Williams and his mother, however, as of an imaginary figure defending order and equally imaginary figures trying to evade it. An Amsterdam matron supervises her housemaids. But they are restless; they sing while they work and wish they weren't working: "Speak of your Amsterdam and the whitest aprons and brightest doorknobs in Christendom. And I'll answer you: Gleaming doorknobs and scrubbed entries have heard the songs of the housemaids at sun-up and—housemaids are wishes." The housemaids then invoke in Williams' imagination the image of a loiterer to seduce them away from their labors, a vagabond leaning against a lamppost in the posture of a waiting lover or girl watcher: "Whose [wishes]? Ha! the dark canals are whistling, whistling for who will cross to the other side. If I remain with hands in pocket leaning upon my lamppost—why—I bring curses to a hag's lips and her daughter on her arm knows better than I can tell you—best to blush and out with it than back beaten after." Williams' imagining himself as a loiterer suggests an appropriate landscape, and in a wonderfully deft move he transforms Holland's orderly canals into an emblem of mystery, darkness, and seduction. Instead of dawn it is dusk, and instead of being dominated by a Dutch matron who personifies the work ethic and sexual repression, Williams' piece describes a prostitute's madam's proposition to a young man loitering by a lamppost on the other side of the canal. The desiring, id-dominated self that began to emerge as Williams fantasized about the housemaids' songs and secret wishes has by the end of the paragraph conjured up a sexual invitation.

The italicized commentary upon Improvisation I.3 retells the story of the housemaids, the daughter, and the older woman, but with significant differences. In the introductory clause, we are given a distinct place and time for the action: "*In Holland at daybreak, of a fine spring morning.*" Unlike Williams' automatic writing, his commentary respects the unities of place and time. We then meet a third-person narrator, whose objective point of view unifies the scene: "*One sees the housemaids beating rugs before the small houses of such a city as Amsterdam, sweeping, scrubbing the low entry steps and polishing doorbells and doorknobs.*" When the commentary shifts to cover the rapid time change that occurs in the middle of the Improvisation, the

change is clearly indicated at the beginning of the next sentence—
*"By night perhaps there will be an older woman with a girl on her arm,
whistling and whistling across a deserted canal to some late loiterer trudging
aimlessly on beneath the gas lamps."* As readers, we are not suddenly
pushed into darkness, as we were in the Improvisation; we are duly
warned. The objective commentary, furthermore, carefully dis-
tinguishes between present and future, actual and hypothetical, as
the dreamlike voice of the Improvisation does not, and it rigorously
presents all its figures in the third person, using nouns and adjectives
with comparatively little connotative meaning ("old woman" versus
"hag"). This not only expunges the hypnotic animism of the Im-
provisation, in which the whistling is done by the dark canals, a
whole terrain in the city of the mind; it also rewrites and largely
represses the sexual tension in the scene. In the commentary, the
loiterer is never tempted to cross to the other side, his responses do
not provoke anger, and the girl herself does not think the same
thoughts about the scene that the poet does. The Improvisation's
aura of sexual invitation is thus almost completely dispelled in the
commentary. Moreover, the dream narrative that came out during
Williams' free writing has had its material changed to conform to
aesthetic as well as social conventions. Its multiple, shifting points of
view have become unified, objects are distinct and whole, the sur-
rounding space is made unambiguous, and the narrative that in-
volves them is sequential, reserved, coherent.[43]

The changes in the material of Improvisation I.3 that Williams'
commentary on it made are paradigmatic of those made by later
commentaries as well: multivalent, ambiguous possibilities tend to
be restricted in favor of a single, univocal interpretation, and the
action is frequently displaced from the present tense to the past and
from the first person to the third. In Freud's terms, Williams' com-
mentaries represent secondary (or even tertiary) revision rather than

43. This process of translation is observable in an even more extreme form than in the
commentary to Improvisation I.3 in a letter on the same subject that Williams wrote to Robert
Lowell in 1952: "I remember Holland as a place through which I passed in 1910. . . . I also,
remember a girl with her 'mother' who whistled at me from across a canal. What strange things
we remember, they must have been important to us. That one was to me then" (SL, 312). By
the 1952 version, time and place are rigidly fixed in the past, and the incident has been reduced
to a simple fact. Perhaps because of the distance from the memory that Williams felt, he was
able in the letter to concede that the woman was a prostitute's madam rather than her real
mother. But such explicitness entirely discharged whatever sexual tension remained in the
incident for Williams. In an Improvisation, however, the ambiguities and disguises invented by
Williams release desire rather than suppress it.

a pure transcription of the automatic state itself: They act as a censoring mechanism, defusing, ordering, assigning meaning.[44] In the context of *Kora in Hell*, then, Williams' commentaries do not have more authority than the texts they paraphrase. They are simply another voice in the rich cacophony that is *Kora in Hell*, paragraphs whose principles of construction usually respect the aesthetic and social conventions that the Improvisations flout.

The first three paragraphs of *Kora in Hell* name two opposing themes prominent in the rest of the book. First is the "Amsterdam" theme—Williams' invention of characters like the farmhand and the Dutch matron who defend the virtues of order, shelter, and tradition. Second is the "dark canals" theme. Its heroes are all creative wanderers, outcasts in one way or another from correct Amsterdam society, such as Jacob Louslinger, Williams' mother in Rome, or many of the children, lovers, old people, and women who figure prominently in the later Improvisations. All these figures either reject or are unfit for the social roles that middle-class Amsterdam citizenship requires they play. They enjoy teasing Amsterdam's good citizens by giving them puzzles they cannot solve, and by daydreaming, lusting, singing, and tossing out provocative boasts like "There's more sense in a sentence heard backward than forward most times" (Improvisation XIII.1) when they should be working. No wonder the citizens of that city are threatened by them. But because the child, the grandparent, and the wanderer live apart from the Amsterdam world, they become the heroes and heroines of *Kora in Hell*, the figures whose "rigor of invention" and disdain for society's conventions serve as an example to Williams. Collectively, they may be said to be the Kora-figure of *Kora in Hell*; they represent the buried life-giving energy that Williams the Orpheus-hero hopes to rescue.

If Williams' debate between imaginative freedom and social restrictions was partially influenced by Dada, it also owed much to Whitman's *Leaves of Grass*, which Williams had reread just four years before he began *Kora in Hell*.[45] "Song of Myself" (1855), "The Sleepers" (1855), "Spontaneous Me" (1856), and "Song of the

44. For two prominent uses of the term "secondary revision," see *The Interpretation of Dreams* (London, 1953), 488–508, vol. V of James Strachey (ed.), *The Standard Edition of the Complete Psychological Works of Sigmund Freud*, 24 vols., and *Introductory Lectures on Psycho-Analysis* (London, 1953), 182–83. Vol. XV of *The Standard Edition*.
45. Noted by Breslin, "William Carlos Williams and the Whitman Tradition," 153. Breslin's essay is still the best short discussion of Whitman's influence on Williams, but see also Breslin, *William Carlos Williams: An American Artist*, 3–49; Tapscott, *American Beauty: William*

Open Road" (1856) are particularly relevant. The influence of these poems upon Williams is on the deepest level of all, that of metaphor. When Williams sought emblems for conventional and revolutionary definitions of selfhood, he often reworked Whitman's own tropes. In "Song of Myself" and "Song of the Open Road," for example, Whitman depicts his past selves, especially his proper social ones, as fixed, encircling, and blocking things that impede his spiritual progress. "The Sleepers" includes these but focuses on death, the most frightening blockade of all. Each of the acts of release that Whitman invents to escape being trapped—burrowing, wandering, flying, lovemaking—also plays a major role in *Kora in Hell.* But these motifs are often handled ironically by Williams, who thus questions Whitman even as he borrows from him.

One of Whitman's metaphors for his fear that he will not be able to break away from the restrictions of his social self is the image of the blocked road or passage. It appears in "Song of Myself," Sections 3 and 4, for example, in which Whitman compares the demands of that social self to a circle of people closing in around him. But Whitman does not exempt himself from criticism; his description of the tightening social circle includes portraits of himself as well as portraits of others:

> Trippers and askers surround me,
> People I meet, the effect upon me of my early life
>   or the ward and city I live in, or the nation,
> The latest dates, discoveries, inventions, societies,
>   authors old and new,
> My dinner, dress, associates, looks, compliments,
>   dues
> . . . .
> These come to me days and nights and go from me again,
> But they are not the Me myself.

Others may pressure Whitman to act conventionally, but the syntax of this passage makes it clear that some of the pressure comes from himself; he too is interested in the infinite number of things that ground him to a particular place and time—to the nineteenth century, to Brooklyn, to the social history of one's dress, actions, and conversation. In "Song of the Open Road," Whitman converts this instance of being surrounded by one's history into that of being

Carlos Williams and the Modernist Whitman; Roy Harvey Pearce, *The Continuity of American Poetry* (Princeton, 1961), 111–30, 335–48; Guimond, *The Art of William Carlos Williams,* 225–30; and Mariani, *William Carlos Williams: A New World Naked,* 519–47, 598–600.

trapped underground. The figures surrounding him are much more threatening, and no escape seems possible:

> Allons! from all formules!
> From your formules, O bat-eyed and materialistic
>   priests.
> The stale cadaver blocks up the passage—the burial
>   waits no longer.

Later, Whitman defines those nameless "formules" as including social as well as religious strictures for shaping identity. This "duplicate self" threatens to block Whitman's access to "the Me myself," to bury its voice beneath false voices:

> Another self, a duplicate of every one, skulking
>   and hiding it goes,
> Formless and wordless through the streets of the
>   cities, polite and bland in the parlors
> . . . .
> Keeping fair with the customs, speaking not a
>   syllable of itself,
> Speaking of any thing but never of itself.[46]

Most of *Kora in Hell* can be read as an argument between Williams' undiscovered or buried "Me myself" and his blockading "duplicate selves." "Leave yourself at the door," he advises in Improvisation XII.2; "walk in, admire the pictures, talk a few words with the master of the house, question his wife a little, rejoin yourself at the door. . . . Or if dogs rub too close and the poor are too much out let your friend answer them." This persona, like Whitman's, is a social one, highly adaptable to what others ask and eminently employable. From its first appearance in *Kora* as the respectable farmhand to its later incarnations as a matron, a housewife, or a conventional artist (see especially Improvisations II.1–3, XXI.1–3, and XXII.1–3), it represents both society's own image of what is respectable and Williams' own tendencies to agree with that image.

When Whitman imagines a visionary self that may escape entrapment, he tends to describe it in terms of a descent, a flight, or a sexual release. At the end of Section 4 of "Song of Myself," Whitman imagines himself high in the air above the oppressive crowd. He seems to be standing on a balcony or floating in midair:

> Apart from the pulling and hauling stands what I am,
> Stands amused, complacent, compassionating, idle,
>   unitary,

46. Whitman, *Leaves of Grass*, 27–28, 128, 130–31.

> Looks down, is erect, or bends an arm on an impalpable
>   certain rest,
> Looking with side-curved head curious what will come
>   next,
> Both in and out of the game and watching and wondering
>   at it.

In the next section, he redraws this picture of himself at rest: "Loafe with me on the grass." But if he is now lying on the earth, the imagery subtly retains the suggestion of both floating and flying. The nautical language—his head is "athwart" his lover's hips, and love is the "kelson" (keel) of Creation—suggests that the lover's body is like a boat sailing through the sky. But this is also mixed in with a sharply focused depiction of an American landscape, described as it could be seen by someone lying in a field:

> And limitless are leaves stiff or drooping in the fields,
> And brown ants in the little wells beneath them,
> And mossy scabs of the worm fence, heap'd stones,
>   elder, mullein and poke-weed.[47]

One of Williams' most persistent metaphors in *Kora in Hell* for the social self is that of a rock or a wall that blocks his way. His solution, like Whitman's, often involves a sudden change of course, a vagabond's feint. The very first Improvisation compares society's expectations of what an artist should create to a wall, and Williams, consoling himself, argues that if he goes along that wall a little further, working out his frustrations in the free-form Improvisations, he may be rewarded with something more than a mere record of his anger. In Improvisation IV.1b he undertakes another strategic evasion. "Here's a brutal jumble. And if you move the stones, see the ants scurry. But it's the queen's eggs they take first, tax their jaws most. Burrow, burrow, burrow! there's the sky that way too if the pit's deep enough—so the stars tell us." Burrowing is in fact one of the central tropes of *Kora in Hell;* Williams combines the image of the underground ant colony, not unlike the one Whitman contemplated in Section 5 of "Song of Myself," with two different stories of descent from classical mythology, Kora's capture by Pluto and Orpheus' descent into Hades to rescue Eurydice. Instead of studying to achieve "the perfection of a tiger lily or a china doorknob"—note the echo of the housewives in Improvisation I.3—Williams asks "why not try to follow the wheel through—approach death at a walk, take in all the

---

47. *Ibid.,* 28–29.

scenery [of the underworld]. There's as much reason one way as the other and then—one never knows—perhaps we'll bring back Eurydice—this time!" (II.1). The second paragraph of Improvisation XII.2 also suggests an underground escape route, and in XX.1 and XX.3 Williams puns on the phrase "cast down" and then throws himself on his belly, alluding to Sections 5 and 52 of "Song of Myself" ("look for me under your bootsoles"). Williams writes: "One need not be hopelessly cast down because he cannot cut onyx into a ring to fit a lady's finger. You hang your head. There is neither onyx nor porphyry on these roads—only brown dirt. For all that, one may see his face in a flower along it—even in this light." This light is not the clear noon sunshine in which Whitman strolled, however; the poet wanders through smog and the night. The price he pays for not being at the center of an admiring circle of trippers and askers—for refusing to turn his art into an onyx ring to amuse the rich—is greater for Williams than for Whitman. Even as Williams improvises songs to freedom, he remembers that the carefree camerado of "Song of Myself" or "Song of the Open Road" may very well end up as Jacob Louslinger did. Nevertheless, Williams gets up, dusts himself off, and plods on ("Oh, keep the neck bent, plod with the back to the split dark! Walk in the curled mudcrusts to one side, hands hanging"). And as he foretold in the first Improvisation, bitterness does indeed become sweet, and burrowing ends in discovery: "Ha, ha, ha, ha! Leaves load the branches and upon them white night sits kicking her heels against the stars." The tired wanderer, plodding bent-backed, discovers a frisky child, and some of her energy becomes his. He is reborn. The dark underworld has been "split" to give birth.

In Improvisation XX.1, similarly, Williams implies that for the twentieth-century poet Whitman's aerial resting-places are not as "certain" or as easy to get to. If Whitman in "Song of Myself," Section 4, simply and unselfconsciously imagined himself above the crowd ("Apart from the pulling and hauling stands what I am, / . . . / Looks down, is erect, or bends an arm on an impalpable certain rest"), Williams must work a good deal more violently to escape. The pace of change in this century allows for no loafing in the sky; Williams wittily and ironically shows how Whitman's favorite "impalpable" lounging spots among the cumuli have been destroyed: "Where does this downhill turn up again? Driven to the wall you'd put claws to your toes and make a ladder of smooth bricks. But this, this scene shifting that has clipped the clouds' stems and left them to flutter down; heaped them at the feet, so much hay, so much bull's fodder." Despite such difficulties, Williams' optimism remains undefeated. He transforms the "fallen" clouds in the above passage into "fodder" for a homemade, improvised Pegasus, a creature half-horse and half-bull whose strength and stubbornness Williams hopes will allow him to compete with Whitman's unselfconscious confidence. "([Y]ou cannot deny you have the clouds to grasp now, *mon ami!*) Climb now? The wall's clipped off too, only its roots are left. Come, here's an iron hoop from a barrel once held nectar to gnaw spurs out of." By Improvisation XXVI.3, near the end of *Kora*, Williams reckons that the authority of social and intellectual conventions may, just may, be broken by his Improvisations: "All that seem solid: melancholias, *idees fixes*, eight years at the academy, Mr. Locke, this year and the next and the next—one like another—whee!—they are April zephyrs, were one a Botticelli, between their chinks, pink anemones." Here the rock in Williams' path is not dug under, skirted, or flown over, but slowly split in two by flower and wind.

When we see Williams journeying along a skyway rather than a road, as in Improvisation XX.1, we ought to recall Whitman's "The Sleepers." Once that poem is reread with *Kora in Hell* in mind, it becomes clear that it provided strong support—perhaps even stronger than that of "Song of Myself"—for Williams' faith that his exploration of his inner, unconscious self would bear fruit. The major action of *Kora in Hell* and "The Sleepers" is the same: the daytime world of reason, social divisions, and the pursuit of wealth is rejected and the power of darkness and irrational vision accepted. Moreover, crucial symbolic events in "The Sleepers" are reenacted, with some changes, by Williams: descents, dances in which all inhibitions are lost, erotic fantasies, and visionary, nocturnal wanderings.

At the opening of "The Sleepers," originally called "Sleep-Chasings," Whitman sees the hiding of "douceurs" and vows to hunt them out by descending both under the earth and into the hidden regions of the mind: "Cache and cache again deep in the ground and sea, and where it is neither ground nor sea. // Well do they do their jobs those journeymen divine, / Only from me they can hide nothing." In the very first Improvisation Williams, mercifully, translates "douceurs" as "sweetness" and personifies it at various points in *Kora in Hell* as Eurydice or Kora, but he too searches underground. Whitman also dances as well as descends; he passes his hands "soothingly to and fro a few inches" above the bodies of the imagined sleepers, then suddenly is seized by a dance: "I go from bedside to bedside. . . // And I become the other dreamers. // I am a dance—play up there! the fit is whirling me fast!"[48] One of Williams' portraits of such a "sleeper" in *Kora in Hell* refers to his own wife. In Improvisation IX.2, meditating upon his and her sexual inhibitions and the distance he felt between his nighttime dancing (the Improvisations) and his married life in 1917, Williams writes a paragraph that begins negatively but ends in excited affirmation; he too suspends the passage of time and enters and transforms the sleeper. "The time never was when he could play more than mattress to the pretty feet of this woman who had been twice a mother without touching the meager pollen of their marriage intimacy. What more for him than to be a dandelion that could chirp with crickets or do a onestep with snow flakes? . . . What a rhythm's here! One would say the body lay asleep and the dance escaped from the hair tips, the bleached fuzz that covers back and belly, shoulders, neck and forehead. The dance is diamantine over the sleeper who seems not to breathe!"

Similarly, both Whitman and Williams know that exploring the unconscious means questioning social taboos about sexuality. In "The Sleepers," Whitman turns himself into a woman who is taken once by darkness in the shape of her human lover, then once by darkness directly:

> Double yourself and receive me darkness,
> Receive me and my lover too, he will not let me go
>   without him.
> I roll myself upon you as upon a bed, I resign myself
>   to the dusk.
> He whom I call answers me and takes the place of my lover,
> He rises with me silently from the bed.
> Darkness, you are gentler than my lover, his flesh was
>   sweaty and panting,
> I feel the hot moisture yet that he left me.

Whitman, however, becomes violently ashamed immediately after indulging in this fantasy; he follows it in the 1855 version of "The Sleepers" with a classic anxiety dream, intensified because the taboos which he has violated include those surrounding homosexuality as well as sex in general: "O hotcheek'd and blushing. . . // . . . my clothes were stolen while I was abed, / Now I am thrust forth, where

48. *Ibid.*, 355.

shall I run?" In the succeeding stanzas, his sexually spent "sinews flaccid," Whitman has several visions of death, both peaceful and violent. But by the poem's end, he is able to "trust" the forces that have taken him over; "I am not afraid, I have been well brought forward by you," he says in the last stanza, and we understand why lines about childhood and manhood directly follow those about Whitman's anxiety dream. The lines "a first sweet eating and drinking," the "life-swelling yolks," the "ear of rose-corn, milky and just ripened," and the liquor "spilled on lips and bosoms by touching glasses, and the best liquor afterward" imply that a new self has been born out of Whitman's sexual fantasies, a self whose oral stage of development foretells its sexual maturity. Whitman's desires seem primarily homosexual (thus the phallic ear of rose-corn, and the allusion to the liquor spilled on the lover's lips), but his sense of the deep-rooted connection between childhood and sexual identity— whether homosexual or heterosexual—is far-reaching, universal, and, by the poem's end, trusted.[49]

For Williams, dreams are as electric with sexual energy as they were for Whitman, and one of his most important reasons for writing the Improvisations was to encourage those energies to surface. In most of his Improvisations, Williams acts out his fantasies by displacing them into a mythological world of woods, satyrs, and dryads. As a satyr, Williams may safely pursue objects of sexual fantasy as aggressively as he wants to; the more complete the disguise, the more fully the dreamer can lose himself. In Improvisation XVI.2, for instance, Williams narrates a local story of a young woman in trouble by turning the characters into Greek gods and goddesses; as he becomes increasingly involved in his fantasy, his inhibitions and his intellectual distance from the events gradually disappear. The Improvisation begins with generalities about heroism and artistic responsibility: "The gods, the Greek gods, smothered in filth and ignorance. The race is scattered over the world. Where is its home? Find it if you've the genius." But Williams then adopts the colloquial language of excited males talking to each other about rescuing her: "They will come—the rare nights! The ground lifts and out sally the heroes of Sophokles, of Aeschylus. They go seeping down into our hearts, they rain upon us and in the bog they sink again down through the white roots, down—to a saloon back of the rail-road

49. Ibid., 651.

switch where they have that girl, you know, the one that should have been Venus by the lust that's in her. They've got her down there among the railroad men. A crusade couldn't rescue her. Up to jail— or call it down to Limbo—the Chief of Police our Pluto." In alluding to the Greek myths involving Venus and Kora, Williams neatly reverses their plots: for *this* Kora, her life in the daytime, workaday world, not the underground, is her true imprisonment. Pluto's court holds Kora prisoner in the heart of middle-class society, the chief of police's jail.

Williams' commentary on this Improvisation functions as an act of repression, of ironic distancing; it takes the point of view of the judge and the censuring town gossips. "When they came to question the girl before the local judge it was discovered that there were seventeen men more or less involved so that there was nothing to do but to declare the child a common bastard and send the girl about her business" (*I*, 60–61). Such an act functions in an analogous way to Whitman's anxiety dream in "The Sleepers": in both cases, the speaker shies away from fantasies that have suddenly surfaced. In Whitman's case, however, the withdrawal has all of the physical energy of the sexual act it imagined ("O hotcheek'd and blushing"), and it is only after several sections of the poem that Whitman is able to find a more "proper" and public form for his homoerotic fantasies, by retelling the story of the great affection George Washington's soldiers felt for him. Williams' act of repression in this representative Improvisation seems much colder and harsher, perhaps as a result of the commentaries being written after the Improvisations were completed. Very often the commentaries' acts of interpretation function as "mechanical interference," as Williams himself admitted (*I*, 116). One can well see how divided Williams was toward his own enterprise—he is both the "rescuer" of Kora and one of her imprisoners.

The most complex sexual fantasy in *Kora in Hell*, Improvisation XVII.2, interestingly enough, is about Williams' mother, Elena Hoheb Williams, as much as it is about Williams. In the prologue, Williams imagined her to be the Muse of his Improvisations, the perfect example of the primitive mind that he hoped to rescue, but in Improvisation I.3 he imagined her to be just the opposite, an Amsterdam matron personifying the superego. In Improvisation XVII.2, Williams confronts the contradictions in these two portraits of his mother.

There is some dispute over whether the *I* speaking this Improvisation's monologue is Williams or his mother; Kerry Driscoll, who has given the section its richest reading, believes it is Williams speaking, and that the Improvisation's function is "to strip away from Elena's character the deadening accumulation of many harsh years and so reveal her old time suppleness and true self. The metaphors he uses to describe this undertaking—weaving, spinning, unraveling—suggest the traditional activities of the three Fates, with the crucial difference that the poet is weaving *away*, moving backward in time through the trajectory of his mother's misfortunes, to get to the heart's dark, the secret core of her identity." In doing so, Driscoll argues, Williams finds a way of freeing himself from the repressive Victorian standards his mother taught to both her sons. Driscoll notes:

> [The] image of a dying flower dropping its petals signifies, on one level, Elena's loss of beauty, youth, and vitality, yet it can also be read as a metaphor for the religious and ethical values she passed on to her children. In fact, the phrase "bearing me under" appears to be a double entendre, referring to both the process of birth and a symbolic burial. What is most striking about Williams's statement, however, is its insinuation that his destiny is inextricably enmeshed with his mother's. Although he does not identify the exact nature of the "petals" which have buried him, the remainder of the passage suggests he is alluding to Elena's rigid moral standards. The phrase, "that which kissed my flesh for priest's lace so that I could not touch it," evokes the spiritual legacy of her Roman Catholic upbringing in its insistence on the sanctity and chasteness of the body and absolute denial of sensuality. As Williams told his friend John Thirlwall in 1953, "My poor mother always taught me the highest ideals: to be an artist—to be pure—to be sexless—and that almost tore me apart. . . ." It is only by "weaving" backward and imaginatively recreating the vagaries of Elena's sexual experience ("kiss recedes into kiss and kisses into looks") that the poet can escape the bonds of her repressive influence and acknowledge his own physicality.[50]

It is also possible to read the monologue as being spoken by Elena. This would make it even more remarkable, for in it Williams would be imagining how she is responding to her husband's (Williams' father's) death. (We cannot be sure whether the Improvisation was written before or after William George Williams' death in 1917: the crucial fact, though, is that the piece is pervaded by his passing.) As Williams imagines his mother, she secretly admits some of the same doubts about "proper" refusal to acknowledge sexuality that Williams was also experiencing. Memories of her marriage's early

---

50. Kerry Driscoll, "Mother Tongue, Mother Muse," 73–74; John C. Thirlwall, "Portrait of a Poet as His Mother's Son," in Charles Doyle (ed.), *William Carlos Williams: The Critical Heritage* (London, 1980), 324–25.

days and regret for "venomous words" and "honeymoon's end" quickly surface, and she imagines herself growing young and making love again. The paragraph, really a prose poem, then ends with an ecstatic image of the old woman transformed into a plant made of light breaking through earth's winter crust to bring spring. The Improvisation thus argues that Williams' mother is really Kora, not a repressive Amsterdam matron, and in the process it gives us the most detailed picture in all of *Kora in Hell* of how repression operates and of what kinds of healing may occur when the mind's censor is temporarily checked. To escape the sanitizing influence of his mother's genteel ideals, Williams imagined an alternative self for her in *Kora in Hell*, turning this other, secret self attributed to her into the very Muse of the book.

In general, Williams' daily Improvisations, like "The Sleepers," imply that such a recovery of visionary confidence is essential for sanity and health. But Williams tends not to have Whitman's oracular faith that visionary wandering may circumvent all acts of repression and heal all wounds. Hence *Kora in Hell* does not end quite as "The Sleepers" or "Song of Myself" (or even Improvisation XVII.2) does, with a triumphant victory over the forces of inhibition and a passing on of the poet's quest to his reader. "The Sleepers" closes with a stirring invocation to the powers of night and the unconscious; although they seemed threatening at the beginning of the poem, they are now maternal and nurturing:

> Why should I be afraid to trust myself to you?
> I am not afraid, I have been well brought forward by you,
> I love the rich running day, but I do not desert her in whom
>   I lay so long,
> . . . .
> I will duly pass the day O my mother, and duly
>   return to you.[51]

A maternal figure representing the healing powers of the unconscious is also at the heart of the Improvisations in *Kora in Hell*, in the person of Williams' own mother. And admittedly the last Improvisation in the book (and even the final commentary) are full of visionary confidence. Yet the true equivalent in *Kora in Hell* for Whitman's epilogue to "The Sleepers" is Williams' obstreperous prologue and the whole of his commentaries. (Many years later Williams suggested that the prologue—and, by implication, the commentaries as well—

---

51. Whitman, *Leaves of Grass*, 361.

are *Kora*'s "epilogue" [*IWWP*, 30]). Therefore, since even at their
best the commentaries represent classic examples of repressive "sec-
ondary revision," Williams' experiment with free association seems
to end on a decidedly more ambiguous and unsettling note than
Whitman's. Whitman implies that every night he will return to his
unconscious and that its forces will inevitably overcome all kinds of
physical and mental "congestion" and "stiflings," both in the indi-
vidual's and in the country's body politic. Williams in the end ap-
pears to be rather less sanguine, despite all his exuberant theorizing
about the methods and aims of his Improvisations. For if there is
automatic writing, Williams admits, there is also "automatic" repres-
sion or "mechanical interference" (*I*, 16), both in the Improvisa-
tions themselves and, particularly, in the later interpretations. Every
reading of his own Improvisations perhaps "brings forward" the vir-
tues of that piece, as Whitman would say, but it also inevitably
misreads and oversimplifies it; Kora-Eurydice can never be fully
rescued.

If Williams recognized this rather grim truth, his faith in the
importance of automatic writing remained unshaken. For this reason
the fate of Columbus haunts *Kora in Hell*: "The virtue of it all is in an
opening of the doors, though some rooms of course will be empty, a
break with banality, the continual hardening that habit enforces.
There is nothing left in me but the virtue of curiosity, Demuth puts
in. The poet should be forever at the ship's prow" (*I*, 28). "Ku-whee!
Ku-whee! It's a wind in the look-out's nest talking of Columbus,
whom no sea daunted, Columbus, chained below decks, bound
homeward" (*I*, 49). Note the contrast between the heroic de-
claratives of the first passage (from the prologue) to the complex
syntactic ironies of the second (from an actual Improvisation), where
freeing and enchaining occur within a single motion, a single twist of
syntax. This contrast is crucial to *Kora in Hell*: through it, Williams
discovers that every act of liberation inevitably involves an act of
enchaining as well. For him as well as for the Dadaists and Whitman,
the challenge of free writing is both impossible and indispensable. Its
wanderings, feints, and descents must always be beginning again,
forever liberated and forever condemned to be in midsentence, try-
ing "in desperation" to "cut across current" (*I*, 17).

FOUR/THE AGGREGATE IS UNTAMED
Williams' Dadaist Poetry

I didn't originate Dadaism but I had it in my soul to write it.
Spring and All shows that.

—William Carlos Williams

Searching to recover a spontaneous state of creativity, Francis Picabia, Marcel Duchamp, and other European Dadaists decided that Americans had just the prehistorical, naïve virtues they were looking for. They gleefully saw the decomposition of European cultural traditions grotesquely magnified in Americans' efforts to adopt many European tastes at once regardless of their mutual incompatibility and different historical contexts. And they took native American culture, both urban and rural, to be a chance for the European artist to explore a "primitive" or folk culture that had developed largely in ignorance of European canons of taste. In a revealing interview Duchamp gave just as he stepped off the boat in New York City in 1915, he said that "from the very instant one lands one realized that here is a people yearning, searching, trying to find something. . . . If only America would realize that the art of Europe is finished—dead—and that America is the country of the art of the future, instead of trying to base everything as she does on European traditions!"[1] Dickran Tashjian has pointed out that Duchamp's attitude toward America is a particularly Modernist version of a recurrent quest by Europeans "for the primitive in a flight from a presumably corrupt civilization."[2] That quest was initiated by Montaigne, popularized during the Enlightenment by Voltaire, Rousseau, and others, and more recently has motivated the pioneering field expeditions of French structuralist anthropology and the average French-

1. Duchamp quoted in Tashjian, *Skyscraper Primitives*, 50.
2. For Dada's primitivist strain, particularly its attitude toward America, see Tashjian's *Skyscraper Primitives*, especially ix–x; and Evan Maurer, "Dada and Surrealism," in William Rubin (ed.), *"Primitivism" in Twentieth-Century Art* (2 vols.; New York, 1984), II, 535–93.

man's fascination with energetic but *naïf* American heroes in denim such as John Wayne or Clint Eastwood. Duchamp and Picabia developed Dada's distinctive contribution to this age-old European myth: they sought their redeeming savages in the hitherto unexplored urban wilds.

But rather than expressing Dada's optimism that a pristine form of unconscious creativity could be recovered, many Dadaists were instead drawn to defining how the collective unconscious of an urban population is controlled through mass advertising. For the New York Dadaists, the best examples of America's folk culture were her industrial products and her advertising; they recognized that in an urban society mass production and mass communications represent the equivalent for the folk tradition in preindustrial societies. Their exploration of the workings of mass consumer culture was unmatched by European Dada—in fact, it is the one area in which New York Dada may be said to be clearly in advance of its European counterpart. Such leadership was only natural: by the 1920s America was in the vanguard of both commercial advertising and assembly-line production.

Three aspects of Dada's critique of commercial culture particularly influenced Williams' poetry. The first two are associated with New York Dada: Duchamp's "readymades" (sculptures that turned industrial products into art), and the subversive Dadaist elements that Williams' friend Charles Demuth inserted into many of his paintings in the 1920s. The third aspect, collage, was brought to its fullest development in Europe but crossed the Atlantic in time to influence *Spring and All,* which contains Dadaist collage poems whose techniques and ideas differ markedly from Williams' Cubist poems.

Both Picabia and Duchamp thought of themselves as connoisseurs of the new phenomena of American consumer society. Picabia copied ads for products like spark plugs and Model T windshields and drew a series of imaginary erotic machines with swivels, spirals, nodes, and rods, giving them satiric names like *Prostitution universelle* or (for a spark plug ad) *Portrait d'une jeune fille americaine,* thus comically connecting commercial abundance with sexual license.[3] Duchamp also copied ads and commercial window displays and invented sexual machines, but he was most notorious for his readymades. The rejec-

3. For excellent discussions of Picabia's New York period, see Tashjian, *Skyscraper Primitives,* 35–38; and Jan Thompson, "Picabia and His Influence on American Art," 14–21.

tion by the jury of the New York Independent Artists' Exhibition of one of his readymades, a men's urinal entitled *Fountain* and signed "R. Mutt, 1917," prompted his most influential statement on American technology, an anonymous defense of the piece in the New York Dada magazine *The Blind Man* in 1917.

Duchamp's statement may appear to be simply in praise of American industry, but in fact it is one of Duchamp's most ingeniously wry pronouncements: it affirms and negates with equal measure. On one hand, it defends Mutt's actions and succinctly defines Duchamp's criteria for ready-made art: "Whether Mr. Mutt with his own hands made the fountain or not has no importance. He CHOSE it. He took an ordinary article of life, placed it so that its useful significance disappeared under the new title and point of view—created a new thought for that object." On the other hand, Duchamp had special reasons for choosing a piece of American bathroom plumbing for his new readymade. In answering the charge that his *Fountain* was not art but merely "a plain piece of plumbing," Duchamp said: "That is absurd. The only works of art America has given are her plumbing and her bridges."[4] However positive this statement may seem at first, upon rereading it slowly negates itself if *only* is allowed to receive more emphasis than *art*. Moreover, if Duchamp's position is to reject art history, then it is easy to see that the motives for his praising America are double-edged. He lauds her not for the art that she will contribute but because she has been the one country to accord art and artists *less* status than industrial engineers.

Duchamp's own readymades reflect his rejection of the belief that the artist is a craftsman creating unique objects. For one of his first readymades, created in France in 1913, Duchamp took an item familiar to every French bourgeois kitchen, a bottle-drying rack, and proclaimed it to be a sculpture. In doing so, he chose an object that still reflected the craftsmanship of the artist; although the metal of the rack was mass-produced, the rack itself was assembled by hand. Having arrived in America, however, Duchamp was impressed with the rate at which handicraft was being replaced by mass-production techniques, and several of his American readymades—particularly a snow shovel (1915), a machine-made ball of twine (1916), and the urinal (1917)—reflect that change. Duchamp implies that machine-made objects may compete with the oeuvre of the greatest artist; they

4. Lippard (ed.), *Dadas on Art*, 143.

are *the* representative art created by America's "democratic" culture of mass production and mass consumption. Thus they are truly the art of the age of mechanical reproduction.

Duchamp's persona R. Mutt alludes both to the gambler Mutt in the Mutt and Jeff comic strip (which had recently become popular) and to a then well known local plumbing manufacturer, the J. L. Mott Iron Works Company.[5] As the supposed creator of the *Fountain*, Mr. Mutt, a corporate man, becomes America's artist-laureate, for he and his work reflect most accurately the revolutionary changes for the workman caused by industrialization. Yet "R. Mutt" is apparently also a pun on the German word *Armut* (poverty).[6] Duchamp therefore remains ironically detached from his alter ego, seeing him as modern but impoverished or, at best, primitive. Not only are readymades the only art America has given the twentieth century but, Duchamp caustically implies, the only truly representative art this century's workers can ever create. Machine-made objects are an industrial culture's version of the primitive, irrational art created by artists in touch with their gods. In our case, the divine force is electricity; the machines it runs and the hardware those machines produce are our century's true icons, and the engineers and admen who make and promote them are our true technicians of the sacred.

Duchamp's ironic use of the language of mass production and advertising had a catalytic effect on artists and intellectuals living in the New York area. Of particular interest for the student of Williams' work is the writing of Walter Arensberg, Duchamp's patron, for along with the writing that Duchamp, Man Ray, Matthew Josephson, and others did for the New York Dadaist magazines it provides an important precedent for Williams' own experiments in *Spring and All*. In 1919, for example, Arensberg published a piece of comic Dadaist prose in the New York Dadaist magazine *TNT*, en-

5. See Naumann, "The Big Show: The First Exhibition of the Society of Independent Artists," Part I, 39n, for both the Mutt and Jeff and Mott and Co. connections. Duchamp's allusion to the plumbing firm explains Williams' otherwise inexplicable slip in his autobiography, in which he mentions that the urinal was signed "Mott and Co." (134). Afterward, apparently everyone in Arensberg's circle was in on the joke. *Marcel Duchamp in Perspective*, a collection of essays edited by Joseph Masheck, contains much useful discussion of Duchamp. However, the most relevant essay for analyzing the ways in which Duchamp's readymades are icons of consumer culture is not explicitly on Duchamp: it is Walter Benjamin's "The Work of Art in the Age of Mechanical Reproduction," in Hannah Arendt (ed.), *Illuminations* (New York, 1969), 217–51. For more on the connection between Williams and Duchamp, see Marling, *William Carlos Williams and the Painters*, 55–67; and Sayre, "Ready-mades and Other Measures," 3–22.

6. This was first noted by Lucy Lippard. See Lippard (ed.), *Dadas on Art*, 140.

titled "Vacuum Tires: A Formula for the Digestion of Figments." Its
deadpan use of jargon, non sequiturs, and run-on syntax anticipates
many of the best Dadaist poems in *Spring and All*, especially works
such as "At the Faucet of June," whose lines "a song / inflated
to / fifty pounds pressure" may be an oblique homage to Arensberg.
Here is Arensberg's first paragraph:

> When the shutter from a dry angle comes between the pin and a special
> delivery it appears blue. Likewise in concert with strings on any other flow the
> clock of third evenings past Broadway is alarming, because it is written in
> three-four time to chewing gum; if you upset the garter, the r remains west, or
> to the left of flesh, as in revolving or Rector's. The whole effect is due to blinds,
> drawn in arithmetic to a sketch of halves, which are smoked into double disks.
> By such a system of instantaneous tickets a given volume of camera, analyzed
> for uric acid, leaves a deposit of ten dollars, and the style decrees that human
> surfaces be worn for transparencies, the price mark being removed from the
> lapel. 7

The Dadaists' satire of European art and their ironic endorsement
of American commercial art gave Williams many of the satiric tools
he needed for *Spring and All*. And yet he knew that Dada's nihilism
was as simplistic as it was eloquent: American commercial culture
was simply a more complex mixture of virtue and vice than the
Europeans supposed. Williams would use Dadaist rhetorical strat-
egies in his prose and poetry when he wanted to satirize European
culture and American commercialism, as he does in the Dadaist
poems in *Spring and All*. But when he felt it necessary to provide an
antidote to such satiric nihilism, he turned to Cubism and (particu-
larly) to the tenets of Precisionism, which allowed him to depict the
inventive intelligence and moral virtue of American craftsmen and
engineers, not their naïveté.

In Charles Demuth, Williams' closest friend among the Precisionists,
Williams found an artist who could strike a wry balance between
Precisionism and Dada. Although they promote the Precisionist
virtues of clarity, monumentalism, and optimism, Demuth's paint-
ings of the early 1920s also have subversive Dadaist ironies encoded
in their titles and in the fragments of words (often from advertising)
that they reproduce within the pictures. These Dadaist elements
offer what is arguably an even more trenchant critique of commercial

---

7. Walter Arensberg, "Vacuum Tires: A Formula for the Digestion of Figments," *TNT*
(1919). Quoted in Naumann, "Walter Conrad Arensberg," 22.

American culture than Duchamp's *Fountain* and were a crucial form-
ative influence on the Dadaist poems of *Spring and All.*[8]

Consider four paintings of Demuth's that were part of his shows at
the Daniel Gallery in New York City in 1920 and 1922, *End of the
Parade: Coatesville, Pa. (The Milltown), Nospmas M. Egiap Nospmas
M., Business,* and *Spring.* All were known to Williams, and he owned
End of the Parade. The paintings display Demuth's interest in intro-
ducing the harsh colors and repetitive geometric forms of industrial
and commercial subjects into landscape painting. *End of the Parade*
depicts the buildings and smokestacks of the Lukens steel plant in
Coatesville, Pennsylvania. The composition is ordered by objects in
groups of three: smokestacks, ventilators, and windows replicate
themselves before our eyes, as if off of an assembly line (see Illustra-
tion 7). Most of the windows in the building receding into the
distance in the lower right are merely sketched in, implying that the
buildings as well as the things they make are serially mass-produced.
Nospmas depicts grain elevators in Demuth's hometown of Lan-
caster, Pennsylvania, that had been built just two years before. (The
same buildings provided the subject for one of Demuth's late master-
pieces, *My Egypt* [1927]). Imposing white silos and conveyer-belt
sheds rise above short reddish buildings in the foreground, occluding
any view of the sky and compressing the entire space of the painting
toward the picture plane. Larger fragments of letters dominate the
edges of the canvas, with one group—FLOU—apparently taken from
a billboard advertisement for flour.[9] *Business* reproduces a similarly
two-dimensional space, as if the serial factory windows receding into
space at the left side of *End of the Parade* had been turned frontally
toward the viewer and transformed into a calendar chronicling the
working week (see Illustration 8). In *Business* the rigid geometry of
the buildings has now become the fixed grid of the business week

8. My discussion of the Dadaist elements in Demuth's painting is indebted to Fahlman,
Pennsylvania Modern, although I place more emphasis on the importance of Demuth's Dadaist
titles than Fahlman does. For other discussions of Demuth, see Milton W. Brown, "Cubist-
Realism: An American Style"; Brown, *American Painting from the Armory Show to the Depres-
sion,* 114–16; Friedman, *The Precisionist View in American Art;* Dijkstra, *Cubism, Stieglitz, and
the Early Poetry of William Carlos Williams;* Tashjian, *William Carlos Williams and the American
Scene;* Davidson, *Early American Modernist Painting;* Marling, *William Carlos Williams and the
Painters;* and Sayre, "Avant-Garde Dispositions: Placing *Spring and All* in Context."

9. For background on *The End of the Parade* see Fahlman, *Pennsylvania Modern,* 42–43.
Nospmas and *My Egypt* are also illustrated and discussed *ibid.,* 46, 58–59. *Nospmas* has been
analyzed by Alvord L. Eiseman, "Charles Demuth: His Life, Psychology and Works" (Ph.D.
dissertation, New York University, 1976), who points out the possible connection to the story
of Sampson's pride and self-destruction (362; quoted by Fahlman, *Pennsylvania Modern,* 46).

Charles Demuth, *End of the Parade: Coatesville, Pa. (The Milltown)*
The Regis Collection, Minneapolis, MN

Charles Demuth, *Business*, c. 1929, oil on canvas, 50.8 × 61.6 cm, Miss Georgia O'Keeffe Gift, 1949.529 © 1987 The Art Institute of Chicago. All Rights Reserved.

Courtesy of the Art Institute of Chicago

which Demuth then wittily suggests has even more *substance* than the buildings themselves: the buildings appear only as shadows on the calendar, while the grid of the working week—the mental organization that invented mass production in the first place—dwarfs in importance the buildings it created. *Spring* also equates two-dimensionality with the unlimited, springlike "bounty" of industrial design: in this case, the products are shirt-fabric samples; the industry, New England's textile business. The samples are spread out before us on the flat space of the picture plane, as if on a table for a customer.[10]

In many ways these paintings of Demuth's are as celebratory as any painting of Sheeler's or any of Stieglitz's photographs of skyscrapers. And yet the works' use of language and their insistent, slightly claustrophobic two-dimensionality suggest a hidden skepticism about their subjects. The title *End of the Parade*, for example, refers to the fact that the annual Fourth of July parade in Coatesville would end at the factory gates, but its dominant blacks and grays also imply that any festival in a company town ends in—and is dominated by—assembly-line regimentation. Demuth's inscription gives a more foreboding edge to the painting than if, as Sheeler often did, he had merely named it after the owners or the location of the plant. *Nospmas M. Egiap Nospmas M.*, as several scholars have noted, reads "M. Sampson Paige M. Sampson" when read backwards and may be a calculated sample of Dadaist mockery as well as an allusion to the biblical Sampson. The name reads like a parody of a tycoon's name, reproduced *ad infinitum* to give a false sense of monumentality. Such Dadaist subversion may be thought of as the painting's subtext, causing it to speak against itself even as it constructs forms of praise. *Business* and *Spring* also push the two-dimensionality of *Nospmas* to its furthest extreme. The latter's ironies are more lighthearted, but the former painting, witty as it is, may also be the most subversive work in all of Demuth's oeuvre. In *Business*, the repetitive forms and "force-lines" (the ruler-straight lines that often streak across Demuth's industrial paintings) that suggest modern industry's power and plenty in other works become a domineering grid that structures all human life, all time. The work is a meditation on how assembly-line organization creates a new form of serialized, repetitive, "industrial time" rather than the "natural" time associated with performing

10. *Business* is illustrated and discussed in Fahlman, *Pennsylvania Modern*, 48; *Spring* is illustrated and discussed in Sayre, "Avant-Garde Dispositions: Placing *Spring and All* in Context," 28–29. Sayre emphasizes the painting's wit and its patent two-dimensionality.

most nonindustrial tasks.[11] In it, the force-lines that so empower
Demuth's other paintings have become imprisoning. The figure 5 in
Demuth's *I Saw the Figure 5 in Gold*, for example, leaps out at the
viewer filled with the vigor and brassiness of urban life,[12] but in
Business the figure 5 is shut within the drab seriality of the grid and its
work ethic. Demuth's title for the painting, interestingly, is uniquely
deadpan, as if the painted forms were so subversive that he did not
need to use his title as he commonly did, to introduce irony.

In addition to Duchamp's and Demuth's multiple ironies, one other
Dadaist technique—collage—proved indispensable for Williams'
work in the 1920s. The collage techniques employed in the 1921
Dada manifesto in *The Little Review* and other Dada pieces differ
significantly from Cubist collage techniques. Although Dada art and
poetry borrowed the tricks that both Picasso and Apollinaire used,
Dada artists spurned what they thought was the calculating way that
Cubist artists and writers deployed their techniques to create witty,
self-referential art. Picasso and Apollinaire may have seemed icono-
clastic to more traditional artists, but to the Dadaists, ironically, they
represented the epitome of decadence—the admiration of technique
for its finesse and market value. Dadaists' assessments of Cubism may
have been blinded by rivalry, but their understanding of their dif-
ferences with that movement was quite correct. Cubism meditated
upon order; Dada sought to scramble the faculty of reason and cap-
ture the convulsive, ephemeral, and fundamentally asocial creations
of the unconscious. Thus in Tzara's 1918 manifesto, he proclaimed
that "we have enough cubist and futurist academies: laboratories of
formal ideas," and *The Little Review* manifesto referred to the careful
construction and gray tonality of Analytic Cubism as "a cathedral of
artistic liver paste."[13]

Roger Shattuck has defined most cogently the differences between
Cubist and Dadaist collage. He shows that both share the techniques
of fragmentation and juxtaposition, but in Cubist art, "the fragmen-
tation of visual unity did not at the start introduce any theme totally
alien to the composition. The painted bottles and pipes as well as
scraps of newspaper and playing cards belong to an enlarged percep-

11. The classic article on this subject is E. P. Thompson's "Time, Work-Discipline, and
Industrial Capitalism," *Past and Present*, XXXVIII (1967), 56–97.
12. Illustrated in Dijkstra, *Cubism, Stieglitz, and the Early Poetry of William Carlos Williams*,
Plate VII.
13. Lippard (ed.), *Dadas on Art*, 15, 163.

tual unity. . . . German Dada and French surrealism, on the other hand, often juxtaposed fragments of a world that display no apparent relation to one another unless one detours through the underground channels of chance and unconscious association. They put practically anything into the picture."[14] In other words, Analytic Cubist works dissect their subjects from many angles, while Synthetic Cubist collages juxtapose the language of art with objects that it might depict—such as newspapers or playing cards—that were part of the artist's life while he was working on the picture. Although Cubist collages therefore give a radical critique of mimesis, they nevertheless respect the unities of place, time, and individual consciousness. Many of the items in one of Picasso's Synthetic Cubist collages are meant to remind the artist and his friends of specific events in their lives; the words and objects are self-consciously autobiographical as well as iconographic. In a Dadaist collage, conversely, the presence of a unifying, individualistic consciousness must not be strongly felt. The associations that the collage's objects evoke are schizophrenic and cryptic, with no sense of order derived from the unities of place, time, subject matter, and private memory. In a Cubist work the controlling intention of the artist sooner or later must emerge as the dominant factor in the composition. Thus, as the Dadaists understood, the Cubist artist celebrates analysis, invention, revision, balance, and wit. Cubist works are indeed "laboratories for formal ideas," not the bomb factories the Dadaists wanted. Dada's materials are not remembered and arranged so much as dismembered and deranged.

Shattuck does not extend his distinction between Cubist and Dadaist art to literature, but such a distinction does seem possible and useful. Apollinaire's poem "Lundi Rue Christine," as the title

14. Roger Shattuck, "The Mode of Juxtaposition," in Caws (ed.), *About French Poetry From Dada to 'Tel Quel,'* 20. Also relevant are Perloff's book, *The Poetics of Indeterminacy,* and her article, "The Invention of Collage," in *Collage,* New York Literary Forum, Volume X–XI (New York, 1983), 5–47. Perloff's book emphasizes the similarities rather than the differences between Cubist and Dadaist collage. But in her article on collage, she defines Cubist collage in such a way as to differentiate it from Dadaist collage. For Perloff, Cubist collage has a discernible "radius of discourse"; Dada, presumably, does not: "Malevich underestimates the play of signifiers, the equivocation of cubist collage, but he rightly discerns that in a work like Picasso's *Violin and Fruit,* items like newspaper fragments, violin shapes, fruit, table, female forms, and wine glasses are metonymically related, that they belong, in other words, to the same radius of discourse and are synthesized insofar as they lose their separateness in the process of integration" (34–35). Other important general discussion of collage in the visual arts are Hanna Wescher, *Collage* (New York, 1968); William C. Seitz, *The Art of Assemblage* (New York, 1968); and Rosalind Krauss, "In the Name of Picasso." Krauss' deconstructive reading of the collage form has had considerable recent influence.

suggests, is a collage of many things seen, heard, and thought as the poet spent part of a Monday on that street in Paris. An identifiable place and time unite the poem's otherwise comically incongruous details:

> Three gas lamps burning
> The boss's wife has TB
> When you're through we'll have time for a fast
>   game of backgammon
> An orchestra conductor with a bad sore throat
> If you ever get to Tunis you'll have to have
>   some kief
> That seems to make sense sort of [15]

Leroy Breunig has recently argued that a Dadaist poem must resist any such integration; it should not suggest that it was inspired by a particular place and time and that its details were chosen by a discriminating intelligence. Perhaps alluding to Tzara's call in his 1918 manifesto for a poetry of "indominable madness, decomposition," Breunig states that a truly Dadaist poem must obdurately remain in fragments: "If upon successive readings the poem resists all efforts to discover its coherence, it remains Dada; it is a 'destruct.' If the apparently disconnected fragments gradually communicate a convergence of diverse but interrelated meanings, it becomes cubist; it is a 'construct.'"[16]

The 1921 Dada manifesto that Williams saw in *The Little Review* meets such criteria for being Dadaist. Disdainful and cacophonous, the piece dispenses with an identifiable speaker, a single setting, or a unified tone; it is filled with non sequiturs, run-on sentences, contradictions, crude jokes, mixed metaphors, and cultural references that mix the highbrow and the lowbrow. In one passage, for example, the text mentions in quick succession accordions, women's pants (unheard of in the early 1920s, of course), the fatherland, sardines, art, Verlaine, salads, genius, the Holy Virgin, and the eight-hour day. It concludes with a warning about forgeries: "Imitators of DADA want to present DADA in an *artistic* form which it has never had"; such forms cannot have "the PURE IDIOCY claimed by DADA."[17]

It is clear from Williams' poetry and his essays in *Contact* that he

---

15. Translated by Michael Benedikt, in Benedikt (ed.), *The Poetry of Surrealism*, 25.
16. Leroy C. Breunig, "From Dada to Cubism: Apollinaire's 'Arbre,'" in Caws (ed.), *About French Poetry from Dada to 'Tel Quel,'* 39. See also Eric Sellin's article "The Esthetics of Ambiguity: Reverdy's Use of Syntactic Simultaneity," *ibid.*, 112–25, in which he discusses the influence of Cubism on Reverdy; and Perloff, *The Poetics of Indeterminacy*, 109–54.
17. Translated by Lucy Lippard, in Lippard (ed.), *Dadas on Art*, 162–63.

well understood the tenets of Dada's collage anti-aesthetic—its cal-culatedly irrational use of Cubist fragmentation for the purposes of parody and satire. Perhaps one reason why it captured his imagina-tion was that it contrasted so sharply with the aesthetic of the care-fully composed "composition" that Williams was simultaneously adapting using Precisionist and Cubist ideas. Indeed, in an introduc-tory essay for his first issue of *Contact*, Williams praised Dada's meth-ods and (using Tzara's very word) called Dada's art one of "decom-position" rather than composition. He saw such methods to be particularly applicable to satirizing American materialism and its hypocritical worship of European high art. "This America," he said scornfully, "is a bastard country where decomposition is the preva-lent spectacle." To criticize it, Williams would adopt Dada's ironic mimicry of chaos and write work that was as "decomposed" and irrational as its subjects.[18]

As a result, of all the American writers whose art reflects the disgust and disenchantment of the postwar years—including Eliot, Pound, and Hemingway—only Williams fully captures the demoli-tionist's art that was Dada. The anger of *Mauberley*, "In Another Country," or *The Waste Land* is more distanced and ironic than the convulsive, exorcistic energy of French and German Dada. In Williams' Dadaist poems, Dada is able to do with the English lan-guage what it did with French and German—startle, shame, teach, and make us laugh and grimace.

Evidence of the influence of Dada's disgust with reason, social mores, and history can be found in the middle phases of Williams' poetic career, from "March" (1916) to the first four books of *Paterson* (1946–51). Metaphors of violent destruction occur repeatedly in this period, including that of a flood, as in *Paterson*, Book Three, Section II; a car wreck, as in "Romance Moderne" and "To Elsie"; a dangerous underground journey, as in "Sub Terra," *Kora in Hell*, or

18. *Contact*, I (December, 1920), 10. Williams adds that the "decomposition" of which he speaks does not compare with that satirized by French Dada: "the contour [of the spectacle of decomposition in America] is not particularly dadaesque and that's the gist it." Williams' offhand qualification here seems designed to affirm his independence of the Dada movement even as he borrows from it. For another reference to Dada by Williams, see *Contact*, V (June, 1923), 2, in which he compares the "disjointed dada composition" with Spenser's "Epithala-mion," "a most beautiful thing, all of one piece." I do not know whether he knew of Tzara's special use of the word *decomposition*, but by 1920 the word had become commonly associated with all Dadaist work. I use this key word differently from Perloff, who applies it to Williams' Cubism. See Perloff, *The Poetics of Indeterminacy*, 109–54.

Paterson, Book Three, III; a firestorm, as in the poem dated "10/21" from *The Descent of Winter* or in *Paterson,* Book Three, II; or an apocalypse like that in the opening pages of *Spring and All.*

The violent force that appears to have most fascinated Williams was the March wind. He wrote poem after poem about it, starting with "March," in which he lets the winds loose, and ending with the moving late lyric "The Lady Speaks" (1955), in which he finally shuts the wind out. This group of stormy Dadaist poems may be called Williams' "black wind" lyrics, after the poem of that title in *Spring and All.* As a whole, the group well shows one way in which Williams expressed Dadaist disgust in his poetry. Beginning with *Spring and All* (and *The Great American Novel,* also composed in 1922), however, such random Dadaist violence is merged with an angry analysis of mass commercial culture that reflects the influence of Duchamp, Demuth, and *The Little Review* manifesto.

In Williams' black wind lyrics the poet is usually pictured walking alone, often at night, in a sour or even violent mood. Williams' use of the wind was in part merely destructive, a need to fill his poems with invective, but it also helped him to clear the air and discover new possibilities for seeing and writing. March was Williams' favorite month because its weather alternates so rapidly—often within minutes—between winter's turbulence and spring's calm.

In "March," Williams uses the wind's violence to help him uproot the influence Pound had on his second volume, *The Tempers* (1913). "March" was written concurrently with many of the poems in Williams' next volume, *Al Que Quiere!,* but its awkward, transitional style, which ricochets between being formal and informal, distinguishes it from the other poems in that book. (It was eventually published in *Sour Grapes* in 1921.)[19] If "March" is a failure, however, it is a most interesting one, for it accurately reflects Williams' struggle to pull up some of his own most rooted mannerisms. Williams' Dadaist disgust thus was not merely self-righteously directed at literary history or contemporary society; it involved a harsh judgment of his own earlier work.

Half of "March" reflects the influence of Pound, written in the allusive style of *The Tempers.* It mentions artworks, artists, and pagan and Christian myths, and dutifully stands in awe before the splendors of the past. But the other half of the poem is a barbaric yawp that

19. See Wallace, *A Bibliography of William Carlos Williams,* 10–12, 169.

Pound in 1916 would have deplored; its creative energy is less like the hushed perfection of Fra Angelico, whom Williams at one point says he hopes to use as a model, than like the roar of the March winds that periodically interrupts the poem's decorous aestheticism. This is telling: the black winds first appear in Williams' work when he is trying to free himself from Pound's image of the poet as a cultured cosmopolitan. With one blast, the winds seem to offer release, escape, and the discovery of a new identity. This split personality in "March" particularly disturbed Hilda Doolittle, the poet H. D., who wrote to Williams expressing her admiration for parts of the poem, correctly seeing them as being "in the tone and spirit of your *Postlude,*" the poem in *The Tempers* that contained the most classical allusions. But she was also shocked by the civil war occurring within Williams. "I trust you will not hate me for wanting to delete from your poem all the flippancies. . . . It's very well to *mock* at yourself—it is a spiritual sin to mock at your inspiration."[20] Yet that mocking is central to the poem—is in fact its strongest source. With it, Williams is able to exorcise one self and begin making another.

Williams seeks "the flowers of March," the products of his violent, "third" springtime. These are fundamentally different from those of his "second" springtime, which were painted by Fra Angelico and thus stood for all the riches of European artistic tradition that so awed Williams in his second book of poems. Williams now both mocks his second book's style and laments his present poverty:

> I spring among them,
> seeking one flower
> in which to warm myself!
> I deride with all the ridicule
> of misery—
> my own starved misery.
>
> (CP1, 140–41)

Williams then attempts to set his own (largely imaginary) band of American bohemian geniuses against the established London circle of Pound, Eliot, Yeats, and other young poets appearing in *The Egoist* and promoting European art. Williams' vagabonds will "cut" Europe:

> Come, good, cold fellows!
> Have we no flowers?
> Defy then with even more
> desperation than ever. . . .

20. H. D.'s letter was printed as part of Williams' prologue to *Kora in Hell.* See *Imaginations,* 12–13, and the notes on "March" in *CP1,* 493–95.

> But though you are lean and frozen—
> think of the blue bulls of Babylon.
>
> Fling yourself upon
>   their empty roses—
>   cut savagely!
>
> (*CP1*, 140–41)

Strangely, however, in the poem's last lines Williams suddenly re-
tracts his challenge to Europe. The lines may reflect revisions sug-
gested by H. D.,[21] but they certainly also reflect Williams' fear in
1916 that if he defied Europe he would have nothing left to write
about: "But— / think of the painted monastery / at Fiesole," he con-
cludes (*CP1*, 141). As the poem's opening shows, the Williams who
had already launched his career as an obstetrician feared that he
might not be able to bring about his own birth as an artist. March,
the season of birth, is "a flower or two picked / . . . / . . . against
treacherous / bitterness of wind, and sky shining / teasingly, then
closing in black / and sudden, with fierce jaws" (*CP1*, 137).

By 1918, only two years later, Williams was more confident. In the
prologue to *Kora in Hell*, he prints the letter H. D. sent him about
"March" and then replies that the derision to which she objected
actually "filled a gap [in the poem] that I did not know how better to
fill at the time." Further, he implies that his poem's violence cleared
the ground, in typical Dada fashion, for the systematic experimenta-
tion of *Kora in Hell*: "It might be said that that touch is the prototype
of the improvisations" (*I*, 13). "March," like Williams' more well
known poem, "The Wanderer," is thus a pivotal poem in his career;
it leads him away from *The Tempers* and toward *Al Que Quiere!*, the
volume with which he enters literary history as his own man.

"Spring Strains" (1916) rewrites "March" from the point of view
of the newly confident Williams who is everywhere in evidence in *Al
Que Quiere!*. The straining, grappling energy of the poem is similar
to that of "March," but it uses only plain American materials—
birds, a tree, and the March weather—and it ends with a reference
to a successful birth. True, the labor contractions are violent ones:
the wind seeks to uproot the tree, the taproot determinedly anchors
the tree to the ground, and all are interrupted by screaming birds
giving chase to each other in a mating dance. But the poem ends

---

21. See *Imaginations*, 12, where Williams says that "thanks to her own and her husband's
friendly attentions," "March" appeared in *The Egoist*, III (October, 1916) "in a purified form."
Compare Fredman, *Poet's Prose*, 41.

with a clear reference to Williams delivering his "third" springtime
(and his third book of poems) from the womb:

> (Hold hard, rigid jointed trees!)
> the blinding and red-edged sun-blur—
> creeping energy, concentrated
> counterforce—welds sky, buds, trees,
> rivets them in one puckering hold!
> Sticks through! Pulls the whole
> counter-pulling mass upward. . . .
> (CP1, 97–98)

Williams' later "black wind" poems show their maturity by com-
bining and complicating the rhetoric of "March" and "Spring
Strains." In "The Farmer" in *Spring and All* (Poem III), for example, a
solitary figure strolls through the March landscape; the last season's
growth is killed, uprooted, and plowed under, leaving the fields
"blank." Unlike the figure in "March," though, the poet-farmer has
finished his work of derision; his mind has cleared away the past's
dead stalks, and new thoughts may now break through the earth. But
his work remains twofold, one of uprooting as well as planting. His
double roles are emphasized by Williams' use of the dash in the
poem's concluding lines: "the artist figure of / the farmer" is a "com-
posing / —antagonist" (CP1, 186).

In another poem in *Spring and All*, "The Black Winds" (Poem V),
we get a few glimpses of the artist's role as composer, but the poem
emphasizes his role as antagonist or "decomposer." Of all the poems
in the volume, it is the most angry and disarrayed. Strident voices
interrupt, mock, and contradict each other. and there is no progres-
sion toward a resolution, only a heightening of noise. The poem's
divisions dangerously approach those of schizophrenia, and this
makes it not only difficult but harrowing to read. Its opening lines
recall "March." One wonders how H. D. would have reacted:

> Black winds from the north
> enter black hearts. Barred from
> seclusion in lilies they strike
> to destroy—
> Beastly humanity
> where the wind breaks it—
>
>   strident voices, heat
> quickened, built of waves
> Drunk with goats or pavements
> (CP1, 189–90)

Here, humanity is a beast, and genteel culture is shown to be unknowingly governed by the same brute competitiveness that Theodore Dreiser depicted in his parable of the lobster and the squids in the first chapter of *The Financier:* " 'How is life organized?' Things lived on each other—that was it. Lobsters lived on squids and other things. What lived on lobsters? Men, of course! Sure, that was it! And what lived on men? he asked himself. Was it other men?"[22] Williams' poem gives us lightning-flash glimpses of such blind, unthinking violence. We see mobs in action and perhaps labor strife but certainly also the anger and anxiety provoked by pedestrian crowds and traffic jams in a heat wave. And "Drunk with goats" elaborates the earlier adjective "beastly," adding a suggestion of sexual violence as well.

In the next lines of the poem, Williams refuses to seek obscurantist excuses for this violence. He argues that it is found not only in the unconscious mind (the "night") but also in the sunlight of reason itself, in the "day / of flowers and rocks":

> Hate is of the night and the day
> of flowers and rocks. Nothing
> is gained by saying the night breeds
> murder—It is the classical mistake
> . . . .
> Sold to them men knock blindly together
> splitting their heads open
> (*CP1*, 190)

The mazelike modern city is a shambles, both a vast ruin and a slaughterhouse where beasts and men have their skulls split open before they are butchered. The violent collisions of pedestrian crowds and traffic jams in the poem's opening lines have become even more horrific. Near the poem's end, the poet's despair at this spectacle has left him exhausted: "Black wind, I have poured my heart out / to you until I am sick of it—" (*CP1*, 190).

Yet some hope does emerge, tentatively, amid the holocaust of "The Black Winds"—perhaps the equivalent of the announcement that "SPRING IS HERE" in the prose. Immediately after the image of men knocking blindly together comes another image of collision:

> That is why boxing matches and
> Chinese poems are the same—That is why
> Hartley praises Miss Wirt
> (*CP1*, 190)

At first the stanza may seem like a further example of the destruc-

22. Theodore Dreiser, *The Financier* (1912; rpr. New York, 1967), 8–9.

tiveness of both high and low culture. But both Chinese poems and boxing matches (ideally) exhibit well-timed, controlled energy, whereas traffic jams, fighting, and drunkenness do not. This impression is confirmed when one searches Marsden Hartley's *Adventures in the Arts* (mentioned again later in the prose of *Spring and All* [I, 150]) for a Miss Wirt. It turns out that Hartley devotes an entire chapter to praising a "May Wirth," an Australian equestrienne-acrobat, saying, "I have always been a lover of these artists of bodily vigour, of muscular melody."[23] Moreover, a single figure unites the seemingly disparate interests of poetry and boxing, a figure who despite all the reservations Williams had about his art still stood in Williams' mind for the artist's ability to synthesize order. That figure is Ezra Pound, the "inventor of Chinese poetry in our time" and (perhaps less importantly) an earnest student of boxing under Ernest Hemingway.[24]

Pound returns as a model for ordering chaos near the poem's end, where Williams refers to Pound's poem, "Exile's Letter," that he translated from the Chinese for his volume *Cathay* (1915) using Ernst Fenollosa's notes. Williams no longer imitates Pound to praise him, however; in fact, he rewrites Pound's poem:

> The grief of the bowmen of Shu
> moves nearer—There is
> an approach with difficulty from
> the dead—the winter casing of grief
> (CPI, 191)

Pound used the bowmen fighting at the Mongolian frontier to allude to the European soldiers fighting in the trenches in 1915.[25] Their fight is meaningless, their only desire to be home with the ones they are writing to. Not so for Williams. "The Black Winds," it is true, is a kind of exile's letter written by one forced to work in the trenches of the modern city, a desperate telegram sent in sentence-fragments while under bombardment. But Pound's poem is elegiac and dignified; Williams' is harried, angry, and declamatory. And for Williams

23. Marsden Hartley, *Adventures in the Arts* (New York, 1921), 175. See also Dijkstra, 179n, and CPI, 502.
24. The phrase "the inventor of Chinese poetry in our time" is Eliot's. See Kenner, *The Pound Era*, 192. For the story of Pound and boxing, see Carlos Baker, *Ernest Hemingway: A Life Story* (New York, 1969), 86; and Hemingway's own account, "Ezra Pound and his Bel Esprit," in *A Moveable Feast* (New York, 1964), 105–12. Hemingway emphasizes that his student could not learn the left hook.
25. Kenner, *The Pound Era*, 202–203.

the battle is not absurd; he heroically chooses to grieve and fight back. The poem's last stanza notes,

> How easy to slip
> into the old mold, how hard to
> cling firmly to the advance—
> (CP1, 191)

Williams' earlier image of the "winter casing of grief," moreover, implies that the trench warfare of the avant-garde may indeed end in victory, the birth of a new age. So does the startling stanza in which the black winds become a creative rather than destructive power. Williams shows us just a glimpse of the bright form that lies in wait beneath winter's hard brown casing:

> Now I run my hand over you feeling
> the play of your body—the quiver
> of its strength—
> (CP1, 191)

This is spring, not winter, sensuality and "play" rather than hand-to-hand combat in a crowd. Having exorcised Pound in "March," Williams could in "The Black Winds" both pay him homage and rewrite one of his poems because in Spring and All he was at last confident that he had found his own voice.

Yet "The Black Winds" is made up of many different voices—caustic, pleasing, and stubbornly optimistic—and rather than eventually unifying them into a coherent point of view Williams seems to have gone out of his way to create a poem in which identity as well as syntax breaks down. Just one stanza after the speaker has told us he is sick of pouring his heart out in despair, for instance, he excitedly runs his hand over the body of the wind. At first, the poem may seem similar to Williams' Cubist odes in its use of contrasting voices. But unlike poems such as "Overture to a Dance of Loco-motives," "Rapid Transit," "The Rose," or "The Sea-Elephant," "The Black Winds" does not focus on a readily identifiable subject and setting, and its points of view are not carefully balanced. It has neither the confidence in art that "The Rose" does nor the con-trolled use of irony that so animates "Rapid Transit." Rather, as "The Black Winds" develops it becomes increasingly heterogeneous and chaotic—everything is uprooted and blown about by the winds. But the poem's stormy schizophrenia is representative, not solip-sistic. Its "black heart" belongs to all of us. Fighting in the no-man's-land between sanity and insanity, Williams shows that Dada's madness was not a pose: it was heroically self-induced by artists at great risk to themselves. They turned themselves and their art into scapegoats, taking the evil and the violence of their society upon themselves in order (they hoped) to purge them. Like all important Dada art, "The Black Winds" performs emergency therapy.

Williams continued to write black wind poems until 1930, culminating in "April" in the sequence "Della Primavera Trasportata al Morale," one of his most exuberant collage poems in celebration of spring. For our purposes, however, we will concentrate on Williams' other Dadaist lyrics in *Spring and All*, for these are the heart of Williams' Dadaist work of the 1920s and have not been discussed as thoroughly as they should be. They also vary rather remarkably in tone and pace from "The Black Winds" and thus give a good indication of the fairly wide range of effects Williams could achieve with this satiric mode.

When one begins counting the Dadaist poems in *Spring and All* it becomes hard to stop—so many of the poems, even the most sober, have their moments of comic tackiness and black humor. The point, though, is not to turn a reading of Williams' book into an exercise in labeling, so that some poems are pronounced to be definitively Dadaist whereas others are not, but to be able to recognize the Dadaist spirit throughout the lyrics. (In the same manner, we must be able to laugh with the puckish spirit that makes Williams in his prose set a chapter heading upside down even as he is seriously struggling to define why he feels the theory of mimesis is inadequate for modern art.) A great lyric like "To Elsie" is full of feverish Dadaist energy and anger; in fact, it would be hard to think of a more eloquent example of Dada's cry against civilization gone awry than that poem's concluding image of America as a car careening out of control. But "To Elsie" is a mock pastoral against its will, and it can be fruitfully approached through other perspectives as well. The same might be said for most of the other obviously Dadaist poems in *Spring and All*, such as "Flight to the City," "At the Faucet of June," "The Agonized Spires," "Light Becomes Darkness," and others, which are as opaque and as provocative as any of Williams' lyrics. Placing these poems within the context of New York and Paris Dada can make their opacities more transparent—or at least can bring out their reflective surfaces and dark shadows in greater detail.

During the 1920s, popular culture and advertising were touted as America's answers to European canons of taste and respectability, as if America's centuries-long sense of inferiority in the face of European culture was at last to be overthrown. The fact that Americans were convinced that they had rescued Europe from itself in ending World War I had much to do with this new exuberance, as did the fact that American industry and commerce had by 1920 indisputably become the most powerful in the world. But as several historians of American popular culture have recently shown, that transformation of Americans' sense of how to use leisure time had been under way at least since the 1890s, when Victorian forms of urban night life began to break down with the rise of the cafés, cabarets, movie palaces, and, most importantly, new standards defining when and where the classes and the sexes could mix in public.

Williams' poems in *Spring and All* catalog the new mores and enticements as accurately as *Vanity Fair* and *The New Yorker,* sophisticated new magazines that sprang up to chronicle the new forms of conspicuous consumption. "Flight to the City" (Poem IV) includes references to the window displays in a downtown department store; "Young Love" (Poem IX) mentions a popular Parisian singer and dancer and many other details of the new urban night life, all the while recounting memories of a love affair; "Light Becomes Darkness" (Poem XV) chronicles the rise of the urban movie palace; "Our Orchestra" (Poem XVII) journeys to a hot Harlem speakeasy to hear jazz, the most daring adventure for whites in the 1920s; "The Sea" (Poem XX) wittily rewrites the ending of Eliot's "The Love Song of J. Alfred Prufrock" for the jazz age (now the speaker sings *back* to the mermaids and seems to lose all his inhibitions); and a series of poems featuring references to "Gipsies," exotic dark women, and night romance—"Horned Purple" (Poem XIX), "Quietness" (Poem XXI), "Rigamarole" (Poem XXIII), "The Avenue of Poplars" (Poem XXIV), and "The Wildflower" (Poem XXVII)—both celebrate and express some uneasiness with the new sexual freedom of the 1920s.

Williams' greatest Dadaist poems in *Spring and All* are highly ambivalent toward the ways Americans were being urged to spend their leisure time. On one hand, they join the attack on Puritanism that began in the 1920s and delight in violating prohibitions of all kinds; in this, they join those moments in the prose of *Spring and All* when Williams seeks to rise to "drunken heights" (I, 91). On the other hand, they also fear that the newly popular forms of release are not healthy examples of independence but the expression of violence and manipulation. Williams' response to this ambivalence is intriguing. Unlike in "The Black Winds," Williams most frequently expresses his doubts about American culture under a comically deadpan imitation of the typically American exuberance for all things new; he is coolly derisive rather than despairing, somewhat as Duchamp and Demuth were.

"At the Faucet of June" (Poem VIII) is a case in point. Its run-on sentences create classic Dada comedy. The precarious balances of syntax created by each stanza are comically flooded and dismantled by the stanza that follows, reproducing the effect of ceaseless, mindlessly mixed activity. In the following example (the first four stanzas of the poem), the normally separate actions of simple sentences run on into each other like water out of a leaky faucet:

> The sunlight in a
> yellow plaque upon the
> varnished floor
>
> is full of a song
> inflated to
> fifty pounds pressure
>
> at the faucet of
> June that rings
> the triangle of the air
>
> pulling at the
> anemones in
> Persephone's cow pasture—
> (CP1, 196)

In simplified form, this reads as follows: "The sunlight is full of a song by a faucet that rings the triangle of the air that pulls." This intentional run-on flouting of the discriminations and hierarchies normally created by syntax is corroborated by the noun phrases that Williams uses, which calculatedly mix high and low culture in a single sentence. "A yellow plaque" suggests a museum or a monument; "rings the triangle" suggests a Philharmonic concert of European classical music; and in Greek mythology, of course, Persephone is the daughter of Demeter captured in a meadow by Hades and forced to live with him in the underworld for six months out of each year. These allusions to traditional European culture are then mixed in with comically coarse and modern references: floor varnish, the air pressure in a tire, a kitchen faucet, and a cow pasture. It is Williams'

version of the Dadaist gesture of merging references to the Holy
Virgin and sardines.

The later stanzas of the poem wittily satirize modern American as
well as classical European culture. The sublime and the ridiculous
merge as Williams mixes allusions to Zeus and Alexander the Great
along with Henry Ford and J. P. Morgan. His language is similarly
mottled, both mock heroic ("among the rocks leaps J. P. M.," "ex-
traordinary privileges," "to solve the core") and scatterbrained and
cliché-ridden ("the finest on the market today," "And so it comes to
motor cars").

> When from among
> the steel rocks leaps
> J.P.M.
>
> who enjoyed
> extraordinary privileges
> among virginity
>
> to solve the core
> of whirling flywheels
> by cutting
>
> the Gordian knot
> with a Veronese or
> perhaps a Rubens—
>
> whose cars are about
> the finest on
> the market today
>
> And so it comes
> to motor cars—
> which is the son
>
> leaving off the g
> of sunlight and grass—
>
> (*CP1*, 196–97)

Henry Ford is a debased fertility god mating with the Earth to re-
produce the assembly line and the Ford flivver. J. P. Morgan is a
parody of Zeus and Alexander the Great who has seduced and con-
quered America without her knowing it. Like a modern Alexander,
Morgan thinks he can use European art as a sword to cut through that
contemporary Gordian knot, the problem of what to do with all the
money and energy created by the "whirling flywheels" of American
commerce. To solve the problem, he seeks to buy culture and re-
spectability, two things that apparently cannot be mass-produced,
with a Veronese or "perhaps" a Rubens. (The word *perhaps* is as
deadly as any other in the stanza; through it, Williams is able to

imitate a rich American shopping among the wares of European auction houses trying to decide which item to purchase.)

Cutting a knot with a painting is a grotesque action that well captures the naïveté of nouveau riche Americans with little taste. It is also an allusion to Duchamp's Dadaist concept of the "reciprocal." If a Duchamp readymade converts a mass-produced, functional object into a work of art, a reciprocal turns a piece of fine art into a useful object. Duchamp's notorious example of this was his proposal to "use a Rembrandt as an ironing board"; it was recorded in "The Green Box," the notebook that he kept while constructing *The Bride Stripped Bare by Her Bachelors, Even* in Walter Arensberg's apartment from 1915 onward.[26] In Williams' "At the Faucet of June," J. P. Morgan uses paintings as functional objects; their job is to capture and hold "culture" in this country. Williams' allusion to Duchamp's reciprocals is as full of deadpan irony as Duchamp's proposal. But if Williams keeps on his deadpan expression in "At the Faucet of June," his eyes also flash with anger. He clearly thinks that an action such as Morgan's is arrogant and perverse; Morgan and Ford, despite being worshipped in the American press, are parodies of gods and cultural heroes, not real ones.

The influence of Arensberg as well as Duchamp may be involved in "At the Faucet of June," for the poem's run-on style (like that of several others in *Spring and All* and of the Improvisations that Williams wrote during his European trip in 1924) is similar to the comic scrap of Dadaist prose Arensberg published in Man Ray's magazine *TNT* in March, 1919, entitled "Vacuum Tires: A Formula for the Digestion of Figments" (quoted above). Arensberg's prose, like Williams' poem, is a witty concatenation of chic allusions, advertising jargon, sententiousness, and nonsense. But to such a mix Williams adds his allusions to classical and contemporary figures, his wonderful sense of caricature, and a hint of apocalyptic danger.[27]

"At the Faucet of June" ends with a cryptic aside that appears to

26. See Lippard (ed.), *Dadas on Art*, 153; the excerpts from Duchamp's notebook "The Green Box" were translated by Lippard. Williams may have read the notebook at the Arensberg's or, more probably, have heard of Duchamp's idea during one of his many conversations with Arensberg or others in the group. Williams' reference to J. P. Morgan includes both the elder Morgan (1837–1913) and his son, J. P. Morgan, Jr. (1867–1943). See *CP1*, 503.

27. For further discussion, see Marling, *William Carlos Williams and the Painters*, 51–54; and Naumann, "Walter Conrad Arensberg," 20–23, in which a facsimile of "Vacuum Tires" is reproduced. Naumann rightly stresses the connection between Arensberg's style and that of Gertrude Stein's *Tender Buttons*, published in the United States in 1914. But I would expand any discussion of Williams' Dadaist style beyond that of Stein's influence, important as it is.

allude to the natural disasters described in other Dadaist passages in the prose of *Spring and All*:

> leaving off the g
> of sunlight and grass—
> Impossible
>
> to say, impossible
> to underestimate—
> wind, earthquakes in
>
> Manchuria, a
> partridge
> from dry leaves
> (*CP1*, 197)

Williams' juxtaposition of winds, an earthquake, and a partridge suddenly flushed from its hiding place is meant to be a Dadaist puzzle: we must struggle to find a connection. One connection appears to be this: all three elements (with various degrees of seriousness) involve our being suddenly startled by natural forces beyond our control. The implication is that nature may not be as subdued by technology as we think it is—our industrialist gods may be surprised and overthrown.[28] Furthermore, two of the details, the wind and the Manchurian earthquake, seem to be just the sort of thing that might appear together in a newspaper. After all, the juxtapositions of a newspaper are no less absurd and inherently no more comprehensible than those of a Dadaist poem: on a single page we may read articles on an art exhibit, the weather, the death toll of an earthquake in China, and advertising for plumbing and automobiles. Williams argues that it is impossible for us to follow, much less to synthesize, the

---

Incidentally, Arensberg's reference to testing uric acid in the last sentence of the above quotation may be a source for the concluding cryptic stanzas of Williams' Dadaist lyric, "This Florida: 1924":

> I shall do my pees, instead—
> boiling them in test tubes
> holding them to the light
>
> dropping in the acid—
> Peggy has a little albumen
> in hers—
> (*CP1*, 362)

28. A relevant gloss on Williams' reference to the partridge may be the following passage on partridges from *Walden*, "Brute Neighbors": "The young suddenly disperse on your approach, at a signal from the mother, as if a whirlwind has swept them away, and they so exactly resemble the dried leaves and twigs that many a traveller has placed his foot in the midst of a brood, and heard the whir of the old bird as she flew off" (*The Norton Anthology of American Literature*, Francis Murphey, *et al.*, eds. [2 vols.; New York, 1979], I, 1672.

meanings created by such dissociated facts. We cannot find meaningful patterns to accommodate them all, even as we cannot make sense of the run-on syntax of a Dadaist poem. Thus the last lines of "At the Faucet of June" suggest that darker surprises may be in store for us. As a whole, the poem is a rather sunny mock pastoral; unlike "The Black Winds," its satire and slapstick are still relatively good humored. But the references to Persephone and earthquakes suggest that the false pastoral world of American prosperity may not last. It may collapse and be swallowed up, as Persephone was. The poem is dated 1923. How must Williams have read it after 1929?

Several other poems in Spring and All, most notably "Flight to the City," "Young Love," "The Agonized Spires," "Composition," and "Light Becomes Darkness," portray America as a grotesque parody of true pastoral. Like "At the Faucet of June," "The Agonized Spires" uses run-on sentences, mixed metaphors, and rapidly shifting scenes, but its tendency to break a long sentence into many lines, some of them with only a single word to the line, gives the poem a more jagged, violent rhythm than the comically fluid motion of "At the Faucet of June."

Williams begins "The Agonized Spires" (Poem XIII) with a coarse sexual joke: the sea is male, and a collection of seaside resort restaurant kitchens on the rocks are female: "Crustaceous / wedge of sweaty kitchens / on rock / overtopping / thrusts of the sea." The next stanzas abruptly shift the locale from the seashore to an overview of the entire American continent. The "thrusts of the sea" reference becomes a metaphor describing the rising tide of America's industrial culture, which crashes over the countryside and inundates it: "Waves of steel / from swarming backstreets / shell / of coral / inventing electricity—" A city's windows—indented within large buildings, lighted, and infinitely multiplied—remind Williams of underwater coral colonies, just as the resort buildings on the rocks seemed crustacean. But unlike the suspended animation of sea life, urban energy in this poem swarms and smashes. We see the pastoral countryside torn up by road-building crews with trip-hammers, then watch as the cars that follow on those new roads bring their own special kind of violence. And as in "At the Faucet of June," Williams mixes references to modern technology and traditional high European culture. It all happens within the space of a few lines, as if his headlong syntax were trying to capture the unintelligible pace of change in this century:

> Lights
> speckle
> El Greco
> lakes
> in renaissance
> twilight
> with triphammers
>
> which pulverize
> nitrogen
> of old pastures
> to dodge
> motorcars
> with arms and legs—
> (*CP1*, 211–12)

America *is* Dada.

The concluding lines of the poem accelerate the pace even more, adding to its dizzying effect and suggesting that such rapid change penetrates and alters us as aggressively as a surgeon's fingers entering the heart.

> . . . bridge stanchions
> rest
> certainly
> piercing
> left ventricles
> with long
> sunburnt fingers
> (*CP1*, 211–12)

The inspiration for Williams' audacious metaphor is visual. The spires of a bridge's stanchions are metonymous for all technology, and because they are long and thin they remind Williams of fingers. The opening image of the poem, the "thrusts of the sea," has returned, nightmarishly transformed: the human body is invaded by technology even as the earlier "old pastures" were.

"The Agonized Spires" does not end entirely in despair. Williams concedes that "the aggregate" of modern American culture is "untamed" and probably untamable. But a reference to surgery in the penultimate stanza suggests that some sort of peace may be achieved. Where "agonized spires" created wounds, the poem "knits / peace" —or at least tries to—as skillfully as a doctor sutures:

> The aggregate
> is untamed

encapsulating
irritants
but
of agonized spires
knits
peace
(CPI, 212)

Williams' aggressive, fractured, run-on syntax thus tries to conquer and correct the lacerations of the modern world. This imitation of violence is intended to be as radical a cure as emergency surgery's use of violence to fight violence. The poem is a Dadaist decomposition, but against its will.

Another Dadaist poem from *Spring and All*, "Composition" (Poem XII), at first seems like one of Williams' Cubist poems and has been read as if it were.[29] In fact, it may be used to clarify the ways in which Williams' Dadaist lyrics have a different aesthetic from his Precisionist and Cubist poems. The poem presents several different views of its subject, a red paper box, by ambiguously splicing sentence fragments and wittily comparing artifice and nature, à la Cubism: the box is lined "inside and out / with imitation leather." But "Composition" (like "At the Faucet of June" and "The Agonized Spires") retains no unified place and time and no central subject matter, unlike a proper Cubist construction, and its occasional coarse joking violates the decorum of the still life respected by other non-Dadaist poems in *Spring and All* such as "The Pot of Flowers" (Poem II) and "The Rose" (Poem VII). Williams begins by describing "the red paper box" but then quickly creates a series of fantastical landscapes that cannot be directly related to the original box. The poem's box— and its subject matter—are best described as a typically Dadaist contraption, infinitely expandable and lacking a bottom.

"The box," Williams claims near the outset, "is the sun / the table / with dinner / on it for / these are the same." These two images hardly seem linked, except perhaps for the fact that they both represent energy, the sun in its natural, the dinner in its artifical form. The motif of energy is then continued as the poem lists the many jobs using boxes that are being done across the country during an average

29. For this alternative, Cubist reading, see Perloff, *The Poetics of Indeterminacy*, 124–29. Perloff compares the poem's spatial ambiguities to those of a Cubist still life such as Juan Gris' *Still Life Before an Open Window: Place Ravignan*.

working day. We see engineers assembling airplanes and old women
using their sewing kits:

> Its twoinch trays
> have engineers
> that convey glue
> to airplanes
>
> or for old ladies
> that darn socks
> paper clips
> and red elastics—
>
> (CP1, 210)

The engineers and the women, however, are caustically de-
humanized. The tiny trays "have" the engineers as well as the glue
they use; they are both tiny, replaceable parts in a giant assembly
system. And the women are merely "old ladies." The next image in
the poem is even more clearly negative: "What is the end / to in-
sects / that suck gummed / labels?" (CP1, 210). The pure energy of
the sun is steadily debased as the poem progresses, and turned into
mechanical, inhuman activity.

   The last three stanzas of "Composition" return us to the cosmic
perspectives of the opening stanzas, but the tone is even more satiric.
"Eternity" and the heavens themselves are described as if they were
some kind of box-shaped machine with a dial—perhaps an enormous
Dadaist radio capable of picking up the music of the spheres as well as
more earthly wavelengths and their static. But as soon as this pos-
sibility is suggested, it is coarsely undercut. The infinitude of space is
transformed into an endless roll of "transparent tissue"—toilet pa-
per, perhaps.

> for this [the box] is eternity
> through its
> dial we discover
> transparent tissue
> on a spool

In the final two stanzas, Williams transforms his Dadaist assemblage
yet again.

> But the stars
> are round
> cardboard
> with a tin edge
>
> and a ring
> to fasten them

to a trunk
for the vacation—
(CP1, 210–11)

Williams may here be referring to the peephole landscape that a child makes by decorating the inside of a large box and punching a hole in the top for light and a hole at one end for viewing. In such a box, small cardboard stars could be edged with tin (an easy metal to work with the hands) to make them shine. The poem's final stanza represents an "adult" fantasy of using nature for our own pleasure. Like J. P. Morgan in "At the Faucet of June," man in "Composition" thinks he has a godlike power to shape and use nature; the heavens and the earth are made to serve him like a radio, a roll of tissue, a child's toy, an adult's vacation trunk, an artist's "composition." Williams archly pretends to be enthusiastic about his consumer society's simultaneous use of nature as a toy (a radio, a magic box) and a place to store its waste (toilet paper); his Dadaist posing is held as coolly as Duchamp's or Demuth's. But unlike the creative energy associated with the Cubist constructions of "The Rose"—in the next to last stanza of that poem, for example, Williams writes that a "being of steel / infinitely fine, infinitely / rigid penetrates / the Milky Way" (CP1, 196)—the various "boxes" in "Composition" are associated with arrogance, dehumanization, crass consumerism, and defecation.[30]

Poem XV, "Light Becomes Darkness" focuses its satiric eye on yet another target in modern American mass culture, "the phenomenal / growth of movie houses." The poem mixes diction associated with religious discourse ("cathedrals," "catholicity," "sacrifice," "schism," "joy," "darkness," and "passion plays") with both a parody of journalistic boosterism ("without sacrifice / of even the smallest / detail," "Thus the movies are a moral force") and comically Dadaist mixed metaphors that sound impressive but are basically hot air ("schism . . . / . . . is diverted / from the perpendicular / by simply rotating the object // cleaving away the root of / disaster which it / seemed to foster"). Such mixed diction is very unsettling: these different modes of speech undercut as well as reinforce each other's authority, so that language associated with religion comes to sound

---

30. For another poem in *Spring and All* satirizing consumerism, see "Flight to the City." The best reading of this poem is by Breslin, *William Carlos Williams: An American Artist*, 72–73.

like advertising language, while journalese begins to sound homiletic, even sacerdotal. Ultimately, of course, the poem wickedly exposes the debasement of any claim to authority by church or newspaper; neither language is able to comprehend the enormity of the social changes that occurred as viewing movies in the movie palaces (on Sundays as well as other days) came to be as universal a form of popular entertainment, instruction, and reassurance for American culture in the 1920s as passion plays and religious rites were for the Middle Ages.

Recent historians of American movies and mores have confirmed the validity of Williams' startling equation between the cathedral and the 1920s movie palace. Lary May, for example, has argued that although nickelodeons existed throughout northern cities at the turn of the century, it was only by 1914 that "producers widened the audience to include the middle classes" so that movie-going could become "the first true mass amusement in American life." By the 1920s, theaters had become palaces, rivaling any buildings in the country in opulence, including cathedrals and the mansions of the new movie stars, and Sunday afternoon matinees were drawing the largest audiences of the entire week, often outnumbering church attendance. Such unprecedented power of course made the motion picture industry the center of a debate over how best to regulate popular culture so that it promoted rather than undermined traditional virtues associated with work and family. After the mayor closed all of the movie houses in New York City on Christmas Day, 1908, movie producers began to cooperate with reformers, creating the first national censorship board for the movies, eventually called the National Board of Review. The function of the board was to ensure that the new places of entertainment and the features they showed used leisure to teach what the board regarded as proper values of hard work and family responsibility; the censors reasoned that values absorbed freely during a citizen's leisure time would be an even more effective source for absorbing middle-class values than those habits taught during working hours. With the rise of routinized industrial labor, overcrowded urban housing, and increased immigration and what was thought to be the lower standards of immigrant family life, reformers stressed the crucial role that the movies could play in cultural assimilation and homogenization. May quotes one sociologist whose view was representative of those promoting the movies in professional journals and popular periodicals: "Popular art does not precipitate us into the class struggle. The conflict is not so much between the warring classes as it is the two sides of human nature—appetite and will, impulse and reason, inclination and idea. Here if anywhere is the place for ethical considerations. . . . To acquaint young people with the good or ill effects of different varieties of recreation or the higher self is the surest way to wean him [sic] from what is frivolous and debasing." Worried by the specter of class conflict raised by the cycles of urban labor unrest that had plagued the country since the 1880s, reformers were convinced that if the country's most popular form of entertainment were regulated properly, it would be an invaluable agent for securing class and family harmony, not the reverse.[31]

Williams' "Light Becomes Darkness" mimics the self-righteousness and optimism that characterized such a defense of movies as popular entertainment, and his poem also understands the fears of social disintegration that such exhortations hid. He mockingly calls their regulated and sanitized vision of the movies "the supple-jointed / imagination of inoffensiveness // backed by biblical / rigidity." The movie screen is a modern altar, Williams suggests, whose miracle of transubstantiation consists of converting class schisms into homogeneity and conformity:

> passion plays
> upon the altar to
> attract the dynamic mob
>
> whose female relative
> sweeping grass Tolstoi
> saw injected into
> the Russian nobility
> (CP1, 213–14)

The Tolstoy reference may be explained as follows. Williams sees an analogy between Tolstoy's vision of the regeneration of the upper classes through the addition of peasant stock (promoted in *Anna Karenina* and *A Confession,* the former in Williams' personal library) and the modern American determination to preserve traditional American values through the movies. In both cases, according to Williams' analogy, what is new, threatening, and associated with the

---

31. Lary May, *Screening Out the Past: The Birth of Mass Culture and the Motion Picture Industry* (Chicago, 1980), xii, 58–59, 272n. The long quotation is from the sociologist Edward Ross, "Social Control," *American Journal of Sociology,* III (1898), 151–63. Also relevant is Lewis A. Erenberg, *Steppin' Out: New York Nightlife and the Transformation of American Culture, 1890–1930* (Chicago, 1981).

lower classes is assimilated by an older, bourgeois life-style, giving that higher class new vigor and authority but not substantially altering its makeup or its power. A similar analysis was made in another book that Williams owned, Brooks Adams' *The Law of Civilization and Decay.* Adams claimed that once past their prime all civilizations would inevitably decay unless revived "with fresh energetic material by the infusion of barbarian blood." Williams' Dadaist mocking of the language of church, government, and the press thus becomes a mockery of all those who would use the movies to enforce conservative and repressive middle-class values; he sees the movies approved by the review board as a predominantly *repressive* force, determinedly translating dangerous materials into proper ones, class conflict into conformity, resulting in crowds "with the closeness and / universality of sand." The poem satirizes both Tolstoy's optimistic vision of class harmony and its vulgar American version.[32]

Although on the surface "Light Becomes Darkness" is less violent and obviously Dadaist than other poems in *Spring and All,* it can be argued that it is that volume's most disturbing poem. The Dadaists believed that the pleasures of consumer culture would relax repressiveness and release unconscious desires. But Williams' poems in *Spring and All* explore how the collective unconscious of an urban population is thoroughly *controlled* through popular culture and the wish fulfillments it offers. Far from being a utopian return to the primitive that the Dadas at their most optimistic believed it might be, popular culture in the view of "Light Becomes Darkness" and poems such as "At the Faucet of June" seems rather to represent the mass production and regulation of individual desire. Under their charming and brightly colored parody, Williams' Dadaist lyrics are thus more bitter, dark, and unsettling than anything else produced by the short-lived New York Dada movement. They make us uncertain whether the moment of release from "the winter casing of grief" envisioned in "The Black Winds" will ever come.

Grouped together, Williams' Dadaist lyrics and experimental prose

32. Peter Schmidt *et al.* (eds.), "A Descriptive List of Works from Williams' Library Now at Fairleigh Dickinson University," *William Carlos Williams Review,* X (1984), 40, 42; Brooks Adams, *The Law of Civilization and Decay,* 61. An anonymous writer in *Contact,* I—probably either Williams or Robert McAlmon, his coeditor—had expressed a similar view of Tolstoy in 1920, just a few years before Williams wrote "Light Becomes Darkness," using adjectives that from Williams' point of view couldn't be more damning: "the conventional, Tolstoian, mystical concept of faith has never been more of a superficial decoration" (p. 10).

written between 1917 and 1930 appear as the richest and most remarkable literary product of the New York Dada movement, superbly representing all the contradictions at its heart. We see Dada's mixture of envy and abhorrence of the rise of mass urban culture, its exuberant mimicry of American consumers in their native habitat along with an uncannily accurate analysis and debunking of the ideology of that culture. We also see the most distinguished American attempt to capture the idealism that is at the heart of Dada's violence—its attempt to believe that spontaneous creative powers of the unconscious could still remain inviolate in the face of mass advertising. The idealism of the Dadaists was as filled with contradictions as their cynicism. The belief that Dadaist techniques for inducing "spontaneity" could tap the unconscious was at odds with the assurance that the unconscious could resist *other* attempts to influence it as well, particularly the techniques of advertising. Indeed, there are disturbing parallels between Dadaist techniques of automatism and those of their supposed enemy: the highest ambition of both is to work "automatically," largely free from the rational, censoring mechanisms of the conscious mind. Advertising and Dada art therefore both encourage a short attention span and an unmixed delight in the play of visual and aural surfaces. Dada's and advertising's automatism, in short, cannot be as firmly separated from each other as the Dadaists would have liked to believe; they seem mirror images of each other, like the word *ad* and the nonsense syllable that makes up Dada's name.

Williams' considerable irony toward his own methods throughout his Dadaist lyrics and his Improvisations, however, shows that Williams, for one, was as skeptical of Dada's claims as he was entranced by them. This skepticism—a kind of tragic realism—accounts for his ironic handling of Whitmanesque motifs in *Kora in Hell* and his powerful explorations in his Dadaist lyrics in *Spring and All* of the ways in which an artist is *implicated* by the decadence of his culture rather than able to maintain an immaculately critical distance from it. Such skepticism must always be remembered when Williams' apparently enthusiastic endorsement of the "relief" that automatic writing gave him is cited. Like Freud, Williams knew that dreams, Improvisations, and automatic writing were not entirely free from "secondary revision" or (in Williams' phrase) "mechanical interference" (*I*, 16).

Stephen Fredman has eloquently argued that the ideal of automatic writing (and of the Dadaist enterprise itself) is to achieve a "beginning" rather than a point of origin: "The improvisation has about it a certain timeliness, the stamp of a specific moment. It purports to be the farthest thing from a timeless utterance; it is a meditation upon the moment, with the implication that no later revision is possible. First and foremost a beginning, an improvisation begins from the middle, not from the point of origin. And to the extent that the writer is recalled to the task of improvising, the text continues beginning throughout its length, abjuring a sense of finality through contradiction, paradox, and non sequitur."[33] Certainly any reader of *Kora in Hell* or the Dadaist lyrics in *Spring and All* can testify to the unsettling power of these texts to plunge us into the middle of things before we have gotten our bearings and to keep us moving so that recollection (and reorientation) in tranquillity becomes impossible. But it can also be claimed that what Williams' Dadaist work *really* seeks to do is to recover a point of origin outside of time, a moment of absolute spontaneity in which the interferences and repressions taught by history are (however briefly) transcended. The truly spontaneous moment, after all, would be an unprecedented one, an ahistorical one. Such a moment is the moment of "relief" and renewal toward which all Dadaist art aspires. If Williams remained skeptical that such a moment was ever possible, he also could not live without believing in it, in the "rescue" it seemed to offer. That was Dada's Orphean hope and, in a way, its Orphean despair, for Kora-Eurydice, after all, must forever return to hell. All of Dada's efforts to bring something back from the unconscious end like Orpheus'. Despite its relentless forward motion, Dadaist automatic writing must always look backward and lose much of what it seeks to recover.

Williams' interest in using Dadaist collage techniques to criticize American consumer society receded into the background after 1930; he wrote relatively few later lyrics with the compressed vehemence of his Dadaist poems in *Spring and All*. ("It is Living Coral" [1924], "This Florida: 1924," "Della Primavera Trasportata al Morale" [1930], "The Trees" [1930], and "Sluggishly" [1933], among others, did continue the tradition.) Williams may have felt that their irrationalism and their satire (ironically) were too carefully contrived and edited. He appears to have preferred to express his anger in the late 1920s and the 1930s more directly, in his later Improvisations

33. Fredman, *Poet's Prose*, 14.

and his dramatic monologues on political subjects, such as "An Early Martyr" (1934) and "The Yachts" (1935).

When Williams began contemplating writing an epic of his own, however, in response to long poems by Pound, Eliot, Crane, and Stevens, his interest in Dadaist techniques—especially that of collage—revived. One of the many problems that Williams would face in writing *Paterson* would be whether it was at all possible to reconcile the contrasting working principles of his art—particularly the different goals of his Precisionist, Cubist, and Dadaist modes. Could Williams' collage epic be a composition, a "sum" (*P*, 3) of his working principles? Or would it in some fundamental way have to be a Dadaist decomposition, a deconstruction of every epic ambition that his poem expressed?

FIVE/PATERSON AND EPIC TRADITION

At times there is no other way to assert the truth than by stating our failure to achieve it.

—William Carlos Williams

Epic poems are like the cities of Rome and New York: all roads lead to them. Similarly, for a reader of Williams' work, all roads lead to *Paterson,* or away from it. It is impossible not to treat Williams' earlier work in prose and in poetry, despite its diversity, as a prelude to the epic poem that occupied so much of Williams' energy in the 1940s and 1950s. The reader cannot help but see the earlier work as a trying out of various ways of writing that would be rolled up into a sum in *Paterson.* And it is hard not to treat Williams' later work as a response to *Paterson,* even if a few of the poems he published in the 1950s were absorbed in the last installment of *Paterson* in 1958.

Like several of his Modernist contemporaries, in the later decades of his life Williams dreamed of a collection of poems that would form one long poem, "The Complete Collected Exercises Toward A Possible Poem," as he called it.[1] And *Paterson* seems like a (large) scale model that Williams used to work out the possibilities of synthesis. His use of the infinitive tense in setting his goal in the poem's preface ("To make a start, / out of particulars / and make them general, rolling / up the sum, by defective means—" [P, 3]) suggests not only the epic immensity of his task but the fact that this credo does not apply to *Paterson* alone. The challenge of the poem's unity would also be the challenge of the unity of all Williams' work; if, like Sisyphus' attempt to roll a boulder up a hill, the task proved impossible, far more than just the failure of one long poem would be implied. Williams' faith in the coherence of his entire enterprise would be jeopardized.

This chapter approaches the site of *Paterson* from several direc-

1. Wallace, A *Bibliography,* xix.

tions, on the principle that such diversity will give a better sense of the lay of the land. As in the other chapters, Williams' mixture of art and literary traditions is emphasized, on the principle that like the "city" and the "man" in *Paterson*, the poem itself is an "interpenetration, both ways" (*P*, 3). Crucial influences of Dada on the poem are examined first, from the notorious library-burning episode in Book Three and the grotesque mock-pastoral poetry of Book Four, where Dadaist influences surface most dramatically, to other episodes where Dada's subversive pressure is largely hidden underground. The evolving role of Dada's influence for the overall plan of the epic is considered next, with emphasis on how during the course of composition Williams gave the poem two thoroughly different endings, first with Book Four in 1951 and then with Book Five in 1958, thus radically altering our sense of the "plot" of the poem and of its relation to epic tradition. The chapter concludes with a meditation on the meaning of the collage form as Williams uses it in *Paterson*—both the contradictions between Cubist and Dadaist versions of the form and the larger, ideological implications of choosing such a form for an epic about an American industrial city.

In the fall of 1936 a translation of a Dadaist diary appeared in *transition*, one of William Carlos Williams' favorite periodicals at the time, that may have influenced two of the most famous passages in *Paterson*, the flood and the fire episodes in Book Three. The work was excerpted from writings of Hugo Ball published in Germany in 1927 that dated from 1916 and 1917, when Ball and Tristan Tzara were two of the founding members of Zurich Dada. Entitled "Dada Fragments," the *transition* pieces were selected and translated by the editor of the magazine, Eugene Jolas, who had turned his publication into an American port of entry for the French Surrealists, James Joyce, and other European avant-garde writers. Jolas also thought of *transition* as a museum and exhibition gallery for documents relating to the then-defunct European Dada movement. By the 1930s, those manuscripts needed protection: Dada's obstreperous demonstrations had faded from the European scene as suddenly as if they had marched down one of the narrow streets of Paris, Cologne, or Zurich and then vanished around a corner.

The excerpts from Ball's diary that Jolas published in 1936 are not particularly original Dadaisms, for they all lack the telegraphic urgency that was Dada's most arresting feature. Ball's entries read more like private, lapidary epigrams, and one wonders whether he didn't polish them up a bit before publishing them. Several of Ball's statements in *transition*, nonetheless, are of particular interest for the reader of Williams' work. They provide us with a succinct example not only of how Dadaist ideas influenced *Paterson* but also of how Williams struggled to integrate the legacy of his Dadaist work with that of his other writing styles, particularly the reassessment of traditional literary forms that characterized his work in Precisionist and Cubist veins.

Echoing Dada's general determination to scramble all logically ordered syntax, Ball wrote in his June 18, 1916, entry that "We have developed the plasticity of the word to a point which can hardly be surpassed. This result was achieved at the price of the logically constructed, rational sentence. . . . People may smile, if they want to; language will thank us for our zeal. . . . We have charged the word with forces and energies which made it possible for us to rediscover the evangelical concept of the 'word' (logos) as a magical complex of images."[2] This call to disrupt rational sentences ought to have reminded Williams of "Dada Soulève Tout" in *The Little Review*. That tract had also called for the derangement of syntax, but unlike Ball's it practiced the heresies that it preached. Such works served as precedents for Williams a decade later, when he composed the jumble of broken sentences in *Paterson*, Book Three, to represent the debris of dead clichés that blocked his search for a living language (see Illustration 9). Williams calls this page "a sort of muck, a detritus, / in this case—a pustular scum, a decay, a choking / lifelessness" (*P*, 140). This excerpt from *Paterson*, Ball's diary entry, the *Little Review* announcement, Tzara's 1918 manifesto, and other similar Dada pieces all have the same motive for disordering syntax and linear reading: they spit out a flood of things once known and believed but now thrown up in disgust and despair.

A later entry of Ball's in *transition* bears even more directly on *Paterson*, particularly the library-burning episode in Book Three. At that point in the poem, the local Paterson library is an Inferno packed with dead thoughts, "books / that is, men in hell" who "reign over the living." To overthrow their rule he proposes to fight their deadly hellfire with a fire of his own, writing that will obliterate the

---

2. Hugo Ball, "Dada Fragments," *transition*, XXV (Fall, 1936). Republished in Motherwell (ed.), *The Dada Painters and Poets*, 52.

Hi, open up a dozen, make
it two dozen!   Easy girl!

You wanna blow a fuse?

All manner of particularizations
     to stay the pocky moon   :
                         January sunshine   .

                    1949
Wednesday, 11
               (10,000,000 times plus April)

—a red-butted reversible minute-glass

               loaded with
salt-like   white crystals
          flowing

                    for timing eggs

Salut à Antonin Artaud pour les

     lignes, trés pures   :

          "et d'évocations plas-
          tiques d'éléments de"
                                   and

"Funeral designs"
               (a beautiful, optimistic
word   .   .   )   and
          "Plants"
                    (it should be explained that
in this case "plants" does NOT refer to interment.)

     "Wedding bouquets"   .
                    —the association
     is indefensible.

Page 137 of William Carlos Williams' *Paterson*
Paterson Copyright © 1946, 1948, 1949, 1951, 1958 by William Carlos
Williams. Reprinted by permission of New Directions Publishing Corporation.

past in a great firestorm: "The writing / should be a relief, // relief from the conditions / which as we advance become—a fire, // a destroying fire." The spark that will start the conflagration is laughter: "A drunkenness of flames . . . a multiformity of laughter." The past is mocked and then cremated, thus clearing space for the myriad new examples of beauty:

>   Papers
>   (consumed) scattered to the winds. Black.
>   The ink burned white, metal white. So be it.
>   . . . .
>   Hell's fire. Fire. Sit your horny ass
>   down. What's your game? Beat you
>   at your own game, Fire. Outlast you:
>   Poet Beats Fire at Its Own Game! The bottle!
>   the bottle! the bottle! the bottle! I
>   give you the bottle!
>   (*P*, 113–18)

The birth of spring in *Spring and All* (1923) was similarly preceded by a drunken, violent upheaval: "The imagination, intoxicated by prohibitions, rises to drunken heights to destroy the world. Let it rage, let it kill" (*CP1*, 179).

The following excerpts from Ball's diary in *transition* may have inspired Williams to make the library in Book Three a synecdoche for the vaguer world of *Spring and All* and to shift his symbolic liberating action from murder to arson: "*January 9, 1917*—We should burn all libraries and allow to remain only that which every one knows by heart. A beautiful age of the legend would then begin . . . *March 30, 1917*—The new art is sympathetic because in an age of total disruption it has conserved the will-to-the-image; because it is inclined to force the image."[3] Admittedly, in *Paterson* Williams does not advocate a return to oral formulaic literature and innocent audiences, as Ball does; he stresses what Ball calls the "will-to-the-image," the difficult necessity of inventing or seeking out new forms of the Beautiful Thing, the "radiant gist that / resists the final crystallization" (*P*, 109). But other assumptions in the Williams and Ball passages seem similar, most notably the premise that no search can be begun until the ground is violently cleared. Moreover, the use of a library by both writers to represent decadent traditional culture is a striking parallel, because the usual examples of such decadence for the

---

3. Motherwell (ed.), *The Dada Painters and Poets*, 53.

Dadaist were public monuments, art museums, churches, govern-
ment buildings, and the marketplace, not libraries.

When precedents for Williams' symbolic destruction of the library
in *Paterson* have been discussed, the Dada movement has been men-
tioned casually, if at all, and then usually in reference to Antonin
Artaud, who came to Paris in 1920, followed Dada street theater, and
joined the Surrealists in 1924, publishing articles in *La Revolution
Surréaliste* and making a living as a stage and film actor.[4] The Artaud
connection is stressed because Williams mentions him in *Paterson*
during the flood scene and its Dadaist jumble of textual fragments.
Williams praised Artaud for the purity of his Dadaist principles; like
Ball, Artaud had demanded that masterpieces be "broken apart" and
"destroyed" to allow literature to become more "plastic" so that it
could take on the imprint of contemporary life: "Masterpieces of the
past are good for the past: they are not good for us. . . . We must get
rid of our superstitious valuations of texts and written poetry. Written
poetry is worth reading once, and then should be destroyed. Let the
dead poets make way for others. Then we might even come to see
that it is our veneration for what has already been created, however
beautiful and valid it may be, that petrifies us, deadens our responses,
and prevents us from making contact with that underlying power,
call it thought-energy, the life force." Elsewhere, Artaud had writ-
ten, "The library at Alexandria can be burnt down. There are forces
above and beyond papyrus: we may temporarily be deprived of our
ability to discover these forces, but their energy will not be sup-
pressed. . . . [A] culture without space or time, restrained only by
the capacity of our own nerves, will reappear with all the more
energy."[5] Striking as these passages are for their parallels with

---

4. See especially Margaret Glynne Lloyd, *William Carlos Williams' "Paterson": A Critical
Reappraisal* (Cranbury, N.J., 1980), 254; Miller, *Poets of Reality,* 338–39; and Anne Janowitz,
"*Paterson:* An American Contraption," in Carroll F. Terrell (ed.), *William Carlos Williams:
Man and Poet* (Orono, Maine, 1983), 317. Mike Weaver, in *William Carlos Williams: The
American Background,* does mention Artaud and other Surrealists in the context of *Paterson,*
but his handling of Artaud's relevance to the poem is rather oblique (he doesn't discuss *The
Theatre and its Double* or the flood episode, for example), and he gives little background on
Williams' earlier contact with Dada.

5. Antonin Artaud, *The Theatre and Its Double,* trans. Mary Caroline Richards (New York,
1958), 74, 78, 10. The book was originally published in Paris by Gallimard in 1938. See also
Lloyd, *William Carlos Williams' "Paterson,"* 254. Mariani, in *William Carlos Williams: A New
World Naked,* 574, notes that Williams later denied Artaud's relevance to *Paterson,* implying
that he included the quotation from *The Theatre and Its Double* in the flood episode because he
thought it was merely a cliché. In view of what happens in *Paterson,* Book Three, however, I am
not sure that we can take Williams at his word.

Williams' thought (Artaud's ideal of "contact," for example, must have been particularly intriguing for Williams), the importance of Artaud's influence on *Paterson* is easy to overstate, given the fact that the above passages were published in 1938 and that Williams had had much earlier contact with these same Dadaist principles through *291, 391, The Little Review, transition,* and other magazines. Artaud did not give Williams new ideas so much as eloquently recall old ones.

Williams acknowledged his debt to the founders of Dada throughout Books Three and Four of *Paterson,* though always in a more oblique way than his citation of Artaud. Of the destroying fire in Book Three, for example, he says that it gives "relief" from the oppressive past that the library represents (*P,* 113). This recalls the definition of Dada that Williams improvised in *The Great American Novel* in 1923: "It is the apotheosis of relief. Dadaism in one of its prettiest modes: *rien rien rien*" (*I,* 173). That definition was in turn inspired by Francis Picabia, who published a tract in *391* in 1920 declaring that all Dadaists desire to know "*rien rien rien*" so that their art will be truly spontaneous; it was quoted in *New York Dada* in 1921.[6]

What may be another buried tribute to Picabia and the early Dadaists in *Paterson* Three alludes to a little piece Picabia brought out in André Breton's proto-Surrealist magazine *Littérature* in 1923. "What I like," Picabia boasted, "is to invent, to imagine, to make myself a new man every moment, then forget him, forget everything. We should be equipped with a special eraser, gradually effacing our works and the memory of them."[7] Similarly, in *Paterson,* Book Three, Section III, Williams hoped that the flood would destroy the past and allow him to begin afresh: "how to begin to find a shape—to begin to begin again, / . . . / . . . The leaf torn from / the calendar. All forgot" (*P,* 140). This description may seem like a general paraphrase of Dada's belief that memory should be obliterated, but mixed in with Williams' Dadaist praise of amnesia is what may be a specific reference to Picabia's analogy of erasure: "It is dangerous to leave written that which is badly written. A chance word, upon paper, may destroy the world. Watch carefully and erase, while the power is still yours, I say to myself, for all that is put down, once it escapes, may rot

6. Picabia quoted in Lippard ed., *Dadas on Art,* 166.
7. Picabia quoted in Lippard ed., *Dadas on Art,* 171.

its way into a thousand minds, the corn become a black smut, and all libraries, of necessity, be burned to the ground as a consequence" (*P*, 129). At first it may seem that only the badly written is to be erased, but when Williams' fire storm appeared in Book Three it consumed the library's treasure and trash alike.

Most deeply buried of all the allusions to Dada in *Paterson*, however, is perhaps the most personal of all the sources of inspiration for Williams. In 1916 three American poets, Marjorie Allen Sieffert, Harold Witter Bynner, and Arthur Davison Ficke, were involved in a quintessentially Dadaist literary hoax, when under the pseudonyms of "Emanuel Morgan" and "Anne Knish" they published a parodic volume of avant-garde verse called *Spectra: A Book of Poetic Experiments* and then, a year later, participated in a special issue of the little magazine *Others*, edited by Williams and Alfred Kreymborg. Williams became a correspondent with Sieffert, who used "Elijah Hay" as a pseudonym, and when in 1918 the Spectric hoax was exposed, Williams greatly enjoyed the joke, even though it had partly been at his own expense. One of the Spectric manifestos in *Others* is particularly relevant to *Paterson*; it is the single most important source for Williams' library-burning episode:

> Prism on the Present State of Poetry
>
> *Knish:*—
>
> Out of a cradling has there come a sunset?
> Oh for the fellowship when once in Alexandria
> The world of learning burned!
>
> *Morgan:*—
>
> Laughter, dear friends, will do for kindling;
> And we shall wear ridiculous beads of flame
> To tinkle toward the corners of the world.
> Slapping with light the faces of old fools.[8]

Not only does this passage connect laughter and fire, as *Paterson* does, but it also raises the issue of violence, an attempt to disrupt the decline of all ideas in time, from the promise of their "cradling" to the decadence of "old fools."

The American sources for the poem's satire become much more strongly emphasized in Book Four, Section I, which presents a mock pastoral (complete with attempted homosexual seduction) staged by

---

8. For more on the Spectric hoax and Williams' friendship with Sieffert, see Barbara Herb Wright (ed.), "Fourteen Unpublished Letters by William Carlos Williams," *William Carlos Williams Review,* XII (Spring, 1986), 22–38. This quotation is from page 24.

Dr. Paterson's alter ego, the lesbian poetaster Corydon. Several crit-
ics, especially Paul Mariani and Jay Grover-Rogoff, have noted the
many allusions to Hart Crane's epic *The Bridge* in this section, as if
Williams were simultaneously paying homage to an earlier attempt to
render Manhattan in epic poetry and stressing that rival's decadence
and failure.[9] Just as relevant for a reading of this section, however, is
the parodic machine art of Picabia and Duchamp, particularly its
emphasis on sterility, greed, and meaningless repetition:

> While in the tall
> buildings (sliding up and down) is where
> the money's made
>   up and down
>   directed missiles
> in the greased shafts of the tall buildings .
> They stand torpid in cages, in violent motion
> unmoved
>   but alert!
>   predatory minds, un-
> affected
>   UNINCONVENIENCED
>   unsexed, up
> and down (without wing motion)   This is how
> the money's made   .   using such plugs.
>   (*P,* 165)

Passages such as this one overlay allusions to Crane (especially the
"Proem" in *The Bridge*) with references to Picabia's and Duchamp's
work, most notably Duchamp's *The Large Glass* and Picabia's *Prostitu-
tion universelle* and *Portrait d'une jeune fille americaine,* the latter two
satiric portraits of Americans as a spark plug and various kinds of
pistons (see Illustration 10). Voices upon voices from Williams' con-
tacts with the Dadaists in the 1920s and 1930s echo in Books Three
and Four, with the most important influence, New York Dada, being
the most thoroughly disguised, and the most recent influence, Ar-
taud, given more prominence.

Excavating such buried allusions within *Paterson* should not become
an exercise in critical treasure hunting but should be undertaken
because it allows us to pose the following crucial question: granted
Dada's pervasive presence underneath the surface of the poem, es-
pecially in the third and fourth books, to what degree can it help us

9. Mariani, *William Carlos Williams: A New World Naked,* 615–18; Jay Grover-Rogoff,
"Hart Crane's Presence in *Paterson,*" *William Carlos Williams Review,* XI (Spring, 1985), 20–29.

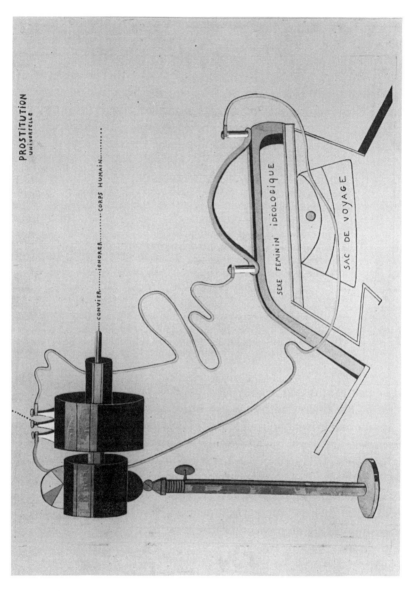

Francis Picabia, *Prostitution universelle*   *Yale University Art Gallery, Gift of Collection Société Anonyme*

better understand the structure of the epic as a whole? By recalling Dada's most colorful slogans, of course, Williams involves himself in an inextricable paradox: he shows that he can't forget Dada's ideal of forgetfulness. Furthermore, Williams' very act of attempting an epic is a profound reenactment of literary tradition, an affirmation of the past's enduring power. Hence Williams' allusions to Dada in *Paterson* not only raise the question of what role Dadaist ideas could play in the overall organization of his poem, particularly its use of collage; they also require us to consider how Williams' long poem *remembers* epic tradition even though it may also give the illusion of erasing or repressing it.

In the traditional epic, the action begins *in medias res,* with the hero and his companions farthest from their goal. The narrative approaches its end as the hero approaches his home: Odysseus' re-formed Ithaca, mankind's Christian paradise regained, William Wordsworth's mature retrospection, Whitman's transference of his quest for the union of body and soul to the reader. Conventionally, epic narrative also has two points of view. One is prospective and dramatic, recreating the past adventures of the book's hero. The other is retrospective and (relatively) static, magisterially framing the action to let us know not only that its events have previously occurred but also that their meaning and their part in the larger story of the hero's race have already been defined. This retrospective point of view can be said to operate even in epics like Vergil's *Aeneid* or John Milton's *Paradise Lost,* which seem at first glance to end still in the middle of their stories. In both cases, the endings allude by their self-conscious incompleteness to the larger story of which they are a part. For Vergil, this story is the rise of Augustan Rome, which had already occurred when he composed the *Aeneid;* for Milton, it is God's judgment of man, which will occur at the end of time. From Augustus Caesar's point of view in history or God's point of view above history, the epics are retrospective. In the romantic period, the epic's prospective and retrospective points of view began to dis-solve into one, creating an epic without a frame in which the poet's developing consciousness became the one subject in romantic art that had the nobility and universality traditional epic narratives required. Some indication of this redefinition of epic retrospection by romanticism can be seen in Wordsworth, who planned a four-part epic describing his growth as a poet but was able to finish only its prelude. As the opening lines of *The Prelude* make clear, however, the poem is narrated retrospectively, from the vantage point of the poet's mature consciousness. It is English romanticism's version of the retrospective epic. American romanticism was more radical. Whitman's egotistically sublime "Song of Myself" is also a poem about the poet's developing consciousness, but unlike Wordsworth's it is brazenly ahistorical and open-ended and thus carries to an extreme the process of conflating the twin points of view that had been begun by Wordsworth. Whitman's poet-protagonist does not have a past and a present identity so much as two selves perpetually in flux, the natural "Me myself" and the artificial (or social) "the other I am." And as is well known, the last sentence of the poem in the 1855 edition did not end with a period. This was because Whitman's quest itself could not end; it was *periodic*, to be continued by each reader who takes Whitman up on his challenge to make himself the hero of his own life. Twentieth-century epics, most notably Pound's, have now generally made these unfinished and unfinishable histories of the growth of the poet's mind the norm for the epic, so that any firm separation between retrospective and prospective points of view becomes impossible. Eliot's *Four Quartets* and James Merrill's *The Changing Light at Sandover* are calculated exceptions to this generalization; they both pointedly try to reestablish the extratemporal perspective and formal closure of Dante's long poem as a model.

Recently several critics have tied *Paterson* firmly to romantic epic tradition by stressing that the protagonist, Dr. Paterson, gradually matures during the course of the poem. In their account, Dr. Paterson possesses an idealized, mythic vision of the Beautiful Thing at the opening of the poem, but he loses it and then slowly learns to search instead for a humbler, more time-bound vision that concedes that in modern Paterson beauty will necessarily be imperfect and impermanent. James Breslin in particular has drawn our attention to the implications of the scene involving Dr. Paterson and a poor black woman that follows the fire storm in Book Three. Dr. Paterson encounters the woman in a basement and suddenly recognizes in her all the primal power that the library lacked—power for which he has been searching since the beginning of the poem. The woman becomes a battered Kora or Persephone figure, imperfect and even filthy but carrying within her all of nature's powers of renewal. "I can't be half gentle enough, / half tender enough / toward you," he says, humbled and awed, and then sings, "BRIGHTen / the cor / ner / where   you   are!" (*P*, 128). ("Corner" is split by a line break

here to emphasize the parallel with "core" and "Kora.") As Breslin
has shown, Dr. Paterson in this scene has changed markedly since
the previous section of Book Three. When he encountered the same
woman then, he first turned her into a virgin in a "white lace dress,"
and then when she did not conform to his idealized fantasy self-
righteously treated her as if she were a whore:

> (Then, my anger rising) TAKE OFF YOUR
> CLOTHES! I didn't ask you
> to take off your skin   .   I said your
> clothes, your clothes. You smell
> like a whore. I ask you to bathe in my
> opinions, the astonishing virtue of your
> lost body (I said)   .
>
> (P, 104–105)

Williams here unflinchingly records Dr. Paterson's brutal treatment
of the woman but also includes key phrases in parentheses that
separate Williams the narrator from Dr. Paterson the protagonist,
therefore encouraging us to criticize Dr. Paterson's actions and rhet-
oric. Such ironic asides in parentheses are absent from the later lyric
rhapsody sung by the contrite Dr. Paterson to the woman (P, 128)
and help to portray Dr. Paterson's partial regeneration, his new will-
ingness to find beauty in this world, not an ideal one of his own
making. Much of the drama of *Paterson* can therefore be uncovered if
we attend to Dr. Paterson's own struggle to change and the many
successes and reversals he undergoes.[10]

Despite many instances of Dr. Paterson's growing self-knowledge,
however, the examples of anger, despair, and divorce that surround
Dr. Paterson at the start of the poem become dominant in Books
Three and Four, thereby changing the overall mood of Books One

10. James Breslin, *William Carlos Williams: An American Artist*, 192–95; for a more general
discussion of the significance of "reversal" in the poem, see 178–82. Mariani first pointed out
the core/Kore pun in *William Carlos Williams: A New World Naked*, 581–82. Other critics
besides Breslin who stress that *Paterson* is an ironic epic in which the hero continually has to
redefine what he is searching for include Walter Sutton, "Dr. Williams' *Paterson* and the Quest
for Form," *Criticism*, II (Summer, 1960), 242–59; Guimond, *The Art of William Carlos
Williams*, 153–200; Todd M. Lieber, *Endless Experiments: Essays on the Heroic Experience in
American Romanticism* (Columbus, Ohio, 1973), 191–241; Joseph Riddel, *The Inverted Bell:
Modernism and the Counterpoetics of William Carlos Williams* (Baton Rouge, La., 1974), es-
pecially 255–301; Paul Bové, "The World and Earth of William Carlos Williams: *Paterson* as a
'Long Poem,'" *Genre*, XI (Winter, 1978), 575–96; James E. Miller, *The American Quest for a
Supreme Fiction* (Chicago, 1979), 126–60; Lloyd, *William Carlos Williams's "Paterson"*; and
Tapscott, *American Beauty: William Carlos Williams and the Modernist Whitman*, 177–225.
None of these critics, however, explores the role played by Dada in the poem. A reading that
dissents from the critics who stress the "descent" of *Paterson* is M. L. Rosenthal and Sally M.
Gall, *The Modern Poetic Sequence: The Genius of Modern Poetry* (New York, 1983), 233–68.

through Four from celebratory to satiric. Book One began in pre-history, with Dr. Paterson witnessing the male and female principles of the poem interpenetrating perfectly.

> Paterson lies in the valley under the Passaic Falls
> its spent waters forming the outline of his back. He
> lies on his right side, head near the thunder
> of the waters filling his dreams!
> . . . .
> And there, against him, stretches the low mountain.
> The Park's her head, carved, above the Falls, by the quiet
> river; Colored crystals the secret of those rocks
> (P, 6, 8)

This mythic and timeless union is immediately counterpointed by a vision of modern spiritual, sexual, and intellectual dysfunction, as represented by "automatons" living in the cities,

> Who because they
> neither know their sources nor the sills of their
> disappointments walk outside their bodies aimlessly
>   for the most part,
> locked and forgot in their desires—unroused.
> (P, 6)

At the start of *Paterson*, the theme of marriage predominates, and the passages introducing the poem's examples of divorce are kept clearly subordinate. The later books shift their focus downstream from the Falls (first to the park by the Falls, then to the areas of Paterson below the Falls such as the library, then to New York City and the Atlantic Ocean), and examples of spiritual and physical divorce play an increasingly prominent part in the poem. The economy is shown to be more usurious, the language more corrupt, the communication between people—especially between lovers—more sterile. In Book Four, Section II, admittedly, Madame Curie emerges as a heroine, and as such represents an advance beyond the grim frustration of the lesbian Corydon in the poem's previous section. But viewing Madame Curie in the context of all of Book Four, we see that she is surrounded by figures representing self-destruction rather than self-discovery: Corydon, the murderer Jack Johnson, the "blood-red" Atlantic, and the shark that snaps at his own guts (P, 200), among others. Even Curie's own important discovery of how to split the uranium atom and release energy (P, 175–78) is parodied in the same section of the poem by another kind of splitting, in which a corrupt evangelist accepts "27 Grand" for his efforts to divide striking Paterson mill workers by "calling them to God" instead (*P*, 172–73). Book Four, Section II, in other words, is not a "visionary" answer to Corydon's mock pastoral in the first section; its hopeful vision glows strongly at times, but most often in this particular section and in Book Four as a whole we feel the leaden oppressiveness of history.[11] In general, Book Four reads like a long mock pastoral with few truly pastoral or visionary interludes. It is dominated by figures in historical and modern Paterson who distort pastoral's traditional celebration of love, fertility, labor, and honor, and by beasts like the shark, which eats its own guts and thus is a grotesque parody of the interpenetrating River and Mountain at the beginning of Book One.

Book Four also represents the sharpest reversal in the poem of Dr. Paterson's epic quest to discover the Beautiful Thing. At the end of Book Three, he was hoping to make a fresh start. And, indeed, the homage he paid to the black Kora figure had suggested that he might succeed. But by the opening of Book Four, Dr. Paterson seems as far as he has ever been from his goals of reforming society, language, and himself. The liberating clearing of the ground accomplished by the flood and the fire in Book Three has been lost; Book Four is set in the most congested locale of the entire poem, the shores and the mouth of the polluted Passaic River as it enters the Hudson and then the Atlantic. As Corydon says at the start of the book, the three guano-stained rocks in the East River that she sees out of her window are "all that's left of the elemental, the primitive / in this environment" (*P*, 152). Even Dr. Paterson himself is apparently not immune from this corruption. At one point the poem's narrative comments sardonically,

> Oh Paterson! Oh married man!
> He is the city of cheap hotels and private
> entrances . of taxis at the door, the car
> standing in the rain . . .
> . . . .
> Goodbye, dear. I had a wonderful time.
> Wait! There's something . but I've forgotten.
> (*P*, 154)

"He is the city": Dr. Paterson as a sleazy city is much closer to the "automatons" in Book One or to the exhausted Tiresias of *The Waste Land* who imitated the clichés of conversation ("Goodnight ladies,

11. Breslin, *William Carlos Williams: An American Artist*, 201.

goodnight, sweet ladies") than he is to the mythic giant Paterson in the poem's opening pages or to the humble but resolute poet at the end of Book Three. Moreover, despite Dr. Paterson's discovery of Madame Curie, Social Credit, and so on, in the later episodes of Book Four, he is largely reduced to satirizing stale literary conventions rather than finding ways to make those conventions new: like Corydon, his alter ego, he writes a long mock-pastoral poem. Compared with his deliriously successful obliteration of tradition in Book Three, this attack on tradition in Four seems labored and ineffectual. The "white-hot man" (*P*, 123) of Book Three reshapes and invents; the exhausted man of Book Four largely resigns himself to parody, documentary, and nostalgia.

Dr. Paterson's tragic descent seems consistent both with the topography of the Passaic River valley, which descends toward the sea, and with certain general principles of Dada that appear to have influenced the structure of *Paterson*. The Dadaists believed that art and ideas petrify and therefore have to be discarded soon after they are invented. This is why they urged artists to forget everything they learned; the memory of what they and others have done would impede their efforts to do new things. Dada thus made artists martyrs to the impossible ideal of perpetual self-renewal. As J. Hillis Miller has noted, Williams consistently discriminated between creative shaping energy and the passive forms created by that force and then left to congeal as the force passes on.[12] In Book Four of *Paterson*, Williams calls this shaping force "the radiant gist," while the stale forms of beauty that congeal after the creative force passes on are called both "the final crystallization" and "lead" (*P*, 109, 178). In Williams' earlier volume *Kora in Hell*, he imagined creativity and decadence as a wheel cycling between upturn and downturn: "When the wheel's just at the up turn it glimpses horizon, zenith, all in a burst, the pull of the earth shaken off, a scatter of fragments, significance in a burst of water striking up from the base of a fountain. Then at the sickening turn toward death the pieces are joined into a pretty thing, a bouquet frozen in an icecake" (*I*, 71). The beginning of *Paterson* draws on this passage from *Kora in Hell* to represent the buoyant creativity of the Falls. Its waterdrops, Williams shows us, are suspended against gravity and against time: "fall, fall in air! as if / floating, relieved of their weight" (*P*, 8). But this energy gradually

12. Miller, *Poets of Reality*, 328–44.

succumbs to its natural fate, to gravity and time; *Paterson* becomes dominated by references to blockage, divorce, decay, murder, and "pretty things" such as the stale literary parody used by Corydon in her *Corydon, a Pastoral* (*P*, 159–62). The shift in the epic's overall tone from sweet to sour is thus emphatic. All we need do is compare the first few pages of Books One and Four to see that the pure, spontaneous energy of the Falls has run its course. The free water of the Falls is now, Williams puns, "sea-bound" (*P*, 200).

At the conclusion of Book Four, Dr. Paterson awakens from this suicidal nightmare of modern history: "Waken from a dream, this dream of / the whole poem   .   sea-bound" (*P*, 200). If the descent of Dr. Paterson imitates the fate of creativity in time (inevitably declining into decadence, parody, death), at the very end of Book Four Williams' hero eludes such a fate by refusing to be either sea-bound or tradition-bound. He audaciously stands the traditional conclusion of the epic on its head:

> I say to you, Put wax rather in your
> ears against the hungry sea
>   it is not our home!
>   .   draws us in to drown, of losses
> and regrets   .
> (*P*, 201)

Books One through Four do not conclude as a traditional epic does, when the hero arrives home, but when the hero realizes that he is *farthest* from home, from the Passaic Falls and their unending creative power. And when Williams wittily alludes to Odysseus' blocking his sailors' ears from the Sirens' song, he reminds us that as the wily pilot of his own epic craft he hears the beautiful music of epic precedent, the temptation to follow the "correct" way of ending an epic, but refuses to give in to it.

For Dr. Paterson, discovering how far he is from home is the first step toward a successful Odyssean escape from the forces that entrap him. During the very last pages of Book Four images of cleanliness and fertility dominate the poem once more. After swimming in the sea, Dr. Paterson is greeted joyfully by his dog (one of his alter egos throughout the epic), spits the seed from a beach plum out onto the dunes, and then heads inland with the "steady roar, as of a distant / waterfall" on his mind (*P*, 203). In doing so, he reverses the direction of the entire poem and begins a new quest to recover the creative powers he has gradually lost. Williams, of course, originally

planned to have his epic be only four books long. He thus intended to
conclude the poem at the moment that his hero, after a pause,
renews his quest. Such an ending is a prospective or "open" one,
despite Williams' references to "the eternal close" and "the end" on
the book's last page. We leave Dr. Paterson as he stands on the dunes
contemplating an endless series of other Odyssean descents into
history—and, consequently, an endless series of further losses and
self-defeats. Williams emphasizes this pessimistic, Dadaist truth by
interrupting Dr. Paterson's lyrical meditation on rebirth with a refer-
ence to the eternal violence of history: "John Johnson, from Liver-
pool, England, was convicted after 20 minutes conference by the
Jury. On April 30th, 1850, he was hung in full view of thousands who
had gathered on Garrett Mountain and adjacent house tops to wit-
ness the spectacle" (P, 203). This juxtaposition of a rebirth and an
execution contains in miniature the entire descent of Books One
through Four.

When Book Four was published in 1951, Williams thought he was
done. But after recovering from several strokes, he conceived and
wrote Book Five, inspired by his harrowing of death. By adding it to
the first four books of Paterson in 1958, he makes us read the ending of
Book Four differently from how we read it when considering Books
One through Four alone. The ending of Book Four implies that a
sequel to the epic does not need to be written because any further
adventures of Dr. Paterson would inevitably be other descents made
up of gradually increasing despairs and diminishing awakenings. But
if Books One through Five are taken as a unit, it seems that when Dr.
Paterson walks on the dunes at the end of Book Four he meditates not
just on another descent but on Book Five, which thoroughly revises
the role played by descent in Williams' poem.

In Book Five the destructive and creative principles that had been
at war throughout the previous books are wrested at last into equi-
librium, so that each creative "upturn" and the decadent "down-
turn" are fiercely held in balance. If the mythical nature-goddess the
Mountain dominated the opening of Book One and the decadent
Corydon the opening of Book Four, in Book Five Williams intro-
duces a paired or doubled image of women: "The moral // proclaimed
by the whorehouse / could not be better proclaimed / by the virgin"
(P, 208). This doubling continues throughout the book as Williams
counterpoints references to powerful women (including Mary in
Brueghel's Nativity painting, the Virgin in the Unicorn tapestries,

Sappho, and the anonymous passerby on pages 219–20 to whom
Williams impulsively dedicates all his poems) with those to barren or
self-destructive women (such as the whores in Gilbert Sorrentino's
letters on pages 214–15, or the poignant old woman on the penulti-
mate page of the poem who wore "a china doorknob / in her vagina
to hold her womb up"). Similarly, if Dr. Paterson migrates in Books
One through Four from expressing the comic realm of mythic cre-
ative power free from time (the Falls and the Mountain) to the tragic,
degenerative fate of all that is born into history (Paterson the city), in
Book Five fallen history and the eternal world of art are interwoven
into a harmonious, tragicomic design. The descent motif no longer
controls the poem: its powers are continually counteracted by motifs
of ascent and recovery.

In Book Five, moreover, Williams gives Dr. Paterson the home-
coming denied him in Book Four:

> Paterson, from the air
>   above the low range of its hills
>   across the river
> on a rock-ridge
>   has returned to the old scenes
>   to witness
> What has happened
>   since Soupault gave him the novel
>   the Dadaist novel
> to translate—
>   *The Last Nights of Paris.*
>   "What has happened to Paris
> since that time?
>   and to myself?"
>   A WORLD OF ART
>   THAT THROUGH THE YEARS HAS
>   *SURVIVED!*
> (*P*, 209)

Dada's principles guided Dr. Paterson during his descent into dec-
adence in Books One through Four. But in Book Five Williams puts
Dada in its place, satirizing it and carefully restricting its destructive
energy. The movement that was to end all art has survived, as have
the works it meant to destroy. The apocalyptic Surrealist novel *Last
Nights of Paris* (written in 1929 by Philippe Soupault, who
coauthored *Les Champs magnétiques* with André Breton) has been
translated into another language, and Paris itself has survived two
European wars. Dada's pessimistic view of the fate of art is now

counterpointed by a faith that creative power is perpetually able to escape from the forces that try to destroy it. As Williams caustically says near the very end of Book Five, alluding to Duchamp's celebrated announcement (which later proved untrue) that he was rejecting art for chess: "Equally laughable / is to assume to know nothing, a / chess game" (*P*, 239). Book Five of *Paterson* thus restores the traditional epic conclusion that Williams excluded from his earlier ending for the poem. That is, if we take Books One through Four as a unit, we find that the epic ends with the hero realizing that he is farthest from home. But if we consider Books One through Five together, the poem ends classically, with the hero symbolically returning to the Falls, to a world where the eternal and the time-bound, the creative and the decadent, may be held in balance.

Williams acknowledges in the last lines of *Paterson* that this balancing act characterizes Book Five as it does no other book in the poem. The lines describe a satyr's dance. The "tragic" beat of the satyr's foot represents history as a tragedy in which creativity is lost and the artist is inevitably reduced to Dadaist satire and erasure ("We know nothing" [*P*, 239]). Because the satyr is half-man, half-goat, he can be seen as an emblem of a grotesque degeneration from the norm of what man should be, and is thus connected etymologically for Williams with satire, the mode of literature, including Dada, that criticizes such deviations. As Williams had said at the end of Book One, quoting J. A. Symonds, "The Greeks displayed their acute aesthetic sense of propriety, recognizing the harmony which subsists between crabbed verses and the distorted subjects with which they dealt—the vices and perversions of humanity—as well as their agreement with the snarling spirit of the satirist. Deformed verse was suited to deformed morality" (*P*, 40). But throughout Book Five Williams also syncopates this tragic, "deformed" beat with what he calls a "pre-tragic" or comic one.[13] It, too, is associated with the satyr, but in this case the satyr represents man's sexual and spiritual potency, his ability to create.

> the Satyrs, a
> pre-tragic play,
> a satyric play!
> All plays
> were satyric when they were most devout.
> Ribald as a Satyr!

13. See also Lloyd, *William Carlos Williams's "Paterson,"* 267–71.

> Satyrs dance!
>   all the deformites take wing
> (*P*, 221)

The complementary meanings of Williams' references to satyrs thus contain in miniature the contrapuntal, tragicomic structure of Book Five itself.

We know that in the late 1950s Williams decided that *Paterson* was to have been an open-ended epic, for drafts for a sixth book survive. As the poem now stands (or dances, rather), it is an epic documenting the history of a locality, Paterson, New Jersey, in which its hero, Dr. Paterson, succeeds when he discovers that local history is both his proper home and his place of exile. He must journey downriver and face the failures of his city and his self—he must, in his own words, look "death / in the eye" (*P*, 106). But by the end of Book Four he is also freed to somersault upstream, aware that his decline into satire, Dadaist disgust, and violence is merely part of an inexorable creative dance that will soon counter its own rhythms. If the first four books of Williams' epic seem to descend from their early poetic heights (as most contemporary critics, comparing the poem to the other epics they knew, saw and protested), Williams would perhaps answer that that is the way time, rivers, and modern epic poems naturally flow. But Book Five countered Dadaist pessimism by describing the fate of art and the body in time without despairing of the mind's ability to rediscover its creative heights. Books Four and Five thus construct two endings for *Paterson*. The first is an open ending, with the poet beginning a new journey. The second is a truly closed ending in which the poet concludes an old journey: as Williams says near the end of Book Five, "The (self) direction has been changed / the serpent / its tail in its mouth / 'the river has returned to its beginnings'" (*P*, 233). In creating two endings for his long poem, Williams fashioned an agitated equilibrium between the impulses toward closure and exposure, retrospection and progression, that have informed epics from the *Iliad* on.

Is *Paterson* a Dadaist or Cubist collage of texts? What does reading a collage of texts in fact entail? Williams critics have only just begun to consider these questions.[14] If we glance at the architecture of Books

14. The best discussion of *Paterson* as a collage is by Henry Sayre, in *The Visual Text of William Carlos Williams*, 93–117. Sayre does not make a distinction between Cubist and Dadaist collage principles, but he does argue that beginning with Book II, *Paterson* begins to

One through Four and then Books One through Five, it seems at first as if they are both Cubist. After all, their use of heterogeneous materials is carefully selected and composed, as can be seen from the following note on his collage techniques that Williams wrote to himself while working on *Paterson:*

> There are to be completely worked up parts in *each* section—as completely formal as possible: in each part well displayed.
> . . . But—juxtaposed to them are unfinished pieces—put in without fuss—for their very immediacy of expression—as they have been written under LACK of a satisfactory form.
> —or for their need to be just there, the information.[15]

Paterson uses "found" materials as Williams' Cubist odes did, except that in his epic Williams greatly increases the variety and length of found materials that he includes in comparison with, say, "Overture to a Dance of Locomotives" or "Rapid Transit." And *Paterson* also combines both improvised sections written quickly with the "mistakes" left in (akin to "The Rose" or Williams' Improvisations) *and* "completely worked up parts" as carefully composed as any of Williams' Precisionist lyrics or dramatic monologues. Further, the many texts in *Paterson* recurrently cluster around central themes and symbols—especially natural versus urban, female versus male, democratic versus totalitarian, among others. Finally, Williams' procedures in *Paterson* require that he select, detach, and order as carefully as his Cubist poems do. As Williams says in his preface, he is rolling up a "sum" of materials to make an ordered aggregate.

Yet Williams' confidence that he can compose such an "identity" for his collage-epic is also seriously undercut. Problems first surface in the preface, in which Williams laments "the defective means" available to him and warns against letting his craft be "subverted by thought," "no more than the writing of stale poems" (*P*, 3, 4). These are early warnings of the Dadaist frustration with being "blocked" (*P*, 72) and forced to write "under LACK of a satisfactory form" that appears more and more frequently as the poem develops. This failure

---

deny its own dream of synthesis. Readers interested in Williams' use of collage should also consult Perloff, *The Poetics of Indeterminacy*, 109–54; Perloff, "The Invention of Collage"; and Margaret L. Bollard, "The Interlace Element in *Paterson*," *Twentieth Century Literature*, XXI (1975), 288–304.

15. These phrases are from a note to himself that Williams wrote while working on *Paterson*. The note is cited by Joel Conarroe, *William Carlos Williams's "Paterson": Language and Landscape* (Philadelphia, 1970), 26. Conarroe's is the best book-length study of Williams' epic published to date.

emphasizes not the Cubist coherence of *Paterson* but its Dadaist decomposition: Dr. Paterson is increasingly forced to resort to defective means such as parody or mere vandalism. He becomes less and less a composer in the Cubist sense. Book Five, however, appears to reverse this trend and restore Dr. Paterson's ability to create an "identity" out of history's fragments.

In order to be useful, such a distinction between the Cubist and Dadaist energies of Williams' collage method ought to be applicable to *any* section of the poem, not merely as a way to describe the poem's "closed" and "open" endings. As a test case, we may consider, say, Book Two, Section II. If the poem indeed chronicles a kind of epic combat between generation and decay, then such a conflict ought to be dramatically present in each section of the poem, with either "composition" or "decomposition" gaining the upper hand (so to speak), depending on that section's place within the overall plot of the poem. Such a close reading of Williams' use of collage in a particular section also makes it possible to ask whether Williams managed to integrate all the different styles of his earlier writing, particularly those influenced by Precisionism, Cubism, and Dada, or whether Williams was forced to concede that there were inveterate contradictions among those styles.

In Book Two, Section II, we indeed find that Dr. Paterson plays the two roles of composer and decomposer. One is that of Faitoute (*P*, 62), French for "to make everything." The other role (to coin a name) is that of Faitrien, a Dadaist poet of decomposition, irony, and despair. The title of Williams' epic gives us another possible set of names for these two roles: Dr. Paterson plays both the role of a *pater*, an authority figure creating an order, and a *son*, a recreant perpetually dismantling that order and searching for a new one. The section has a representative mix of texts, from raw prose taken from newspapers, history books, a sermon preached in a park, and personal letters to Williams, to poetry both high and low—a bitter satiric ballad, Faitoute's own narration and interior monologues, and three examples of carefully finished, high poetry ("Is this the only beauty here?," "The gentle Christ," and "If there is subtlety," [*P*, 71, 72, 74–75]).

The prose texts are selected, edited, and rearranged according to Cubist principles: they are treated as found objects removed from their original context with enough clues left of that context to allow a complex dialectic to emerge between their original context and the

new one that is created for them. One way to think of these found
passages is to consider them as offspring or "sons" faithful to their
parental texts; through them, many of the original meanings of their
parental texts may be reconstituted. Once those found passages are
also allied with the text of *Paterson*, however, they may act as both
submissive and subversive sons: they may be contained within the
new structure that Faitoute their foster father has built, but they may
also destabilize and revise that structure.

Williams' poetic texts work in a similar way to his found ones,
especially to the degree that they allow him to criticize monopolies of
all kinds in private and public history. Yet since the poems are in-
vented rather than found texts, they may do what found texts usually
do not—function as self-questioning meditations on the methods of
Paterson itself, its successes and failures. In Section II, the poem that
most clearly performs this inquisitorial function is the lyric that
comes at the very end, "If there is subtlety" (*P*, 74–75).

The most prominent event in Section II is Williams' transcription
of and reactions to a sermon on the mount (Mount Garrett) infor-
mally preached in the park by the Passaic Falls by a born-again
German immigrant named Klaus Ehrens. The sermon's topic is a
familiar one: having come to America to pursue the American
Dream, Ehrens finds that the true pursuit of happiness can only be a
pursuit of spiritual, not material, wealth. But Williams' short intro-
duction to the section gives us an outline of the context in which he
will place Ehrens' confession. This section of *Paterson* is to be a
history of failures to find spiritual wealth in America by religious,
economic, artistic, and political figures. The general principle guid-
ing Williams' diagnosis is clear: all monopolies that attempt to con-
trol the means of production and distribution are dangerous, whether
they involve the tangible goods of politics and economics or the
intangible "good" of religion and art. In their place, Williams argues
for what he claims is a more "natural" form of organization—*many*
sources of production and no control of the rights of distribution.
Thus the action of the section properly opens with Faitoute's exem-
plary "wandering" through the park. Dr. Paterson's freedom to see
and think as he chooses (and to organize this section of the poem
around what he discovers) is placed in pointed opposition to all forms
of restriction and control.

Ehrens' sermon provides an example of how to rebel against mo-
nopolies: it is improvised, evangelically Protestant, and spiritualist,

as opposed to ritualistic, institutionally sanctioned, and materialist. It is frequently interrupted, however, as Williams combines a series of examples of monopolistic behavior from American history and (ironically) Williams' own private life. The most obvious of these examples is a series of texts on the economic and ideological importance of the city of Paterson in colonial and nineteenth-century American history. Paterson was named in honor of the governor of New Jersey, who signed the charter granting Alexander Hamilton's Society for Useful Manufactures the right to sell capital stock and create the colonies' first industrial city, and it had America's first textile mills and manufactured its first locomotives and Colt revolvers.[16] In the texts Williams chooses, Alexander Hamilton emerges as the first in a long line of industrialist tycoons. He is for Williams a sort of American Antichrist, a figure who under the guise of rebelling against Britain's political and economic monopolies would have set up new monopolies in America to take their place. Williams focuses on Hamilton's authoritarian Federalism, which envisioned the creation of various systems for the control of the manufacture and distribution of material goods, money, and political power.

> The Federal Reserve System is a private enterprise . . . a private monopoly . . . (with power) . . . given to it by a spineless Congress . . . to issue and regulate all our money. . . .
>   Witnessing the [Passaic] Falls Hamilton was impressed by this show of what in those times was overwhelming power . . . planned a stone aqueduct following a proposed boulevard, as the crow flies, to Newark with outlets every mile or two along the river for groups of factories: The Society for Useful Manufactures: SUM, they called it.
>   The newspapers of the day spoke in enthusiastic terms of the fine prospects of the "National Manufactory" where they fondly believed would be produced all cotton, cassimeres, wall papers, books, felt and straw hats, shoes, carriages, pottery, bricks, pots, pans and buttons needed in the United States. (*P*, 73–74)

An earlier quotation from a history of Paterson stresses the irony of these plans: Hamilton protested against English political and economic policy, but the means with which he chose to make America

16. See Weaver, *William Carlos Williams: The American Background*, 118–19; and Conaroe, *William Carlos Williams's "Paterson,"* 155–56 n. 30, on the important sources for Williams' knowledge of Paterson's history: William Nelson and Charles A. Shriner, *History of the City of Paterson and the County of Passaic New Jersey* (Paterson, N.J., 1901); Nelson and Shriner, *Records of the Township of Paterson, N.J., 1831–1851* (Paterson, N.J., 1895); John W. Barber and Henry Howe, *Historical Collections of the State of New Jersey* (New York, 1894); and Herbert A. Fisher's unpublished manuscript "Legends of the Passaic." The best brief summary of

economically and politically independent *subverted* his dream (in Williams' view, at least) and merely reproduced the oppressive features of English corporate capitalism in the New World.

> The new world had been looked on as a producer of precious metals, pelts and raw materials to be turned over to the mother country for manufactured articles which the colonists had no choice but to buy at advanced prices. They were prevented from making woolen, cotton or linen cloth for sale. Nor were they allowed to build furnaces to convert the native iron into steel.
> Even during the Revolution Hamilton had been impressed by the site of the Great Falls of the Passaic. His fertile imagination envisioned a great manufacturing center, a great Federal City, to supply the needs of the country. Here was water-power to turn the mill wheels and the navigable river to carry manufactured goods to the market centers: a national manufactury. (P, 69)

In Williams' analysis, Hamilton's dream of independence was endangered by the monopolistic forms with which that independence was declared: American workers would become as dependent on the Federal manufacture as they once were on the British system; the means of production and distribution were still to be highly centralized and thus monopolistic. Moreover, since Hamilton defined the American Dream in primarily material rather than spiritual terms, his failure was all the more ignoble. By juxtaposing Hamilton's dream with Ehrens' sermon, Williams helps us see the self-defeating principles of Hamilton's thought more clearly than we could if we read the passages on Hamilton alone.

Other texts interrupting the sermon are similar examples of self-defeat. One is an angry parody of "America the Beautiful" inspired by Hamilton's monopolistic Federalism. Another is an account of the American eagle being forced back into its egg. The most startling of these examples, however, are taken from Williams' private life—two letters from Marcia Nardi, a woman who as an aspiring artist imagined herself to be controlled and blocked by Williams. Her letters emphasize the very things that Williams criticized Hamilton for

---

Paterson's history is in Conarroe, 49–51. The following secondary sources ought to be essential reading for anyone concerned with the historical importance of Paterson and Alexander Hamilton's views on Federalism, banking, and corporate capitalism: Federal Writers Project, *New Jersey: A Guide to Its Present and Past* (New York, 1939); Louis M. Hacker, *Alexander Hamilton in the American Tradition* (New York, 1957), 127–90; Broadus Mitchell, *Alexander Hamilton: The National Adventure, 1788–1804* (New York, 1962), 181–98; Jacob Ernest Cooke, *Alexander Hamilton* (New York, 1982), 58–108; Nancy F. Cott, *The Bonds of Womanhood: "Woman's Sphere" in New England, 1780–1835* (New Haven, Conn., 1977), 19–62, on the transition of New England textile making from cottage-industry homespun to mass production between 1790 and 1830; and Herbert G. Gutman, *Work, Culture, and Society in Industrializing America* (New York, 1976), 211–60.

doing. They accuse him of paternalistic authoritarianism—of un-consciously controlling another person's right to speak and act inde-pendently, and of refusing to admit that such an unfair situation exists. We cannot judge the truth of Nardi's accusations, of course, nor are we meant to. But by including her letters in *Paterson* Williams inevitably challenges his own authority as an interpreter and a maker of history: he may not practice what he preaches.[17]

Williams' collage techniques in Book Two, Section II (as in oth-ers), are Cubist insofar as they force the various meanings of his texts to converge around central principles such as the evils of monopoly in all its forms. They are Dadaist insofar as they subvert these organ-izing principles, ironically revealing contradictions between his ends and means. Williams criticizes Hamilton for creating the monopo-listic Society for Useful Manufactures, for example, but in the same section of the poem is accused of wanting to monopolize another poet's life. Furthermore, Hamilton's "SUM" project is reminiscent of Williams' attempts throughout *Paterson* to make an epic *summa* of his own: "To make a start, / out of particulars / and make them general, rolling / up the sum" (*P*, 3).

This is not to argue that the book's Cubist methods are monopo-listic while its Dadaist ones are heroically subversive. Williams' Cubist collage techniques themselves create a play of various mean-ings throughout the texts that they use, never a single meaning. By placing the passages on Hamilton within the context of Ehrens' sermon, for example, Williams sets up a rich interaction between Hamilton's vision of independence (which Ehrens and Williams would certainly praise) and his failure to realize that vision. The passage can hardly be read "monopolistically," as signifying merely one thing. This is even more clearly seen when we widen its context still further, including in our analysis not only the sermon but, say, the following fragment, which follows immediately after the first passage about the Society for Useful Manufactures quoted above:

> Washington at his first inaugural
> . . . . .   wore
> a coat of Crow-black homespun woven
> in Paterson . . . . .
>
> (*P*, 74)

17. Compare the ground-breaking readings of the Nardi material in *Paterson* by Theodora R. Graham, "'Her Heigh Compleynte': The Cress Letters of William Carlos Williams' *Pater-son*," in Daniel Hoffman (ed.), *Ezra Pound and William Carlos Williams: The University of Pennsylvania Conference Papers* (Philadelphia, 1983), 164–93; and Sandra M. Gilbert, "Pur-

After reading the passages on Hamilton, we must note the irony of Washington's coat being called "homespun," for Hamilton's Society for Useful Manufactures was an organized effort to supplant the cottage weaving industry with modern mass production financed by selling capital stock. Yet the above passage also celebrates American independence, signified by Washington and by his American-made coat, and recalls the many links that were drawn in the late eighteenth and early nineteenth centuries between the rise of American manufacturing and the survival of the republic.[18] In its own way, the passage is as much about spiritual values as Ehrens' sermon. Thus by juxtaposing fragments of three texts (the sermon, the discussion of Hamilton, and the above lines) Williams has created an interlocking system of cross-references and various possible interpretations. It does not merely condemn manufacturing and praise Ehrens' spirituality. And there are many more texts within this part of Book Two, Section II; my discussion has inevitably reduced the Cubist multiplicity of possible readings that Williams has constructed. Their number increases each time the context is broadened and a new fragment introduced into the collage for consideration.

As with Williams' Cubist lyrics, however, the variety of possible readings produced by such a collage in *Paterson* is neither infinite nor self-destructive and wholly indeterminate. The readings suggested by each text check and balance the readings created by the other texts. The result is a reinforcement of our faith in the profundity and authority of the collage method itself. Its creator, Faitoute, is an exemplary master who selects, edits, supplements, and juxtaposes his materials in ways that *celebrate* his ability to create a new order, a rich sum of readings that does justice to the complexity of his materials, enforcing his point about the evils of monopolies and yet also depicting how Paterson played an important role in the birth of an independent American economy.

Dadaist collage techniques, on the other hand, subtract and divide rather than create sums; they destabilize the Cubist play of meaning and question the authority of the composer himself. More than any other piece of material in Book Two, Section II, the Nardi letters perform this Dadaist function. Indeed, they impugn Williams' authority as an interpreter: if he is accused of being me-

loined Letters: William Carlos Williams and 'Cress,' " *William Carlos Williams Review,* XI (Fall, 1985), 5–15.
    18. The best discussion of this topic is by Kasson, *Civilizing the Machine,* 3–135.

chanical and impersonal in his private life, then why does he claim
the right to criticize those qualities in public life? The letters thus
upset the Cubist balance of meanings that I have paraphrased; they
cannot be as easily assimilated into the structure's play of meanings
as, say, the passage about Washington's homespun coat could be. At
the start of his epic, Williams said that his goal was to make particu-
lars "general"—that is, to use his collage techniques to interpret
the meaning of his particular pieces of data. But fragments such as
the letters, or the poem "If there is subtlety," do little to support the
general readings that Williams is elsewhere trying to create. In-
stead, they assert the independence and idiosyncracy of all "partic-
ulars" in the poem and disrupt the authority of all interpreters to
make them signify "general" truths. Dada is an energy of fission, as
Cubism (ultimately) is that of fusion. Together they are as conten-
tious and interdependent in *Paterson* as *pater* and *son*—or (in view
of Nardi's importance) as *pater* and *daughter*.

As Books One through Four evolve, Williams' authority as an
interpreter is increasingly undercut, as is the integrity of the mate-
rials he works with. This loss is the burden of the superb lyric "If
there is subtlety." It is addressed to the Beautiful Thing, the object of
Williams' epic quest through history's fragments:

> how futile would be the search
> for you in the multiplicity of
> your debacle.
>   . . . . . .
>   in your
> composition and decomposition
> I find my   .   .
>   despair!
>
> (P, 75)

In Book Five, in contrast, Dr. Paterson's compositions are not so
violently decomposed; his Cubist will to order masters the Dadaist
demon of irony. Despite the frequent play of irony throughout the
book (as in the placement of the rather inarticulate interview with
Mike Wallace at the end of Section II), that play is always subordi-
nated to Williams' faith that his quest repeatedly succeeds.

Hence it is possible to argue that in the sequence of Books One
through Four each episode aspires to be a Cubist collage but inevita-
bly degenerates into a Dadaist one, with that failure becoming more
obvious and violent as we progress through the books. In the se-
quence of Books One through Five, on the other hand, Williams

tries to reshape the poem into a stable (*not* static) Cubist construc-
tion in which the play of composition and decomposition is
rigorously held in balance. Such critical indeterminacy is necessary
on the reader's part, I think, to appreciate a poem whose twin end-
ings aspire simultaneously to closed and open forms. *Paterson* is an
epic gathering of the multiple and contradictory poetics that
Williams developed since he came into contact with Precisionism,
Cubism, and Dada many years before.

To what degree was such a vision of the modern epic primarily
Williams', and to what degree was it shared with his contemporaries
and his romantic predecessors? A key to handling this question
comes from a surprising source—William Wordsworth. *The Prelude*
of course is the venerable progenitor of all modern epics that present
themselves as honorable failures, unfinishable histories of the growth
of the poet's mind whose gaps and contradictions are as important as
its continuities. Wordsworth was profoundly troubled by the specter
of such lacunae, however, as if he realized that they would be the
high price paid for the romantic era's discovery of the egotistical
sublime as it unfolds in time. One scene in *The Prelude* is particularly
memorable for its dramatization of Wordsworth's fear that all modern
epic quests must be fragmented and unfinished: the famous dream of
the Arab, the stone, and the shell in Book Five, lines 50–191. This
episode holds parallels with the drama of *Paterson* that are especially
worth exploring.

   Reading *Don Quixote* by the seashore, Wordsworth falls asleep and
dreams that a Quixote-like Arab approaches him in a desert carrying
a stone and a seashell "Of a surpassing brightness." The former
symbolizes Euclid's *Elements*, the Arab tells him; the latter, not a
particular book so much as the power of speech itself, for it

> Had voices more than all the winds, with power
> To exhilarate the spirit, and to soothe,
> Through every clime, the heart of human kind.

Yet when Wordsworth puts the shell to his ear, he hears sounds that
are distinctly unsoothing:

> in an unknown tongue,
> which yet I understood, articulate sounds,
> a loud prophetic blast of harmony;
> An Ode, in passion uttered, which foretold
> Destruction to the children of the earth
> By deluge, now at hand.

The Arab tells Wordsworth that he is going to bury the two "books" to save them from the coming flood, and as soon as he says this Wordsworth looks behind him and sees

> over half the wilderness diffused,
> A bed of glittering light: I asked the cause:
> "It is," said he, "the waters of the deep
> Gathering upon us."[19]

There are many reasons to pair *The Prelude* and *Paterson*, not least among them the fact that they have the two most powerful flood scenes in all of modern poetry. Wordsworth's Book Five and Williams' Book Three are primarily about the destruction of books—both the epic poet's guilty participation in such a scene and his deep fears about what such fantasies mean. As J. Hillis Miller, one of Wordsworth's most astute readers, has pointed out, Wordsworth's dream in Book Five centers on his profound ambivalence toward books. They seemed to him both to entomb his living voice and to be the only way that that voice could *escape* permanent entombment. Miller mentions several negative references to printed books in *The Prelude*, especially in some lines in Book Three that could serve as the credo for that same book in *Paterson:* Wordsworth describes all the books he did *not* read while in the library of Cambridge University as "those long vistas, sacred catacombs, / Where mighty minds lie visibly entombed."[20] Yet books also seem to be the only safe bearers of the living voice. When Wordsworth in his dream places the Arab's shell next to his ear, the passage stresses the oral rather than the textual life of the words: it is as if Wordsworth is listening to the archetypal sound of human speech itself, an "unknown" tongue that is the tongue of tongues, their primal source. (This reading is strengthened by the fact that in a seashell, of course, one hears the sound of one's own blood circulating, primal noise—like the sea's—antecedent to all articulate speech.) Wordsworth is so anxious to help the Arab bury his two "books" not (or not *only*) because they seem dead to him but because they seem so alive, so worthy of being preserved from impending destruction.

In *Paterson* Williams is equally ambivalent about books; they represent both the death or "sleep" of living speech and (using imagery identical to Wordsworth's) speech at its most fluid and alive. Yet, as

19. William Wordsworth, *The Prelude*, Book Five, 107–109, 93–98, 128–31.
20. *Ibid.*, Book Three, 341–42.

in *The Prelude,* in *Paterson* that very fluidity makes what the poet
hears frightening as well; it seems a deluge:

> with the roar of the river
> forever in our ears (arrears)
> inducing sleep and silence, the roar
> of eternal sleep . . challenging
> our waking—
>
> (*P,* 18)
>
> The past above, the future below
> and the present pouring down: the roar,
> the roar of the present, a speech—
> is, of necessity, my sole concern .
> . . . .
> I must
> find my meaning and lay it, white,
> beside the sliding water: myself—
> comb out the language—or succumb
>
> (*P,* 144–45)

If texts seem to fix the poet's living voice, water represents a danger of
another kind: speech that is *too* fluid, that drowns individual artic-
ulation, the poet's ability to order.

Ultimately, both Wordsworth and Williams seek texts that myste-
riously are neither too fixed nor too fluid. Wordsworth wants to bury
the shell so that it may survive the deluge and meditates on the frailty
of books and their precious cargo:

> Oh! why hath not the Mind
> Some element to stamp her image on
> In nature somewhat nearer to her own?
> Why, gifted with such powers to send abroad
> Her spirit, must it lodge in shrines [that is, books] so frail?

Williams, similarly, sees the "roar" as "challenging" his waking and
fights to "comb out the language" into lines on the page so that his
particular voice won't be lost. For him as for Wordsworth the flood of
the "real language of men" is as frightening a source as it is indispens-
able; he fears the submergence of his own voice within it, like a
spectator at the Passaic Falls drawn toward the brink, or Odysseus
tempted by the music of the Sirens.[21]

The fact that Wordsworth was reading *Don Quixote* before his
dream in *The Prelude* also has significance for the reader of *Paterson.*
For *Don Quixote* stands for Wordsworth as an example of an epic

---

21. *Ibid.,* Book Five, 45–49.

quest narrative that may be in fragments but nevertheless accomplishes its two most challenging tasks: it vanquishes the dead language of the past and records its own living cadences for posterity. In Miller's words, *Don Quixote* was "supposed to be reproduced from an incomplete manuscript, its lacunae testifying to the fact that it has survived a catastrophe, perhaps like the one which awaits those books the Arab hurries to bury in Wordsworth's dream. An episode of book burning in *Don Quixote* demonstrates that Cervantes, like Wordsworth, was concerned not only for the power to induce madness possessed by books, but also for their impermanence."[22] A flood and a fire: for Wordsworth as for Williams imagining catastrophe forces the poet to explore the dangers of his commitment to living speech and to speech recollected and fixed on the page. Yet the marks of such a catastrophe—the lacunae and fissures in the poet's text—then become its badges of honor, its sign of having been immersed in flood and flame and endured. Wordsworth's dream in Book Five of *The Prelude* at first glance may seem the *opposite* of Books Three and Four of *Paterson* (Wordsworth is, after all, openly reverential toward books and fearful of their destruction), but there is a fundamental agreement among these epics in their imagination of disaster and in their strategies for surviving it. Williams' collage text, rebellious Modernist son though it is, here shows itself to have been sired by romanticism. Its contradictions and lacunae are the identifying marks, the Odyssean scars, of the modern epic form. And if the form of *Paterson* seems even more scored and broken than that of *The Prelude*, it is the result, Williams would no doubt argue, of a deeper plunge into more dangerous waters. Yet both texts emerge from the waters like the Arab's seashell, "Of a surpassing brightness."

22. Miller, *The Linguistic Moment From Wordsworth to Stevens*, 92. Miller's two chapters on Wordsworth and Williams are relevant (59–113 and 349–89, respectively), but with Williams he focuses on the lyrics, not *Paterson*. On the general topic of textual fragments, see Eugenio Donato, "The Ruins of Memory: Archeological Fragments and Textual Artifacts," *Modern Language Notes*, XCIII (May, 1978), 575–96.

SIX/LISTEN WHILE I TALK ON AGAINST TIME
Williams' Late Odes

THINK WHAT A MINOR
PART THE SELF PLAYS IN A WORK OF ART
COMPARED TO THOSE GREAT GIVENS   THE ROSEBRICK MANOR
ALL TOPIARY FORMS & METRICAL
MOAT ARIPPLE! FROM ANTHOLOGIZED
PERENNIALS TO HERB GARDEN OF CLICHES
FROM LATIN-LABELED HYBRIDS TO THE FAWN
4 LETTER FUNGI THAT ENRICH THE LAWN,
IS NOT ARCADIA TO DWELL AMONG
GREENWOOD PERSPECTIVES OF THE MOTHER TONGUE
ROOTSYSTEMS UNDERFOOT WHILE OVERHEAD
THE SUN GOD SANG & SHADES OF MEANING SPREAD
& FAR SNOWCAPPED ABSTRACTIONS GLITTERED NEAR
OR FAIRLY MELTED INTO ATMOSPHERE?
AS FOR THE FAMILY ITSELF MY DEAR
JUST GAPE UP AT THAT CORONETED FRIEZE:
SWEET WILLIAMS & FATE-FLAVORED EMILIES . . .

—W. H. Auden, speaking in James Merrill's *The Changing Light at Sandover*[1]

In 1955 Williams wrote a short poem, "The Lady Speaks," that illustrates many of the characteristic qualities of his late poetry. From the protection of their house, a husband and wife watch a summer storm shake the Spanish moss on the live oak trees outside. The wife speaks for both of them using the first person plural. They watch the violence of the storm and worry that their marriage will also end violently—not through divorce but through the death of one partner before the other. Death is spoken of as a kind of natural force much more frightening than the storm raging outside; it will destroy the carefully built house of their marriage and leave the surviving partner

---

1. Williams' readers should also be aware of Merrill's delightful tribute to Williams in "From the Cutting Room Floor" in his recent collection of poems *Late Settings* (New York, 1985). Consisting of several passages that were cut from *Sandover*, this poem includes ouija-board "interviews" with Williams, Moore, Djuna Barnes, and Elvis Presley, among others.

exposed and alone until he too is swept away. The wife feels sure, moreover, that *she* will be the one left alone, not her husband:

> a storm sends the moss
> whipping
> back and forth
> upright
> above my head
> like flames in the final
> fury.

Despite her fears, the woman faces the future with dignity. For her, the most important thing she contemplates is not the fury of the lightning but the frail permanence of a candle flame in front of her. She and her husband may be standing in front of a window holding two candles (is the electricity out?) or sitting across from each other at their dining room table with the candles between them:

> Two candles we had lit
> side by side
> before us
> so solidly had our house been built
> kept their tall flames
> unmoved

(PB, 134)

The wife keeps this image of her marriage before her mind's eye even as she watches the storm. If the frame of her house and the rituals of the dining room become an emblem for the facts of marriage—its material trials and pleasures, its importance as a shield against the outside world—the paired candle flames stand for its soul. Miraculously, two figures are together yet apart, living separate lives yet sharing the same light. The poem ends with the wife's understated yet resolute prayer that she may keep this image of her marriage before her even when she and her husband are separated by death: "May it be so," she whispers, when the storm destroys their home "in the final / fury."

Unabashedly embodying the virtues of order, protection, and permanence, Williams' "The Lady Speaks" signifies a fundamental shift in his art. In earlier poems such as "March," "Spring Strains," "Spring and All," and "The Black Winds," only violence could free Spring to be born, and even a later poem in praise of shelter, such as "Burning the Christmas Greens," would find that shelter valueless without periodic invasions of what that poem calls nature's "recreant" violence. In Williams' Improvisations, he claimed to scorn composure and composition as a retreat into decorum, a flight from the energy of the present into the sheltering forms of the past. He mockingly implied that anyone who respected order and tradition was not a creator but a homemaker, a lover of "neatness and finish." He compared the stanzas of a poem to the rooms of a house (*stanza* in Italian means "room") and in Improvisation XXI.3 wrote of "the pretension of these doors to broach or to conclude our pursuits, our meetings,—of these papered walls to separate our thoughts of impossible tomorrows and these ceilings—that are a jest at shelter." Real communication here can only occur outdoors, freed from traditional forms and their restrictive divisions and connections. In his commentary on the section, Williams allegorized: "*The young pair listen attentively to the roar of the weather. The blustering cold takes on the shape of a destructive presence. They loosen their imaginations. The house seems protecting them. They relax gradually as though in the keep of a benevolent protector. Thus the house becomes a wine which has drugged them out of their senses*" (I, 71–72). The artistic values of this passage were reversed by the time Williams wrote "The Lady Speaks." In that poem, sheltering forms make communication possible rather than impede it, and the steady, step-by-step progression of Williams' triadic line honors the spiritual willpower of the married couple, not the fury of the storm.

A study of Williams' poetry before 1951, however, shows that he was often less insistent about opposing order and energy than he was in his Dadaist writing. In the non-Dadaist work I have discussed, Williams' synthesis of order and energy, tradition and invention is profound and intricate. Even though such a union may not be the first thing in Williams' writing that captures our attention—the first things, surely, are the extraordinary freshness of Williams' eye and ear and his generosity of spirit—it is one of the qualities that has made his work an endless resource for American poetry. Yet compared to the poems of Williams' late period, his lyrics between *Al Que Quiere!* (1917) and *The Collected Later Poems* (1950) for the most part recognize his debt to literary tradition obliquely and tentatively. Neither "Spring and All" nor "Fine Work with Pitch and Copper" directly ask to be read as pastoral lyrics, nor do "Rapid Transit" or "The Sea-Elephant" immediately call attention to themselves as odes. But by the 1950s Williams was able to affirm the importance of inventing new forms while openly alluding to other art and artists from all periods, ancient and modern.

Williams' last decade of work after Books One through Four of *Paterson* and "The Desert Music" falls into two periods. The first, covered by *The Desert Music and Other Poems* (1954) and *Journey to Love* (1955), is discussed in this chapter; it is marked by Williams' use of the triadic or three-step metrical line and by a much more digressive, generalizing, allusive, and personal voice than he had ever used before. The second period, discussed in the epilogue, represents a reaction to the first; the results are found in Williams' last volume, *Pictures from Brueghel and Other Poems* (1962).[2]

Williams' late odes cannot by any stretch of the imagination be called Cubist, yet their innovations may profitably be placed within the context of his earlier experiments in writing in the form. The rapid transitions and heterogenous textures that marked Williams' earlier odes give way to the sinuous interweavings of the three-step line, which pairs and merges the poems' heterogeneous elements rather than sharply contrasting them. Furthermore, in Williams' late odes the speaker may quickly shift his rhythms, mood, and subject matter, and even occasionally quote others. But a single speaker is ever present, and the cacophony of different voices that enlivened "March," "January Morning," and "Overture to a Dance of Locomotives" is renounced. If "The Drunk and the Sailor" had been written in Williams' earlier, Cubist style, for example, we would hear their angry words interrupting the poet's, as we hear the voices of the crowds in "Overture" or "The Desert Music." Instead, the drunk's actions are described but his words not quoted; the primary focus is on the poet's response as it is remembered. Williams' late odes are thus even less tied to a specific place and time than his Cubist odes were. The result is a dramatic and powerful expansion of the vision-

2. Williams' poems from the 1950s and early 1960s are collected in *Pictures from Brueghel and Other Poems* (New York, 1962). The benchmark discussion of the metrics, diction, and themes of Williams' triadic poems is in Breslin's *William Carlos Williams: An American Artist*, 203–32. Breslin, however, generally dissents from the critical consensus approving Williams' late work. He finds its informality, didacticism, and emphasis on the harmonies rather than the tensions among its parts to be interesting but less powerful than Williams' earlier work, particularly *Spring and All*. See also Guimond, *The Art of William Carlos Williams*, 201–43; Jerome Mazzaro, *William Carlos Williams: The Later Poems* (Ithaca, N.Y., 1973), 1–144; Mariani, *William Carlos Williams: A New World Naked*, 630–770; and, in particular, Rapp, *William Carlos Williams and Romantic Idealism*, 121–48.

ary possibilities inherent in the sublime ode form. This is not to say
that Williams' late odes cut all ties to place and time. The poems may
portray an event exclusively from the perspective of the present, as
with "The Negro Woman," but the majority of the late odes quickly
move from present experience into a world almost entirely governed
by the speaker's memory and fantasy. The structure of "The Sparrow"
is an exemplary case. It begins by referring to a sparrow on a win-
dowsill, but by the second line of the poem the speaker is focusing on
his memories of sparrows, not on the bird in front of him. The poem
seems to end with the poet outside, viewing a dead sparrow on the
pavement at his feet, without giving us any clues (unlike, say, "Janu-
ary Morning" or "The Desert Music") as to how he moved from one
place to another. But the concluding scene may in fact recount a
memory of seeing such a corpse, not an actual journey of the poet
outdoors: the actual time and space coordinates of the poem's "pres-
ent" are thoroughly ambiguous.

To make the interior action of these odes dramatic, Williams
needed a voice more supple than the one that dominates "The
Descent" (1948), the poem in which he said he discovered the
triadic line. Whatever the undeniable importance of "The De-
scent," it has a slight rhetorical stiffness that contrasts with Williams'
mature work in his triadic style. Its diction and syntax are relatively
abstract and uncolloquial, and its principal connectives are drawn
from formal argument: "No defeat is made up entirely of defeat—
since / the world it opens is always a place / formerly / unsuspected"
(PB, 73). Williams soon learned, however, that his new style could
easily mix the particular and the general, the colloquial and the
formal, so that the possibilities for a striking use of enjambment were
dramatically increased.

Consider these lines from "The Sparrow":

> This sparrow
>   who comes to sit at my window
>   is a poetic truth
>   more than a natural one.
>   His voice,
>   his movements,
>   his habits—
>   how he loves to
>   flutter his wings
>   in the dust—
>   all attest it;
>   granted, he does it

> to rid himself of lice
>> but the relief he feels
>>> makes him
> cry out lustily—
>> which is a trait
>>> more related to music
> than otherwise.
>
> (PB, 129)

The phrase "all attest it" is an attempt by Williams to conclude his assertion of the bird's "poetic truth" with a grandly general summation, but this attempt is thwarted in the last foot of the line as the poet qualifies his thought by giving an example of the sparrow's earthy practicality. This qualification is then itself undone as Williams emphatically restates his idealistic truth: the voice of the bird is an emblem of lyric poetry itself. The rest of the poem's lines work similarly. On the one hand, there are many high-sounding and formal words and phrases such as "the poem of his existence that triumphed finally," "a trait related to music," "amours," "profound insight," "minor characteristics," "the aristocratic unicorn," "all attest it," "escutcheon," "effigy," and "wafer." These imply authoritative generalization and appreciation; the speaker seems both a naturalist and a professor of aesthetics who weighs, compares, savors, judges. On the other hand, the poem's diction is peppered with colloquialisms and coarse details, including the following: "granted, he does it to rid himself of lice," "a pity there are not more oats eaten nowadays to make living easier for him," "the air of being always a winner," "What was the use of that?," and references to a "serviceable beak," "droppings," and "yelling" (PB, 129–32). Usually as soon as a formal word or phrase appears in the poem—that is, as soon as the poet attempts to "read" what he calls the sparrow's "poetic" truths for us—it is paired with a colloquialism or a noticeably mundane detail that undercuts the speaker's pretensions. Like the poem's "natural" and "poetic" truths, mundane and refined words are woven together, and the casually formal texture that such mixed diction creates in "The Sparrow" differs from that of "The Descent" and is responsible for the uniquely close-knit combination of casualness and authority that is the signature of Williams' late odes. Instead of the relatively large blocks of materials, each in a different style, juxtaposed in the Cubist odes, the triadic odes intercut and blend such heterogeneous elements, creating odes written in a single voice with a great variety of inflections rather than odes for many

different voices. Williams' triadic odes of the 1950s thus return him
to the early experiments with expanding the dramatic monologue
that he undertook forty years before.

Another source of contrast between Williams' triadic and Cubist
odes lies in their use of meter. The meter of Williams' Cubist odes was
calculatedly irregular, as free as any of his lyrics. It could be quickly
adapted to mime overheard voices or sounds, as in the following
stanzas from "The Waitress" (1934):

> The Nominating Committee presents the following
> resolutions, etc. etc. etc. All those
> in favor signify by saying, Aye. Contrariminded,
> No.
> > Carried.
> > > And aye, and aye, and aye!
> And the way the bell-hop runs downstairs:
> > ta tuck a
> > > ta tuck a
> > > > ta tuck a
> > > > > ta tuck a
> > > > > > ta tuck a

Or the meter could imitate the shifting inflections of the poet's own
thoughts, as in this later, more formal passage from the same ode:

> O unlit candle with the soft white
> plume, Sunbeam Finest Safety Matches all together in
> a little box—
> > And the reflections of both in
> the mirror and the reflection of the hand, writing
> writing—
> > Speak to me of her!

(CPI, 280)

Williams' triadic meter, in contrast, is variable but not irregular.
Most commonly, each line has three such feet, and each foot may
have from one syllable to a dozen or more. But the number of sylla-
bles is determined by how quickly or slowly Williams intends the line
to be read; there is a regular time-pulse governing each triadic part,
regardless of the number of syllables. The fewer the syllables, the
greater the emphasis:

> Be patient that I address you in a poem,
> > there is no other
> > > fit medium.

(PB, 75)

Williams' early experiments with his triadic line, in poems like
"The Descent" and "To Daphne and Virginia," have the greatest

degree of variation between the lines, as if Williams were explicitly testing the dramatic capabilities of his new invention. In the last stanza of "To Daphne and Virginia," for instance, Williams calculatedly collapses the orderly rhythms of the previous lines to imitate an action:

> Men
>   against their reason
>   speak of love, sometimes,
>   when they are old. It is
>   all they can do   .
>   or watch a heavy goose
>   who waddles, slopping
>   noisily in the mud of
>   his pool
>
> (PB, 78–79)

Williams' later poems using the triadic line tend not to use such sharp breaks in decorum, as if Williams had become confident that his line could be dramatic without such extreme measures. Most of the lines of "Asphodel, That Greeny Flower," for instance, vary between two and eight syllables, with important pauses indicated by short lines and sometimes a missing foot, as in this example:

> Give me time,
>   time.
> When I was a boy. . . .
> (PB, 154–55)

Yet even with such shifts of rhythm, Williams' mature triadic odes—unlike his Cubist ones—impress their periodic, emphatic pulse upon our memory. Williams had had a heart attack in 1948, and after a major stroke in 1951 he no longer felt drawn to the dramatic metrical fibrillation of earlier odes such as "Rapid Transit" or "The Waitress." Indeed, the beat of his triadic odes sometimes verges on iambic tetrameter; their regular heartbeat signifies confidence and power:

> Of asphodel, that greeny flower
>   like a buttercup
>   upon its branching stem—
>   save that it's green and wooden—
>   I come, my sweet,
>   to sing to you.
>
> (PB, 153)

Williams' late odes differ from his Cubist ones in one other way. All lyrics celebrate a spot of time in which time's passing is momentarily forgotten in the spontaneous overflow of song. Yet they

remain bound to time, history, and repetition. Each lyric act, to be a
lyric act, must seem unique and spontaneous. But in order to suc-
cumb to such a moment, an artist must also to some degree repress
any knowledge of history; he or she must forget the fact that the
essential topics on which lyric poems are written do not change.
Poems tempt us to forget time yet simultaneously remind us that such
a desire is eternally unsatisfied and, therefore, eternally repeated in
time. The poet must also contend with the fact that as soon as a poem
is done being shaped, it partakes of the aura of eternity that surrounds
all works of art that survive their creators. The poem grows young;
the moment that inspired it passes and its creator grows old. Poems
haunt us perhaps more strongly than any other literary form because
their song's enchantment of time brings this tension between time
and eternity to its sharpest focus. As Wallace Stevens says in "The
Idea of Order at Key West," their music makes "the sky acutest at its
vanishing."[3]

   All lyrics have such paradoxes, but some make them more notice-
able than others, turning them into the occasion that inspires the
poem. This is particularly true of Williams' late triadic odes, which
not only frequently allude to other works of art but also tend to make
us self-conscious about the specific literary traditions they inherit. If
Williams' early Cubist odes (such as "Overture to a Dance of Loco-
motives") tend to celebrate the release of energy that comes when
old forms are strained to the breaking point, Williams' triadic odes
explore the release of energy that occurs when the past seems "us-
able"—when spontaneous acts suddenly appear to flow in eternal
forms. The late odes do not merely assert the importance of tradition
and allude to classic works, as Williams' odes from the 1940s (to their
detriment) tend to do. Rather, Williams' best triadic odes turn such a
discovery of the past in the present into a *dramatic* event: it is only
after we attend to the poem's flow in time, to the ways in which it
imitates the unique rhythms of the poet's thoughts, that we are
suddenly allowed a glimpse of the poem's generic form, the way its
seemingly spontaneous acts repeat an eternal pattern.

   Although almost all of Williams' triadic odes conclude by con-
trasting eternal forms and mortal lives, four odes in particular, "Trib-
ute to the Painters," "The Host," "The Sparrow," and "Asphodel,
That Greeny Flower," stand out for the richness and originality with

3. Wallace Stevens, *The Collected Poems of Wallace Stevens* (New York, 1954), 129.

which they allude to earlier art in the Western tradition. "Tribute to the Painters" is remarkable for the breadth and urgency of its allusions to art and artists in all fields, from painting to literature to music, and it well serves as an example of Williams' late odes, which were strongly in the Pindaric tradition of the sublime ode in praise of heroic feats. The other three poems mentioned are all particularly remarkable for being tributes to the *writers*. "The Host," from *The Desert Music*, is a moving homage to the greatest sublime ode in American literature, Walt Whitman's "Crossing Brooklyn Ferry," a poem Williams had on his mind near the very beginning of his experimentation with the Cubist ode, when he wrote "January Morning" to describe a ferry trip across the Hudson. (Williams' late tribute to Whitman, however, is set in a railway station, not on a ferryboat—perhaps the Penn Station of "Overture to a Dance of Locomotives.") "The Sparrow," one of the least pretentious but greatest poems from Williams' last decade, is a late return to another predecessor, John Keats; its subject is not just sparrows, but "Ode to a Nightingale," "Ode on a Grecian Urn," and the general romantic lyric mode that Geoffrey Hartman has called the "inscription" lyric. "Asphodel, That Greeny Flower," the longest poem Williams wrote using the triadic line, is almost encyclopedic in its absorption of lyric forms—from the sublime ode and the epithalamium to the pastoral courtship lyric, the religious meditation, and the Horatian *carpe diem* ode. Readings of these four odes conclude this chapter, for they show how Williams' late odes brought to full flowering a lifetime of work in the ode form.

"Tribute to the Painters" (*PB*, 135–37) is really a sum of all of Williams' previous tributes to artists, such as "The Rose" (to the Cubists) and "The Crimson Cyclamen" (to Charles Demuth). And like those poems it juxtaposes art's heroic use of "design" with the frightening chaos of twentieth-century history, represented most powerfully in "Tribute" by the bloodthirsty conger eel (an image of violence in nature) and the Nazi mass murderer (an image of social and political violence). The poet's thoughts dance nervously between visions of tyranny, murder, rape, torture, and despair and glimpses of scenes in which "all the deformities take wing"—images of art's power to resist, defend, and even cure. Two critics, Emily Mitchell Wallace and Henry Sayre, have written superbly on the poem, annotating its complex and sometimes bewildering array of allusions and stressing how well the poem integrates an understanding of contemporary and classic art and literary criticism. But new aspects of the poem are revealed when it is read as an ode, in the context of Williams' earlier work in the genre.

As Williams had done four decades earlier in championing the avant-garde, in "Tribute to the Painters" he stresses art's responsibility to deconstruct what he calls the "tyranny" of the images that a culture produces. He fully understands how the tyranny of images is linked to political oppression: all repressive societies try to fix the forms of representation (such as the Nazis' portrayal of the heroic Aryan and the villainous Jew). In comments to others about the poem, Williams linked its fragmentary and restless series of images and references to Cubism's use of fragmentation. As Wallace has written, "When John Thirlwall asked him what this poem means, Williams replied with a question: 'What made the painters deal with the fragmentary presentation of the image? Like the Cubists . . . ' Williams told Walter Sutton about the same time: 'The design of the painting and of the poem I've attempted to fuse.'" Sayre, similarly, has shown that Williams well understood contemporary debate about the proper relation between abstract and figuration in art. Like all Modernists, Williams reaffirmed that art's power and independence come from its self-reflexivity, its ability to abstract. "The exact place where for us modern art began," Williams said, is the following recognition: "it is no longer what you paint or what you write about that counts but how you do it: how you lay on the pigment how you place the words to make a picture or a poem" (*RI*, 218). But Williams, like the Abstract Expressionists and many other Modernists, including Picasso and Gris, was also wary of complete abstraction, absolute self-referentiality. For one thing, the "tyranny of the image" could be combatted most successfully if the artwork *alluded to* images and signs, as Cubism did, rather than eliminated them altogether. As Williams had said in a 1951 essay, "Modern painters . . . have been afraid of the horrible word 'representational,' . . . forgetting that all painting is representational, even the most abstract, the most subjective, the most distorted. The only question that can present itself is: What do you choose to represent?" (*RI*, 197). Design and abstraction could not be all, then, though they were the starting point for any appreciation of modern art. Reference had to be as important as self-reference. Hence "Tribute" alludes not only to numerous other artists, musicians, and writers, but to contemporary events and "images" both public and private. He had alluded to other art and artists in his earlier odes, particularly in the 1940s. However, the scope of reference in "Tribute" is considerably broadened, extending from the revolutionary Modernist artists to progressive art and artists of all kinds in many different centuries.[4]

Despite Williams' comparison of his ode to Cubist collages, however, the design of "Tribute to the Painters," like Williams' other triadic odes, differs markedly from his earlier Cubist ones because it lacks their polyphony and jaggedness. The poem is a swiftly moving interior monologue. Although it contains a daunting variety of material, it is all united by the rhythmic dance of Williams' meter; the poem does not have the sharp breaks in rhythm that mark his Cubist odes. In the following example, images of terror and beauty are interwoven, and the triadic lines that suddenly swerve from right to left to shatter an image of happiness (as in the first four lines below) can also reaffirm the poem's overall optimism, by providing haunting images of happiness in the face of monstrosity at the climactic third beat of the triadic line, the words italicized here:

> I saw love
> > mounted naked on a horse
> > > on a swan
> the back of a fish
> > the bloodthirsty conger eel
> > > *and laughed*
> recalling the Jew
> > in the pit
> > > among his fellows
> when the indifferent chap
> > with the machine gun
> > > was spraying the heap.
> He
> > had not yet been hit
> > *but smiled*
> comforting his companions.
> (PB, 136–37; my emphasis)

The last line above emphasizes the optimistic strain in the poem even more thoroughly: the speaker pauses here, resting for two beats of the triadic line before continuing. But despite the poem's darting shifts between darkness and light, its steady beat (except for dramatic pauses) remains.

4. Emily Mitchell Wallace, "The Satyrs' Abstract and Brief Chronicle of Our Time," *William Carlos Williams Review,* IX (1983), 136–55; Henry Sayre, "The Tyranny of the Image: The Aesthetic Background," *William Carlos Williams Review,* IX (1983), 125–34.

An even more interesting difference from the work of Williams' heroic Cubist phase lies in the poem's open acknowledgement that "design" cannot conquer all. Unlike "The Rose," which ends with a scene of art's ordered intelligence subduing nature, "Tribute" ends with a much more modest image of what art can accomplish:

<blockquote>
the trouble
in their minds
shall be quieted,
put to bed
again.
</blockquote>

(PB, 137)

Art may give us a temporary refuge from tyranny and disorder, a brief respite from nightmares that will always return. The poem's confidence in art is shadowed by its sense of how little art can do: the Jew comforts his companions, yet the bullets still come; the tyranny of one set of images may be shattered, but other oppressive images rise to take their place. The names of Freud, Picasso, and Gris are invoked, but their heroic confrontations with the forces of darkness are juxtaposed with a picture of humanity at the mercy of evil:

<blockquote>
Bosch's
congeries of tortured souls and devils
who prey on them
fish
swallowing
their own entrails
</blockquote>

(PB, 135–36)

The poem's moments of rest and affirmation are temporary and tentative.

One word that is central to the poem, *congeries*, well demonstrates the poem's complex design. *Congeries* is from the Latin *congerere*, meaning to carry or heap together, and in "Tribute" it refers not only to the heaped and tortured bodies portrayed in Hieronymus Bosch and the modern photograph of Nazi atrocities (and, by a wry pun, to the acts of the *conger* eel) but also to the rather haphazard and irregular argument of the poem itself, with its bewildering swerves and reversals, its brief stays against confusion and depression. *Congerere* may also suggest a more ordered design, however, as in the related words *congest*, *condense*, or *gist*. In Williams' one other use of the word in his oeuvre, near the end of Book Five of *Paterson*, he uses it in this latter sense, suggesting the triumphantly orderly Nature in the Unicorn tapestries:

> the yellow flag of the French fields is here
> and a congeries of other flowers
> as well: daffodils
> and gentian, the daisy, columbine
> petals
> myrtle, dark and light
> and calendulas   .
>
> (P, 236–37)

Unlike the tapestries but like Bosch's panoramas, "Tribute to the Painters" includes the deformities even as it imagines their cure. Its beat may be more regular than that of Williams' classic Cubist odes, but underlying it is an even greater anxiety. One of the reasons that Williams' voice in his triadic odes seems so personal is that the poems allow such intimacy: we are allowed to glimpse their creator's doubts and fears, his mind's frightening lapses.

Wallace has persuasively argued that the opening reference in "Tribute" to the satyrs' dance alludes to the satyrs' choruses that were the foundation of Greek drama: "Although none of the early satyr plays has survived, scholars agree that the dithyramb sung by the satyr chorus was irregular, wild, and inspired in its form. 'I . . . wish often,' Williams says in his poem 'Every Day,' 'that Aristotle / had gone on / to a consideration of the dithyrambic / poem—or that his notes had survived.' . . . He wrote to Norman Holmes Pearson that 'the Greek poets, at their best, had always a quality of irregularity which permitted them to vary their lines much as we vary them at our best, today.'" Yet the dance that "Tribute" performs surely also alludes to the history of the lyric ode: some odes were originally danced by a chorus of singers before an audience, with contrasting choreography for the song's strophe, antistrophe, and epode that is reflected in our English synonyms for these parts of the ode ("turn," "counterturn," and "stand"). The dance of Williams' poem indeed incorporates such irregularities and contrasts into its metric structure; it dramatically opposes moments of doubt with epodelike moments of affirmation and stasis, such as the invocation of Freud, Picasso, and Gris in order to distance the memory of Bosch's holocaust. As Williams' understanding of the ode form developed into the 1950s, therefore, he explored even more deeply than he had previously the ode's sources in Greek culture. "Tribute" strives to be both Pindaric and satyric, an Apollonian song of praise and optimism accompanied by a rather irregular, Dionysian dance laced with melancholy and a vivid sense of the grotesque. We may even add a pun to Williams' and say that the poem is a "congeries" because it conjures up the two dominant spirits of Greek culture—Apollo and Dionysius—in order to praise the wealth of art and artists indebted to the Greek tradition. Williams saw a Greek precedent for his experiments with a modern "variable" metric foot as well. "In all probability we shall have to measure the line by elapsed time, as did the Greeks [with their quantitative measure]," he wrote (*RI*, 219).[5]

"The Host" is one of numerous poems in *Journey to Love* that meditate on the miracles commemorated by the Christian sacraments—Christianity's cure, so to speak, for the "deformities" portrayed so graphically in "Tribute to the Painters." The title of "The Host" has several meanings, varying from the secular and ironic to the sacred and visionary. The most literal meaning in the poem for the word *host* refers to the railway restaurant that serves lunch to a Negro evangelist and his assistants, two nuns, an Anglican priest, and the poet. All but the poet are oblivious to each other as they eat. A second meaning for *host* is the familiar sacred one, referring to bread that has been consecrated for the Christian sacrament of communion. The others in the restaurant with Williams say grace before their meals, but what they eat does not become sacramental for them. For the poet, however, the meaning he gives to *host* is consciously at variance with the conventionally sacred and secular meanings of the word. The poet calls their lunch a "witless" act of communion, a partaking of the host in which the participants are not aware of the sacredness of the moment. Yet he sees his form of communion to be essentially no different from the Christian one: if Christian doctrine decrees that specific words may transform a plain wafer into "the body of the Lord," the poet believes that transubstantiation and communion may happen anywhere, with any food— "fried oysters and what not"—as well as communion wafers. As the last lines of the poem show, however, the *real* host that the poet seeks to commemorate is not food at all; it is language, the special words that will allow a random handful of people—if only for a moment—

5. Wallace, "The Satyrs' Abstract," 139–40. On the ode, see Maddison, *Apollo and the Nine*, 4–38. The best discussion of Williams' interest in classical culture is by Emily Mitchell Wallace, "Musing in the Highlands and the Valleys: The Poetry of Gratwick Farm," *William Carlos Williams Review*, VIII (Spring, 1982), 8–41.

to feel the wonder and mystery of their lives. Yet the poet fails as such a host: the poem commemorates Williams' despair and frustration after his stroke, when he had not yet painstakingly taught himself to speak and write again. Williams' celebration of communion in "The Host" remains only a private and tardy act, occurring later in the poem but incommunicable to those present in the restaurant.[6]

> No one was there
>   save only for
>   the food. Which I alone,
> being a poet,
>   could have given them.
>   But I
> had only my eyes
>   with which to speak.
>
> (PB, 94)

Any American poet after Whitman who writes about spiritual communion between a poet and his fellow travelers—especially a poet who knew his Whitman as well as Williams did—cannot have "Crossing Brooklyn Ferry" far from his mind. Whitman's poem is also concerned with bridging the distance between himself and a chance group of travelers, and he too seeks to broaden the meaning of Christian communion. Here are the poem's climactic lines:

> Appearances, now or henceforth, indicate
>   what you are,
> . . . .
> You have waited, you always wait,
>   you dumb, beautiful ministers,
> We receive you with free sense at last, and
>   are insatiate henceforward,
> Not you any more shall be able to foil us,
>   or withhold yourselves from us,
> We use you, and do not cast you aside—we
>   plant you permanently within us,
> We fathom you not—we love you—there is
>   perfection in you also,
> You furnish your parts toward eternity,
> Great or small, you furnish your parts
>   toward the soul.

As the poem progressed, Whitman moved from being closed within himself to an ecstatic sense of communion with all he saw and

6. A fine discussion of "The Host" can be found in Rapp, *William Carlos Williams and Romantic Idealism*, 142–43. Much of my thinking about this poem—particularly the role played by Williams' muteness—has grown out of conversations I had with Paul Mariani during a conference on Williams at Oberlin College in February, 1984.

imagined—with all of the people who will ever cross on the ferry as well as those with whom he is journeying on the particular evening in which the poem takes place. Underneath the "film" of appearances, separate identities share what Emerson called an Over-Soul. The sacred act that reveals such a communion may occur anywhere, at any time (as in "The Host"). The poet must learn to ignore the separateness of others and himself, to transcend difference and absorb union "with free sense at last."[7]

For Williams, the world is also "blessed" and part of "the body of the Lord," but ecstatic declarations such as "only the imagination is real!" are interwoven—as they are not in "Crossing Brooklyn Ferry" —with a simultaneous sense of irony, separateness, distance. The transcendental imperatives of Williams' predecessor are qualified, the communion of the travelers remains a wish rather than something seen face to face, and the primary agent of transformation, the stroke-stricken and mute poet, involuntarily gives a bitter new meaning to Whitman's phrase "you always wait, you *dumb*, beautiful ministers" (my italics). Williams' tragic realism in "The Host" does not reject the majesty of Whitman's visionary mode but makes its affirmations more complex. A representative triadic line such as "chomping with my worn-out teeth: / the Lord is my shepherd / I shall not want" holds both mortality and immortality in heartbreaking tension, as Whitman's lines do not. As a whole, Williams' poem moves in a long arc, gently rising to the ecstatic triad "Only the imagination / is real! They have imagined it, / therefore it is so," then slowly falling away toward the understated but inconsolable irony of the last lines on the poet's muteness—"but I / had only my eyes / with which to speak" (PB, 93–94). As he had done throughout his career, Williams in "The Host" once again revises his Whitmanesque inheritance even as he makes us conscious of it.

"The Host" is part of a sequence of poems in *Journey to Love* in which religious themes (and images of suffering) are never absent: "For Eleanor and Bill Monahan," "To a Dog Injured in the Street," "The Yellow Flower," "The Host," "Deep Religious Faith," "The Mental Hospital Garden," "The Artist," "Theocritus: Idyl I," and "The Desert Music." Williams' friendship with the Monahans, who were Catholic, revived memories of learning about the prayer forms and

7. Whitman, *Leaves of Grass*, 137.

rituals of his mother's Catholic youth. The first poem of the period in which Williams showed renewed interest in the sacraments was "Two Pendants" (1949), written while his mother was dying; it included references to Easter and the meaning of resurrection.[8]

"The Sparrow" is also a meditation on mortality and the sacredness of common things in which a reference to communion plays a crucial role.[9] But in the poem Williams introduces his sacramental imagery much more obliquely than he does in "The Host," during an especially turbulent passage at the very end:

> Practical to the end,
>   it is the poem
>   of his existence
> that triumphed
>   finally;
>   a wisp of feathers
> flattened to the pavement
>   wings spread symmetrically
>   as if in flight,
> the head gone,
>   the black escutcheon of the breast
>   undecipherable,
> an effigy of a sparrow,
>   a dried wafer only,
>   left to say
> and it says it
>   without offense,
>   beautifully;
> This was I,
>   a sparrow.
>   I did my best;
> farewell.
>
> (PB, 132)

Williams uses the triadic line here as adroitly as anywhere in his work. His strongest assertion of the "poetic truth" of the sparrow's immortality is balanced by the dark natural truths of the bird's decay. The details of death consistently appear at the start of the triadic lines—"flattened," "the head gone," "an effigy," and "farewell"—so that Williams' most affirmative phrases—"the poem of his exis-

8. On Williams' friendship with the Monahans, see Mariani, *William Carlos Williams: A New World Naked*, 655–57, and Kathleen N. Monahan, "Williams' 'For Eleanor and Bill Monahan,'" *William Carlos Williams Review*, XIII (Spring, 1987), 14–23.

9. The fullest discussion of "The Sparrow" is Mariani, *William Carlos Williams: A New World Naked*, 679–81. See also Louis Simpson, *Three on the Tower: The Lives and Works of Ezra Pound, T. S. Eliot, and William Carlos Williams* (New York, 1975), 307–309. Mariani claims that Keats stands as "the major presence" behind the triadic poems that Williams wrote in the early 1950s.

tence," "a wisp of feathers," "in flight," "beautiful"—struggle to counter the lines' grim downbeats. As in "The Host," the soaring and plunging lines of "The Sparrow" enact a dance between death's negations and the imagination's need.

The cluster of metaphors that suddenly appears in the poem's last lines is worth examining still more closely, though, for they are highly unusual in Williams' work and contain a clue to what makes his late odes unique. The word *escutcheon* turns the bird's decaying breast into a shield containing emblems representing family traits and personal deeds; *effigy* suggests both secular and sacred symbolism; and *wafer* of course alludes to communion. All are words that would only be used ironically in any of Williams' volumes after *The Tempers*. They appear in "The Sparrow," however, to defend *against* irony; they are employed as the poet is desperately searching for figures of speech powerful enough to transform the bird's corpse into evidence that the spirit survives the body's death.

Williams began "The Sparrow" confidently immersed in life; his tone was a delightful mixture of the bawdy and the reverent, and his powers of recollection seemed limitless—memory after memory returned to him. But his halting by the corpse of the sparrow at the end of the poem recalls the ending (and the beginning) of "The Desert Music." Williams faces the corpse on the pavement in "The Sparrow" as he did in "The Desert Music"—by releasing a burst of tropes that seek to transform the threatening figure into something else. He turns the sparrow's body into an escutcheon on a tomb, a monument that halts a traveler and speaks to him of death and immortality. In doing so, Williams evokes motifs common to both poetry and painting, which have many examples of speaking or inscribed monuments, funereal escutcheons and urns, and halted travelers who read (or imagine) an epitaph such as *Et in Arcadia Ego*. Geoffrey Hartman is the most resourceful historian of these motifs as they appear in eighteenth- and nineteenth-century lyrics, and a brief digression to consider Hartman's work will allow "The Sparrow" (and indeed all of Williams' triadic odes) to be placed in a provocative new context. [10]

10. See Geoffrey Hartman, *Beyond Formalism* (New Haven, Conn., 1970), 206–30. Oddly, Hartman's wide-ranging essay on Wordsworth, inscriptions, and romantic nature poetry does not discuss the most famous of all inscriptions on a monument, *Et in Arcadia Ego*. It was a popular motif in the visual arts in the seventeenth and eighteenth centuries and was usually associated with a classical tomb in a pastoral setting contemplated by one or more passersby. The definitive discussion of the iconography of this slogan in the visual arts is by Erwin Panofsky, *Meaning in the Visual Arts* (New York, 1955), 295–320. Panofsky shows how the

Hartman has shown how Wordsworth adapted the common but minor eighteenth-century form of the inscription poem so that it could play a central role in romantic poetry. The inscription poem was conventionally an epigram or other short poem "conscious of the place on which it was written" and read. Usually set in a country garden or country house, these poems had sites as varied as a "tree, rock, statue, gravestone, sand, window, album, sundial, dog's collar, back of fan, back of painting." The form's popularity paralleled that of the eighteenth-century formal garden. "In . . . The Leasowes, one of the famous show gardens of the time, beautiful prospects were discreetly marked for the tourist by benches with inscriptions from Vergil or specially contrived poems." In the second half of the eighteenth century, inscribed funeral urns and commemorative benches in gardens became particularly popular, exploiting the elegiac possibilities always present in the inscription mode. Such "speaking" monuments urged travelers to contemplate the prospect of time's passing as well as the passing prospect of the landscape. Hartman notes that there was "a general convergence of elegiac and nature poetry in the eighteenth century. Poems about place (locodescriptive) merge with meditations on death so that landscape becomes dramatic in a quietly startling way." The traveler or tourist who

---

meaning of the famous Latin phrase and the role of the "speaking" monument in painting underwent a metamorphosis with Poussin. Before Poussin's famous painting in the Louvre, *Et in Arcadia Ego* (*ca.* 1636), the phrase was commonly understood to be a *memento mori*, a death's-head halting passersby to speak to them of last things: "I too am in Arcadia." But the role played by the tomb in Poussin's Louvre painting has undergone a subtle but crucial metamorphosis. The painting "no longer shows a dramatic encounter with Death but a contemplative absorption of the idea of mortality. . . . The Arcadians [by the tomb] are not so much warned of an implacable future as they are immersed in mellow meditation on a beautiful past." Accordingly, in Poussin the person in the tomb speaks rather than the tomb itself (or a traditional death's-head), and the Latin is taken to mean "I too *was* in Arcadia" (my italics). Such a creative misreading of Latin grammar, Panofsky points out, became more frequent after Poussin's work became widely known, and by the eighteenth century it had become the standard way of interpreting the Latin. Panofsky ascribes such a change not to ignorance of Latin but to a "radical break with the medieval, moralizing tradition" caused by "the more relaxed and less fearful spirit of a tradition which had triumphantly emerged from the spasms of the Counter-Reformation." He notes that Poussin's new reading of *Et in Arcadia Ego* was inspired both by Italian Arcadian literature (which often emphasized a mellow and meditative elegiac vein, following Vergil's eclogues) and by "the principles of Classicist art theory, which rejected '*les objets bizarres*,' especially such gruesome objects as a death's-head" (313). Panofsky's conclusion anticipates Hartman's own reading of Romanticism's debt to the inscription tradition of the eighteenth century: "We can easily see that the new conception of the Tomb in Arcady initiated by Poussin's Louvre picture, and sanctioned by the mistranslation of its inscription, could lead to reflections of almost opposite nature, depressing and melancholy on the one hand, comforting and assuaging on the other; and, more often than not, to a truly 'Romantic' fusion of both" (318–19).

attends such speaking monuments is traditionally induced to medi-
tate with the words, *"Siste viator"* ("Nay, Traveller! rest," as Words-
worth renders it in his inscription poem, "Lines Left upon a Seat in a
Yew Tree" [1798]).[11]

Hartman argues that Wordsworth revised the plot of such poems in
two revealing ways. First, he reversed the order of importance be-
tween the monument and the halted traveler, making the drama of
the poem center on the traveler's response rather than the content of
the monument's inscription. Second, Wordsworth preferred natural
rather than man-made monuments whose inscriptions had to be
imagined, not merely read: rocks and stones and trees could be
transformed into living hieroglyphs that would address the poet who
knew how to find and read them. In Hartman's words,

> What is truly distinctive . . . is Wordsworth's enlarged understanding of the
> setting to be incorporated. This is never landscape alone. He frees the inscrip-
> tion from its dependence, he gives it weight and power of its own, by incorpo-
> rating in addition to a particular scene the very process of inscribing or in-
> terpreting it. The setting is understood to contain the writer in the act of
> writing: the poet in the grip of what he feels and sees, primitively inspired to
> carve it in the living rock. . . . [Wordsworth] transformed the inscription into
> an independent nature poem, and in so doing created a principal form of the
> Romantic and modern lyric. One step in this transformation has already been
> described. When fugitive feelings are taken seriously, when every sight and
> sound calls to the passing poet— "Nay, Traveller! rest"; "Stay, Passenger, why
> goest thou by soe fast?"—then the Romantic nature lyric is born.[12]

Hartman makes a further point that is useful for a reader of "The
Sparrow." Noting that Wordsworth's best and most ambitious poems
disguise rather than emphasize their debt to the eighteenth-century
inscription lyric, Hartman distinguishes between "archaic" and "ar-
chetypal or generic" elements in a literary work. Archaic elements
seem old as soon as we see them; their form is self-consciously anti-
quarian. Archetypal elements exercise their power over us more
subtly: only slowly does an attentive reader realize that there is an
older pattern informing the seemingly modern surface. Hartman
convincingly shows that Wordsworth's greatness lies in his ability to
recover "elemental situation[s]." He does this, paradoxically, by *not*
imitating the outward conventions of specific prototypes or genres.
On the contrary, because Wordsworth recovers the "generic factor,

---

11. Hartman, *Beyond Formalism*, 207–208, 210.
12. *Ibid.*, 222, 221.

we no longer need to recognize the genre which specialized it. Wordsworth's form appears to be self-generated rather than prompted by tradition; and the greater the poem, the clearer this effect."[13]

Wordsworth's poem "Lines Left upon a Seat in a Yew Tree" is an example of an archaic inscription poem. Even in that early work, however, Wordsworth had begun to shift the emphasis of the inscription poem from the content of the written words to the drama of their being written and read. "Tintern Abbey," (1798), "Michael" (1800), and Keats's "Ode on a Grecian Urn" (1819) are some of Hartman's examples of archetypal inscription poems. "Michael" and "Tintern Abbey" do not contain inscriptions, but they achieve much of their power by adapting the crucial moment at the heart of an inscription lyric—the dramatic juxtaposition of a "speaking" monument that does not experience time and suffering with a halted traveler who does.

"Ode on a Grecian Urn" recalls the eighteenth-century inscription lyric more directly than "Michael" or "Tintern Abbey," for the urn is a common garden monument, often associated with a commemorative inscription. (See, for example, Wordsworth's inscription poem, "Written at the Request of Sir George Beaumont, Bart., and in his Name, for an Urn, placed by him at the Termination of a newly-planted Avenue, in the same Grounds" [1815].) In Keats's poem, as in "Michael" or "Tintern Abbey," no words are actually carved; the urn's scenes remain motionless and its voice mute until the halted poet animates them with his imagination. Thus when Keats's monument "speaks" at the poem's conclusion of eternal beauty and truth, the poet's point of view remains distinct from that of the urn even as he gives it voice. He has imagined a "desolate" town not depicted on the urn and has experienced the eternal truths of "age," "waste," and "woe" that belie the urn's assurance that its equation of beauty and truth is "all / Ye know on earth, and all ye need to know." In Keats's transformation of the inscription lyric the monument seems to have the last word, but actually it is the halted traveler who does; his truths of experience are larger than those of the urn and thus quietly criticize them. At the end of the poem, Keats opens a corridor into the infinite future: human time is de-

13. *Ibid.*, 224–25.

scribed in the future tense, chosen because time's pain is eternally impending, while the urn's time is the eternal present ("thou say'st"), secure and untouchable, though still a friend.

> When old age shall this generation waste,
>   Thou shalt remain, in midst of other woe
> Than ours, a friend to man, to whom thou say'st,
>   "Beauty is truth, truth beauty,—that is all
>   Ye know on earth, and all ye need to know."[14]

Williams' seemingly self-generated poem "The Sparrow" may be usefully considered within the context of the romantic inscription lyric and Hartman's sense of archetypal rather than conventional generic form. Williams' use of such words as "the poem of his existence," "escutcheon," "effigy," and "wafer" echo the role traditionally played by inscribed urns, escutcheons, or other "speaking" monuments in the inscription lyric. The sparrow's spotted breast is a heraldic shield inscribed with emblems of his family lineage and character traits, and like the monuments in earlier inscription poetry it catches the traveler's eye and speaks to him of what once was where he is. But as in Wordsworth and Keats the marker is uninscribed (or silent) until the poet appears; what the traveler reads into the site is at least as important as the site itself. Without the poet's sympathetic act of imagination, no inscription, monument, or meaning would exist; both Grecian urn and American sparrow would be mute. But if Williams' emblem, like Keats's urn, does not speak until the end of the poem, it is also less eternal than the urn—or even Keats's nightingale, an "immortal Bird" because his species' song knows nothing of death or pain.[15] Williams' monument, ironically, knows everything of pain and decay; instead of speaking of immortality, the signs on the bird's breast have decomposed so badly that they are "undecipherable." (When Williams used this very same adjective in *Paterson*, Book Five, again to describe plumage, he referred not to the bird's decay but to that of his own senses: he could no longer make out the bird's colors "in the sun's glare" [*P*, 231].)

14. There has been much debate over the placement of the quotation marks in the ode's last lines. I follow the version of the lines accepted by Douglas Bush; Jack Stillinger, among others, adopts the original edition's typography and assigns the phrase "that is all / Ye know on earth, and all yet need to know" to the poem's speaker, not the urn. Even if Stillinger's version is used, however, my point still holds: the speaker's understanding of the urn's "truth" recognizes its limitations. For an introduction to the controversy, see John Keats, *Selected Poems and Letters*, ed. Douglas Bush (New York, 1959), 349–50. For Stillinger's version, see *The Poems of John Keats* (Cambridge, Mass., 1978), 372–73, 653–54. For another, less complex allusion to Keats in Williams' late work, see "To a Dog Injured in the Street."
15. Keats, "Ode to a Nightingale," l. 61.

Williams revises rather than follows romantic inscription poem formulas in two important ways. Instead of requiring the secluded grove, temple, ruin, or garden common in such lyrics (Michael's isolated sheepfold, the ruins of Tintern Abbey, Keats's garden), the motif of the halted traveler in Williams' work can occur even in landscapes that most English romantic poets would have found barren and abhorrent—in, say, the middle of a city street or sidewalk. And the merging of natural objects and monuments in the works of Wordsworth and Keats is extended by Williams to include an object (the bird's breast) that decomposes even as the poet turns it into an emblem of eternity. Such changes increase the kinds of monuments and arrested moments that may figure in an inscription poem and intensify its already acute sense of the contrast between mortality and immortality. The "oracular didacticism" about beauty, truth, art, and mortality that Hartman associates with the romantic inscription lyric sounds no less strongly in Williams' poem for these revisions, but as with Williams' revision of Whitman in "The Host," "The Sparrow" reads romanticism ironically even as it borrows from it.[16] Williams began his career by unsuccessfully imitating Keats in *Poems* (1909). With "The Sparrow" he at last found a way to pay quiet homage to both romantic poetry in general and to his favorite poet, the author of "Ode to a Nightingale" and "Ode on a Grecian Urn," whose odes "were as familiar to me at one time as breath itself" (A, 61).

If "The Sparrow" well represents Williams' genius for reinventing archetypal lyric forms, it also reminds us what Williams and Keats knew—that recovering those forms is not the same thing as reproducing or imitating them. To feel their full power, we must confront them in new configurations rather than recognize them in familiar ones. The most powerful returns *to* tradition often at first seem to be a turning *away* from it. "The Sparrow" reverberates with the elemental power of the romantic inscription lyric because it first seems to be the spontaneous overflow of the speaker's powerful feelings rather than his recollection of an appropriate form for those feelings. Yet throughout the poem (and especially at its conclusion) Williams' flood of memories of the bird in life and art simultaneously releases memories of poems about memory, speaking monuments, and interpretation. Its every sentence tautly pairs "natural" and

16. Hartman, *Beyond Formalism*, 229.

"poetic" truth, object and inscription, spontaneity and imitation, colloquial American speech from the 1950s and the eternal language of art. In the process "The Sparrow" becomes a case study in how a great Modernist poem may covertly recover, revise, and transform romanticism's original power. It does this, however, modestly but insistently—in the manner of most of Williams' best work, and in the manner of the sparrow itself.

"Asphodel, That Greeny Flower" is also a poem about memory, and it too creates its own more secular version of religious rituals—in this case, not merely communion but also confession, the last rites, and (at the poem's end) the sacrament of marriage. If the poet is flooded with memories in "The Host" and "The Sparrow," in "Asphodel" not just speech but memory have almost been destroyed; the poem portrays more fully than any other Williams' agonizingly slow recovery from a series of strokes he suffered in the early 1950s. "Asphodel" is a sublime ode to the healing powers of memory and the imagination.

Readers have been struck by the simplicity and relaxed assurance that characterize Williams' triadic poems, including "Asphodel," but a closer look at the movement of this poem reveals a mood that seems relaxed or assured only on the surface. Each of the three books of the ode moves from fear and uncertainty to a radiant recovery of power, only to have that achievement be lost and a new section of the poem begun. The fears in Book I are the deepest and most uncontrollable of all; they are never thoroughly exorcised, despite the seemingly confident declarations that conclude the book about poetry's ability to teach men how to die peacefully. Dangerously depressed because of the loss of the use of his right hand due to a stroke and the loss of his appointment as Poetry Consultant to the Library of Congress due to McCarthyist jingoism and bureaucratic indifference, Williams was placed by his doctor and his wife, Flossie, in the hospital for the mentally ill at Hillside, New Jersey. He underwent physical and mental therapy for eight weeks in 1953, entirely isolated from the outside world except for a daily letter to Flossie and a weekly telephone call. In his spare time, he got to know many of the patients and staff, worked on his translation of part of Theocritus' first pastoral *Idyl,* and meditated upon "Asphodel." The poem is thus indirectly inspired by the letters he wrote in isolation to Flossie—like them, it is a long monologue to a partner whose presence and responses must be imagined.[17]

17. For the biographical background to "Asphodel," I am indebted to Mariani, *William*

Alone and slowly rehabilitating himself, Williams felt that he had died and then come halfway back from the dead. He had an urgent need to confess his sins and to gather together as many memories of his life with Flossie as he could before they were separated forever. Each memory regained of their life together seemed like a glint of light leading Williams that much farther out of Hades and back to the sunlight of his wife's presence. But often during Book I Williams fears that she has been lost forever. He wants to speak of "abiding love," but twice interrupts himself on the first page of the poem with references to how time is running out. In a sentence that sounds the keynote for the entire book, Williams pleads for Flossie to

> Listen while I talk on
> against time.
> . . . .
> with fear in my heart
> I drag it out
> and keep on talking
> for I dare not stop.
> (PB, 154)

Such moments recall incidents from the last decade of Williams' life described by Paul Mariani: "Others would remember the look that would come into Williams' eyes if, while they were at a gathering of some sort, Floss suddenly got up to leave his side. Then his hand would reach out to her pathetically until she could reassure him of her presence."[18]

The first book of "Asphodel" portrays Williams' hesitations and frightened haltings on the long uphill road to return to his wife and recover his lost powers. He starts and stops, becomes frustrated with what he is saying, pleads for time, tries to establish contact. When he is expansive and confident, it seems as if he and Flossie have already reentered their pastoral world. He could talk of it forever:

> Endless wealth,
> I thought,
> held out its arms to me.
> A thousand topics
> in an apple blossom.

Carlos Williams: A New World Naked, 636–78. I also admire the readings of Mazzaro, William Carlos Williams: The Later Poems, 77–110, and Rapp, William Carlos Williams and Romantic Idealism, 144–48; and Marilyn Kallet's revealing exploration of the poem's original drafts in Honest Simplicity in William Carlos Williams' "Asphodel, That Greeny Flower" (Baton Rouge, La., 1985). The phrase "relaxed assurance" is from James Breslin, William Carlos Williams: An American Artist, 203.
18. Mariani, William Carlos Williams: A New World Naked, 682.

> The generous earth itself
> > gave us lief.
> > The whole world
> > > became my garden!
> (PB, 155–56)

But three times during the course of the book this memory begins to fade, and Williams finds himself back down in the "hell" of the mental ward, alone.

These three crises occur approximately one-quarter, one-half, and three-quarters of the way through Book I. The first two times they occur they are marked by a sharp break in the pattern of Williams' triadic line. The feet are slowed by monosyllables, halted, and then left incomplete:

> .   Give me time,
> > time.
> . . . .
> I did not like it
> > and wanted to be
> > > in heaven. Hear me out.
> Do not turn away.
> I have learned much. . . .
> (PB, 154, 156–57)

The third break comes when Williams tries to bring together the two topics that, discussed separately, have occupied the bulk of the book, Williams' memories of his life with Flossie and his reflections on the meaning of Homer's *Iliad.* It is not so severe an interruption as the other two, however. Williams loses his confidence momentarily, but quickly rebounds: "Silence can be complex too, / but you do not get far / with silence. / Begin again" (PB, 159).

The last pages of Book I are marked by long, sinuous sentences and Williams' renewed faith that Flossie is securely by his side. He and his wife stand together viewing the "storm" of their life in retrospect, like a couple by the shore watching a storm over the ocean.

> It was the love of love,
> > the love that swallows up all else,
> > > a grateful love,
> > a love of nature, of people,
> > > animals,
> > > > a love engendering
> > gentleness and goodness
> > > that moved me
> > > > and *that* I saw in you.
> (PB, 160)

The exuberant middle part of this sentence elaborates and catalogs; there are a thousand topics in Flossie as well as in an apple blossom. But its richly varied meter is contained by the strong iambic pulse of the sentence's first and last lines, which recall the iambic beat of the poem's opening ("I come, my sweet, / to sing to you") and thus make Flossie seem even more radiantly present. As the first book ends, however, the fears that troubled Williams return. The book's last lines are rhythmically uneven; Williams has a bitter edge to his voice and a new sense of the correspondence between his own mental illness and the world's:

> Look at
> what passes for the new.
> You will not find it there but in
> despised poems.
> It is difficult
> to get the news from poems
> yet men die miserably every day
> for lack
> of what is found there.
> Hear me out. . . .
> (PB, 161–62)

In "Asphodel," Williams retells the story of Orpheus' descent into the underworld, casting himself in the lead role. But in his retelling of the myth, it is Eurydice—Flossie—who performs the rescue, not Orpheus, and when Orpheus is returning from the underworld he will be lost if his rescuer *doesn't* turn around to face him.

The second and third books of "Asphodel" do not have so many reversals, although they too have their momentary losses of direction and assaults of bitterness. Hence all three books build slowly but dramatically toward the sustained radiance of the poem's famous Coda, where the violence of the world and the mind are securely contained and countered by the mind's ability to heal itself. Orpheus has returned to the sunlight, and now Eurydice is eternally by his side:

> In the huge gap
> between the flash
> and the thunderstroke
> spring has come in
> or a deep snow fallen.
> Call it old age.
> In that stretch
> we have lived to see
> a colt kick up his heels.

Do not hasten
          laugh and play
in an eternity
          the heat will not overtake the light.
          That's sure.
That gelds the bomb,
          permitting
                    that the mind contain it.
That is that interval,
          that sweetest interval,
                    when love will blossom. . . .
          (PB, 178–79)

A reader of "Asphodel" may also argue that Williams is rescued by poetry as well as by Flossie. Williams' sense of literary tradition, like his love for his wife, is an identity-shaping force that is lost at the start of the poem and must be regained. Historical and literary allusions thus play a crucial role in the poem. Many of these allusions have been insightfully discussed, but what has not been considered is the way the role played by Williams' allusions changes as the speaker's own role in the poem changes.[19] In other words, Williams' allusions play as dramatic a part in his healing process as the other elements of his poem do; they do not merely act as commentary upon the action.

In the first book, Williams' literary allusions center around the *Iliad* and "Helen's public fault" (adultery) that caused the Trojan War. But the allusions are often awkwardly made, as if Williams is unsure of his audience and feels that his references have to be defended and explained: "All women are not Helen, / I know that." Furthermore, some of the explanations that Williams offers for his allusions are misleading and even dishonest, thus revealing his insecure state of mind. Given the biographical circumstances in which the poem "Asphodel" was written, for example, Williams' comparison of Flossie to Helen of Troy is particularly inappropriate. Paul

---

19. Guimond, for example, explains how Williams' allusions reveal the progressive humbling of his masculinity as it evolves from the "crude force" represented by Verrocchio's statue of a mercenary to the emotional loneliness and frustration represented by Williams' friend Hartley to the strong but also sensitive power embodied in the Negro man Williams encounters on the subway. Mariani, conversely, has stressed how important the unregenerate, potent figure of Pan is to Williams throughout the poem; he presides as a god who may restore Williams' power. And Breslin has reflected at length upon how well Williams' copious and casual allusions to history, art, and artists are an essential part of the colloquial and genial style of the poems in *The Desert Music* and *Journey to Love*. See Guimond, *The Art of William Carlos Williams*, 214–16; Mariani, *William Carlos Williams: A New World Naked*, 673–77; and Breslin, *William Carlos Williams: An American Artist*, 203–32.

Mariani has demonstrated that "Asphodel" grew out of actual confessions of pursuing other women that Williams made to his wife (without really thinking how they might affect her) in order to unburden himself when he thought he might not recover from his stroke. In "A Dream of Love," a play written in 1945, Williams was more explicit about his guilt; in it, a husband dies of a heart attack in a hotel room in the arms of his mistress and then returns from the dead to confess and seek absolution from his wife. Hence "Asphodel" can in part be seen as a rewriting and an expansion of the dramatic moment at the heart of "A Dream of Love"; it too (though much more complexly) is about returning from the dead.[20] What Mariani does not discuss is that this parallel between these two works of Williams' makes his comparison of Flossie to Helen of Troy in "Asphodel" quite troubling:

> Always
>   when I think of the sea
> there comes to mind
>   the *Iliad*
>   and Helen's public fault
> that bred it.
>   Were it not for that
>   there would have been
> no poem. . . .
>   . . . .
>   All women are not Helen,
>   I know that,
> but have Helen in their hearts.
>   My sweet,
>   you have it also, therefore
> I love you
>   and could not love you otherwise.
> (PB, 158–59)

Williams' analogy implies that Flossie is the one who must do the confessing, not he. Such a claim that Helen's infidelity represents the latent desires of all women seems to be a classic case of defensive displacement: at this early point in the poem, Williams is unable to speak of his guilt directly and can do so only by transferring it to others.

Similarly, Williams' explanations of why he is in hell in Book I are

20. Mariani, *William Carlos Williams: A New World Naked*, 503–504, 670, 823 n. 119. For a meditation on the ways Williams used a similar moment of isolation and despair earlier in his career, see Peter Schmidt, " 'These': Williams' Deepest Descent," *William Carlos Williams Review*, IX (1983), 74–90.

quite vague. Williams wants to blame things beyond his control for
separating him from Flossie—his strokes, his nervous breakdown—
rather than to admit that he bears some of the responsibility himself.
He concentrates on recent causes for their separation but hedges
about the ways he had earlier hurt his wife deeply. He talks of the
physical separation caused by his stay at Hillside but not the spiritual
division between him and Flossie that *he* has caused. Thus he instinc-
tively does not use an active verb when he describes being in hell ("I
cannot say / that I have gone to hell / for your love / but often / found
myself there / in your pursuit" [PB, 156]); Williams evidently thinks
that he did not "find himself" in hell until he sought to return to
Flossie's love and began feeling guilty, and he seeks to assuage his
guilt by implying that when he chases other women he is still in
"pursuit" of his wife's love. Other allusions to marital storms in Book
I are similarly vague, indicating that much that Williams needs to
confess is still being repressed.

Near the end of Book I Williams is able to edge closer to the truth,
though his line breaks betray his agitation:

> The storm
> has proven abortive
> but we remain
> after the thoughts it roused
> to
> re-cement our lives.
> It is the mind
> the mind
> that must be cured
> short of death's
> intervention. . . .
> (PB, 158–59)

The phrase "death's / intervention" obliquely alludes to the dead
husband's confession in "A Dream of Love." Williams has begun to
admit that *he* is the one with Helen in his heart, not Flossie. But it is
still done under the guise of talking about other crises and physical
illnesses.

By focusing on the buried meanings in these passages in Book I, I
do not mean to discard their primary meaning, which is part of the
entire poem's deliberate meditation on how eros and the fear of death
ruthlessly control men and women. But the way these passages' sec-
ondary meanings are actively in conflict with their primary ones
suggests how deeply the sources for Williams' insecurities in the first

book lie. "There is something / something urgent / I have to say to you," he pleads near the book's beginning, but then concedes that "it must wait" until later books before it can be known and stated fully (PB, 154).

The literary allusions in Books II and III do not contain the dark double meanings in Book I. Not coincidentally, Williams in these books is able to discuss more forthrightly his own responsibility for being in hell. Of the different "deaths" and "public faults" that he describes in Book II, many are not so much faults for which modern culture is responsible (such as the development of the hydrogen bomb) as faults that Williams admits "I have brought on myself" (PB, 169). In Book II the repeated references to the bomb invoke Williams' as well as his culture's acts of violence. "We cannot wait / to prostrate ourselves" before a picture of a mushroom cloud, he says, speaking generally. But then in the next lines he explicitly applies this truth to the explosive role that eros has played in his own private life. In doing so, he gives a sexual connotation to the verb *prostrate:*

> . . . we cannot wait
>   to prostrate ourselves
> before it. We do not believe
>   that love
>   can so wreck our lives.
> (PB, 165)

By Book III, Williams can confess his private faults even more directly, and treat his adulterous yearnings as comic failures, not heroic exploits.

>   It is ridiculous
> what airs we put on
>   to seem profound
>   while our hearts
> gasp dying
>   for want of love.
>   Having your love
> I was rich.
>   Thinking to have lost it
>   I am tortured
> and cannot rest.
> (PB, 170)

Because such passages have none of the warped conjoining of accusation and confession that was present in Book I, we ought to accept Williams' boast in Book III that he can show Flossie the steps

"by which you shall mount, / again to think well / of me" (*PB*, 171).
And the allusions in the "steps" that follow (to Andrea Verrocchio's
statue, Marsden Hartley, the god Pan, and others) have no hidden
meanings undercutting their obvious ones. Williams shows how mas-
culine posturings are connected with male insecurities and then
determinedly applies this truth to his own case, no longer telling his
story indirectly.

> It is winter
>   and there
>   waiting for you to care for them
> are your plants.
>   Poor things! you say
>   as you compassionately
> pour at their roots
>   the reviving water.
>   Lean-cheeked
> I say to myself
>   kindness moves her
>   shall she not be kind
> also to me? At this
>   courage possessed me finally
>   to go on.
> Sweet, creep into my arms!
>   I spoke hurriedly
>   in the spell
> of some wry impulse
>   when I boasted
>   that there was
> any pride left in me.
>   Do not believe it.
>
> (*PB*, 175)

This passage, one of the most moving in the entire poem, beau-
tifully completes Williams' shorter, earlier confession in the book,
when he admitted that men "gasp dying / for want of love."
Williams' confrontation with his own violence and self-deceit is
heroic in a way that his denunciations of the world's atrocities—
important as they are—can never be. Flossie evidently does not
forgive her husband until near the end of the third book, but by
then Williams has earned it.

Literary allusions also play a prominent role in the part of "As-
phodel" that occurs after Flossie has rescued the poet—the last pages
of Book III and all of the Coda. But unlike the earlier allusions in
Book I, they are made confidently and surely. Williams and Flossie
have been reunited, and references to art and literature that they

know are made as unaffectedly as allusions to things they once did together. No more repressions, apologies, or belabored explications are necessary. The allusions also portray not only Williams' new state of self-knowledge but his poem's growing knowledge of itself and the literary tradition to which it belongs. That is, Williams' allusions in the last part of "Asphodel" point to at least four different lyrics that the poem absorbs and transforms. These poems are four of the greatest lyrics about love, memory, and time in the Western tradition: Christopher Marlowe's "The Passionate Shepherd to His Love," Spenser's "Epithalamion" and "Prothalamion," and Horace's *carpe diem* ode, I.xi.

The allusion to Marlowe's poem comes at the very end of Book III and is rather oblique. Marlowe's shepherd offers a series of presents, including "a thousand fragrant posies," to persuade his girl to live with him. Williams also seeks to persuade, only his woman is not a virgin but his wife, and he pleads for her to love him again rather than to love him for the first time. Yet he too seeks to win her love by offering her flowers "for your pleasure" (*PB*, 177), and the couple becomes a king and queen in a pastoral of their own devising, bringing to fruition all the earlier pastoral imagery in the poem.[21]

Williams' allusions to Spenser and Horace are more direct. They both occur in the Coda, Williams' full-throated celebration of the immortality of his love for Flossie despite their impending deaths. Because "Asphodel" has been steadily progressing toward Williams' reenactment of the marriage sacrament, it is fitting that the one direct quotation of another writer in his poem should come near its conclusion and should be from the chorus of Spenser's "Prothalamion," another poem celebrating a marriage: "'Sweet Thames, run softly / till I end / my song'" (*PB*, 181). There is an even deeper affinity between "Asphodel" and Spenser's "Epithalamion," however, for the "Epithalamion" commemorates Spenser's own marriage rather than the marriage of others, and like Williams' poem it is a meditation on the relation between life's "short time" and art's "endless monument."[22]

21. Williams had known the poem since he was a schoolboy, when he treasured Francis Palgrave's poetry anthology *The Golden Treasury of English Verse*; for the importance of Palgrave to Williams, see Mariani, *William Carlos Williams: A New World Naked*, 11. Williams parodied Marlowe's poem (and Sir Walter Raleigh's famous "Reply" to it) in "Flight to the City" in *Spring and All* and "Raleigh was Right" in *The Wedge*.
22. Williams owned a 1903 edition of Spenser's *Poetical Works*. See Peter Schmidt *et al.* (eds.), "A Descriptive List of Works from Williams' Library Now at Fairleigh Dickinson

Spenser's "Epithalamion" is a time-piece constructed of 12 stanzas and 365 long lines, depicting both the workings of eternity and the activities of the 24 hours of Spenser's wedding day during the 16 hours of light and 8 hours of darkness of the summer solstice in Ireland in 1594.[23] The poem is filled with references to time and timeliness, including pleas not to be late for the wedding, but the lines at its very center are given over to the timeless miracle of the sacrament itself:

> Bring her up to th' high altar, that she may
> The sacred ceremonies there partake,
> The which do endless matrimony make. . . .

In the ceremony, the eternal intersects the temporal, and for one brief moment the participants can see how God guides man's history from above. Near the end of the poem, Spenser moves from a description of the bride and groom's lovemaking up through the spheres of the heavens that preside over the spousal bed. He first asks blessings from Cynthia, Juno, and Hebe, then contemplates the

> high heavens, the temple of the gods,
> In which a thousand torches flaming bright
> Doe burne

and then finally moves beyond the constellations to the Christian firmament above it. Praying for the children he hopes his marriage will engender, Spenser asks that they "May heavenly tabernacles there inherit, / Of blessed Saints for to increase the count." The silence surrounding the marriage bed seems to have become the still point of a turning world that includes both the pagan heavens and the Christian firmament.[24]

Flossie at the altar during the climactic moment of "Asphodel" behaves not unlike Spenser's wife Elizabeth; like their husbands, both are awed and shy. And like Spenser, Williams fills his poem celebrating the eternity of marriage with ironic references to the shortness of time, from "Only give me time / time to recall them" in

---

University," *William Carlos Williams Review*, X (Fall, 1984), 35. See also the following reference to Spenser in *Contact*, V (June, 1923), 2: "One does not write a poem to say something, but to write a poem, and this is equally true of a disjointed dada composition and of Edmund Spencer's [sic] EPITHALAMION—a most beautiful thing, all of one piece." In 1955 when Williams sought to turn away from his triadic style, he revealingly associated it with Spenser, still misspelling his name. See Mariani, *William Carlos Williams: A New World Naked*, 689.

23. The classic study of the role played by time and time-keeping in the "Epithalamion" is by A. Kent Hieatt, *Short Time's Endless Monument: The Symbolism of the Numbers in Edmund Spenser's Epithalamion* (New York, 1960).

24. Edmund Spenser, "Epithalamion," in M. H. Abrams *et al.* (eds.), *Norton Anthology of English Literature* (2 vols.; New York, 1979), I, 718, 722–23.

Book I, to his discussion in the Coda of the "sweetest interval" left to Flossie and him now that they have reunited.

But Williams transforms the epithalamion tradition even as he transmits it. "Asphodel" takes place not during the summer solstice but in midwinter (*PB*, 175), and it is not about crossing the threshold of the bridal chamber so much as it is about leaving the grave and recrossing the boundary separating death from life. His references to the shortness of time consequently have an urgency that is largely absent from Spenser's poem, which magisterially clocks the movements of hours, years, and eternity and confidently eases the losses of this world with the promise of eternal rewards in heaven. Williams is nevertheless able to make promises to his wife that in their own way are as valuable as Spenser's. The Coda of "Asphodel" uncannily mixes present and infinitive tenses in delicate homage to Spenser. Williams both rejoins his wife in time and stands with her outside of time, looking back on the "spectacle" of their lives as if they have already crossed the boundary separating this world and the next. Both the "Epithalamion" and "Asphodel" immortalize marriage through the sacrament of art, but unlike Spenser, Williams believes that the imagination's ceremonies are the only sacraments we have, not foreshortened versions of the miracles performed in church. Williams can also unite soul to soul and time to eternity only after a life of travail—and after the sometimes tortured evolution of his soul that occurs even as his poem fights its way toward its conclusion.

Art is long, life is short. Williams' Coda to "Asphodel" also alludes to another poem, Horace's Ode I.xi, the most famous classical poem about love, memory, and time. Called the *carpe diem* ode, it gave us the phrase "seize the time." Williams perhaps had Horace on his mind in the mid-1950s because he had corresponded with Cid Corman about translations of Horace that Corman was doing. But he had also owned a Modern Library translation of Horace's works since the 1930s. In Horace's ode, the speaker and Leuconoe, his companion, feel the pressure of time as strongly as Williams does, and they too move from restlessness and distress to stoic transcendence. Here is Ezra Pound's matchless 1963 translation:

> Ask not ungainly askings of the end
> Gods send us, me and thee, Leucothoë;
> Nor juggle with the risks of Babylon.
>   Better to take whatever,
> Several, or last, Jove sends us. Winter is winter,
> Gnawing the Tyrrhene cliffs with the sea's tooth.
>
> Take note of flavors, and clarity's in the wine's manifest.

Cut loose long hope for a time.
We talk. Time runs in envy of us,
Holding our day more firm in unbelief.[25]

"We talk. Time runs in envy of us": the situation of "Asphodel" is
similar, except that Williams and Flossie are at the very end of their
lives while Horace's speaker and Leuconoe seem still in the middle of
theirs. All, however, contemplate the spectacle of time from a van-
tage point above it. Williams' voice has all the spacious calm of
Horace's:

But love and the imagination
    are of a piece,
            swift as the light
to avoid destruction.
    So we come to watch time's flight
            as we might watch
summer lightning
    or fireflies, secure,
            by grace of the imagination,
safe in its care.
(PB, 179–80)

In Book I, Williams had pleaded for time and treated it as his antag-
onist: "Listen while I talk on / against time." Now, time is van-
quished; as in Horace, it enviously flees from, or tries to catch up to,
the eternal. From the terror of amnesia that opens "Asphodel, That
Greeny Flower"—Williams' "fading memories" of Flossie, flowers,
names, and literature itself—Williams creates an ode that remem-
bers not only his own life and his specific memories of Marlowe,
Spenser, Horace, and Homer but also, symbolically, the entire West-
ern poetic tradition; it renews its voice through him even as he
speaks in praise of it. The eternal fields in which "Asphodel" blooms
are Williams' American version of the Elysian Fields. And as in
Greek mythology, those fields are filled with the sound of voices
conversing. "Asphodel" thus represents a superb conclusion to the
tribute to the past that is the theme of all of Williams' triadic odes.

25. Schmidt et al. (eds.), "A Descriptive List," 32, and, for the Cid Corman reference,
Mariani, William Carlos Williams: A New World Naked, 710. I wish to thank Gordon Braden for
sharing his thoughts about Horace's poem with me. For Pound's translation, see Ezra Pound:
Translations (New York, 1963), 406; Pound changed the standard spelling of the lover's name,
Leuconoe, to Leucothoë. Could Williams' publication of "Asphodel" and its allusion to Horace
in 1955 have ironically sent Pound—the poet who was incessantly recommending the classics
to Williams—back to the classics? Pound did not translate Horace's carpe diem ode until 1963,
the year of Williams' death. Given the allusion to Horace in "Asphodel," it may be that we
should read Pound's translation as a veiled tribute to his old friend.

EPILOGUE/RETROSPECTIVES FROM BRUEGHEL

After having developed the triadic line and the collo-
quial, generalizing, and digressive style that suits it, Williams in the
mid-1950s began to feel the need to cut across the grain of a devel-
oped style once again: "The poems that [Williams] had written in the
[triadic] step-down style seemed 'forced' to him now, as he told Cid
Corman on November 1 [1955], at least in 'the way I have spread the
lines on the page to make my point on the meter.' They were too
'overdone, artificial, archaic—smacking of Spencer [sic] and his final
Alexandrine.' "[1] The new voice that Williams invented in response
to his dissatisfaction with his triadic odes marks the new poems
included in *Pictures from Brueghel and Other Poems* (1962). These
poems seem an exercise in minimalism in contrast to the cornucopia
of rhetorical effects in Williams' two preceding volumes. Several of
the poems have astringent titles like "Fragment" or "Exercise in
Timing"; lines and stanzas are taut and curt, in direct contrast to the
sinuous, loquacious texture of the poems written using the triadic
line; and Williams' figures of speech, especially his use of simile,
metaphor, apostrophe, and allusion, are curtailed and dissected
rather than indulged. Restricted also is the role played by Williams'
own private thoughts and opinions in *The Desert Music* and *Journey to
Love*. As indicated by the title of his last volume, Williams' concern
is less to make his own life the subject of his poetry than to adopt the
part of being a dispassionate and sharp-eyed witness to the times; he
no longer seems to be living almost entirely within the world of his
own memory. This is not to say that Williams is not present in the last
poems, but only that he no longer tends to be the principal dramatic
figure. He describes things and events for themselves, and his own
reasons for choosing to describe those things and his own opinions

---

1. Mariani, *William Carlos Williams: A New World Naked*, 689. Mariani is especially helpful
in giving the biographical information behind Williams' restlessness with the triadic style in
the mid-1950s and his return to earlier, more overtly avant-garde styles. (He did not com-
pletely reject the style, however; he continued to use it in two poems in *Brueghel*, "The Gift"
and "The Turtle.")

about their importance—all questions the reader must face after a preliminary reading of the poems—are implied rather than stated. In general, in *Pictures from Brueghel* Williams is everywhere present but nowhere seen.[2]

Such an aesthetic recalls Williams' Precisionist ideals, and if we browse through *Brueghel* listening for echoes of some of Williams' earlier styles, we discover that much of this volume's understated power comes from his inventing a new "late" style for himself even as he recollects his own earlier modes of writing. For the Precisionist strain in *Brueghel,* for example, consider "Iris," as lovely a poem as "The Pot of Flowers," written years before for *Spring and All* in honor of Charles Demuth's still lifes. Although "Iris" was probably inspired by irises suddenly blooming one summer morning in the Williamses' garden at 9 Ridge Road in Rutherford, New Jersey, the poem employs characters who are identified solely by their actions and the pronoun *we;* they are as universal and as abstract as any of the figures in his Precisionist lyrics. Williams' line and stanza breaks at first may seem so terse as to stifle the ostensible drama of the poem, the excitement of search and discovery, but in fact they heighten it. The poem opens with a sentence fragment announcing with its crisp play of sibilants, hard consonants, and long vowels the iris' smell bursting upon the Williamses' consciousness as they wake. For a brief moment there is no time, no syntax, no verb tense—only the pure presence of the iris expressed by Williams' noun phrase. Then movement begins and the poem enters time, following the Williamses as they search through all the rooms of their house for the source of the smell. As this occurs, the line and stanza breaks build suspense by breaking units of meaning apart. The phrase "come down for / breakfast" is separated from the subject it modifies, "we," and the description of the people searching is separated by stanza breaks from the direct references to what they are looking for (the "sweetest odor" and "source"):

> a burst of iris so that
> come down for
> breakfast
>
> we searched through the
> rooms for
> that

2. For an intriguing discussion of the intimate impersonality of Williams' late style, see David Walker, *The Transparent Lyric: Reading and Meaning in the Poetry of Stevens and Williams* (Princeton, 1984), 157–77. Several critics have particularly acute things to say about Williams' *Brueghel:* Joel Conarroe, "The Measured Dance: Williams' 'Pictures from Brueghel,'" *Journal of Modern Literature,* I (1971), 565–77; Mazzaro, *William Carlos Williams: The Later Poems,* 145–79; and Steiner, *The Colors of Rhetoric,* 71–90.

sweetest odor and at
first could not
find its

source then a blue as
of the sea
struck

startling us from among
those trumpeting
petals
(PB, 30)

The poem's fourth stanza celebrates the Williamses' discovery of the irises; unlike the others, it does not run on to the next but ends, exquisitely, with the verb *struck*. Aside from the noun *burst* in the first line, the poem's rhetorical figures have been plain and the line and stanza breaks have had to do most of the poem's work. But the buried figurative energy held within the earlier noun *burst* now erupts with a rich surf of sibilants, the ocean simile, and the implication that the iris' beauty strikes the Williamses' senses as strongly as the sea's waves do the shore. The last stanza holds this spot of time together for a moment longer by introducing yet another metaphor, that of the trumpeting petals announcing the importance of the Williamses' discovery. For all its understated effects and minimalist aesthetic, "Iris" is Paterian in its intensity; it is a world of pure discovery and absolute freshness, of sudden sensation and then of chasing down the source of that stimulation. Habit's dullness and time's decay are rigorously excluded; it is a pure pastoral, as pungent and clean as a sea breeze.

"Metric Figure" is another exercise in dramatic understatement and discovery, but its subject matter and style are delightfully Dadaist. The poem opens as abruptly as "Iris," yet its outburst of gutturals and slurred syllables contrasts with the crisp articulations of "Iris":

gotta hold your nose
with the appropriate gesture
smiling

back of
the garbage truck
as the complex

city passes
to the confession
or psychiatric couch or booth
(PB, 36)

The stanza breaks here work just as effectively as in "Iris," dramat-

ically introducing us to the larger and larger implications of the
seemingly trivial observation with which the poem opens. First, we
find the cause of the stink, and then in the third stanza Williams
turns the entire event into a symbolic action depicting a city's dis-
posal of its psychic garbage, its complexes. (Williams' pun on *complex*
would not work nearly so neatly without his line break giving the
word special emphasis.) The verb *passes* becomes similarly fecund,
referring both to a casual event on a street and to the necessary
elimination of wastes, the opposite of *blockage*. The joking coarse-
ness of the opening lines is thus transformed by the end of the poem
into an argument for the necessary link between cleansing inner
refuse—what the Dadaists had called "relief"—and keeping health
and sanity. The Williams who had turned to psychiatry in the early
1950s to cure his depression knew what he was talking about, but
could also laugh at himself: *he* was that lumbering, stinking truck.[3]
"Metric Figure" is a slight poem, but it nevertheless absorbs and
transforms a good deal of complex matter. And although its subject
may be waste, it does not waste a word.

    As for Williams' Cubist style, its presence is never more strongly
felt than in "To Be Recited to Flossie," which opens with a reference
to "The Rose" and Cubist fragmentation. Now, however, Williams
casts Cubism in a rather different light:

> Let him who may
> among the continuing lines
> seek out
>
> that tortured constancy
> affirms
> where I persist
>
> let me say
> across cross purposes
> that the flower bloomed
>
> struggling to assert itself
> simply under
> the conflicting lights
> (PB, 35)

The sentence beginning with the phrase "Let him who may" is left
incomplete, but it is not hard to imagine a whole: "Let him who may
seek out my constancy (that is, my determination to create the best
art I can) be my ideal reader." The phrase that ends the first fragment

---

3. Mariani, *William Carlos Williams: A New World Naked*, 659–66.

then begins a second: "that tortured constancy / affirms / where I persist." Williams implies that although he may sometimes seem a creator of arresting failures, an artist at cross purposes with his own talent, his determination still remains; it will eventually affirm his strength and make his purposes clear. His saying that "the flower bloomed" "under / the conflicting lights" is thus Williams' confession of the soul's torment embodied in his work. His active verbs (*seek out, affirm, persist,* and *bloomed*) suggest a buried force belied by the broken grammar, a force seeking but not yet finding its form. The pure energy of the verbs struggles to order the fragmented syntax and the line breaks that "cross" and block it, just as Williams says that he strains to find the right words but fails.

In the last stanza of the poem, however, Williams is exultant; a complete sentence frees itself from the clot of sentence fragments, becoming a stanza unto itself. After the tortured false starts and warped syntax in the first four stanzas, Williams has at last found the *right* words, and can speak them freely:

> you will believe me
> a rose
> to the end of time
> (*PB,* 35)

By addressing his *wife* in these lines rather than an "ideal" reader as he did in the poem's opening, moreover, Williams gives new shades of meaning to important earlier phrases in the poem—"tortured constancy," "cross purposes," and "conflicting lights." They no longer refer merely to Williams' art but also to his marriage and to his volatile mixture of fidelity and infidelity. It is a plea for forgiveness and also a proud declaration that he *has* fundamentally remained faithful to his wife despite moments when he acted at cross purposes to that love. Williams' sudden introduction of private rather than public meanings into the poem at first may seem arbitrary, as may Williams' switching from addressing a third person ("him") to addressing Flossie. But the beauty of Williams' birthday present to his wife is that it shows that his public career has been firmly rooted in his private life and that his ideal reader is and has always been Flossie, the radiant source (even when he didn't know it or couldn't admit it) for all his art's energy. His birthday gift thus recasts, in miniature, the drama embodied at length in "Asphodel, That Greeny Flower": under Flossie's guiding presence, Williams' art breaks free from its self-destructiveness and blooms. The poem is a fine example of the large-scale ambitions and personal references covertly present within Williams' contracted and "impersonal" style in *Pictures from Brueghel.*

"To Be Recited to Flossie" may also be considered as an old man's ironic glance back at the ostentatious ambitions of his youthful avant-garde poetics. The credo of Williams' most famous Cubist poem, "The Rose," was "the rose is obsolete" because in it Williams had sought to capture the bravado of Modernism—its belief that the basic visual and linguistic vocabulary and syntactic structures of the arts were out of date. From the perspective of almost forty years later, however, Cubism's lofty ambitions seem touching—noble, yes, but also arrogant and rather innocent. The great tradition of Western still life painting and portraiture was hardly replaced by Cubism, just as traditional literary rhetoric did not vanish because a few poems had used rhetoric to argue that some rhetoric was obsolete. Seen from the vantage point of the late 1950s, Cubist work had ironically been canonized as an enduring part of the great tradition that it had sought to overthrow. Williams' allusion to his poem "The Rose" in "To Be Recited to Flossie" is similarly ironic; it shows that his attempts to build new images for love and roses in that poem were inspired by a woman who was, simply, a rose in the traditional sense. The rose is not obsolete as an image of love but eternal: Williams' audacious attempts in "The Rose" to construct new images of love using suitably man-made materials such as majolica and steel merely gave the rose new identities, thereby showing how immortal it was. Similarly, Williams now admits that Modernism's tortured fragmentation of the whole image and the complete sentence was legitimate and necessary and, ironically, representative of a nostalgic desire for the time when traditional images and syntax could suffice. By ending "To Be Recited to Flossie" with an unfragmented, radiantly "complete" sentence, Williams wryly admits that his most aggressively fragmented styles had all the time been longing for the ability to write authoritative complete sentences. Such irony, however sharp, does not dismiss Williams' earlier styles. It just treats them as necessary phases on the way to a style that incorporates and transcends them—the style that Williams believed he has at last found in *Pictures from Brueghel.*[4] This is why terms such as *Precisionist, Cubist,*

4. See also "The Rewaking" (*PB,* 70) and the intriguing summary by Weaver of Williams' views in the late 1950s on how fragmentation in poetry is related to dysfunction between the sexes in *William Carlos Williams: The American Background,* 155. Weaver quotes from an essay by Williams entitled "The Broken Vase" (1957), which is reprinted in Dijkstra (ed.), *A Recognizable Image: William Carlos Williams on Art and Artists,* 206–209.

and *Dadaist*, whatever their usefulness, are too limiting for the late styles of *The Desert Music, Journey to Love,* and *Pictures from Brueghel.* For in Williams' poems of the 1950s he takes the multiple, contradictory poetics of his earlier styles and creates a new synthesis—not once but twice, first with his triadic line and then with *Brueghel's* stricter (though still variable) metrics.

At the end of Williams' life he saw that his rebellious interest in the visual arts and his cries for the new were all actually examples of his tortured constancy to literary tradition. He may appear to work at cross purposes to that tradition, but that is his way—and, he implies, the requisite way for all modern artists—of reconciling the usable past and the individual talent. "To Be Recited to Flossie," like Williams' work as a whole, seeks readers who can understand both the conflict and the constancy at the heart of his genius.

BIBLIOGRAPHY

BOOKS AND ARTICLES

Adams, Brooks. *The Law of Civilization and Decay.* London, 1896.

Adams, Henry. *The Education of Henry Adams.* Edited by Ernest Samuels. Boston, 1973.

Ades, Dawn, ed. *Dada and Surrealism Reviewed.* London, 1978.

Altieri, Charles. "Picasso's Collages and the Force of Cubism." *Kenyon Review,* VI (Spring, 1984), 8–33.

Apollinaire, Guillaume. *The Cubist Painters.* Translated by Lionel Abel. 1949; rpr. New York, 1970. Vol. I of *The Documents of Modern Art.*

Artaud, Antonin. *The Theatre and Its Double.* Translated by Mary Caroline Richards. New York, 1958.

Bakhtin, Mikhail. *The Dialogic Imagination: Four Essays.* Edited by Michael Holquist. Translated by Caryl Emerson. Austin, Texas, 1982.

Balakian, Anna. *André Breton: Magus of Surrealism.* New York, 1971.

Barber, John W., and Henry Howe. *Historical Collections of the State of New Jersey.* New York, 1894.

Benedikt, Michael, ed. *The Poetry of Surrealism.* Boston, 1975.

Benjamin, Walter. "The Work of Art in the Age of Mechanical Reproduction." In *Illuminations,* edited by Hannah Arendt. New York, 1969.

Bercovitch, Sacvan. *The Puritan Origins of the American Self.* New Haven, Conn., 1975.

Bollard, Margaret L. "The Interlace Element in *Paterson.*" *Twentieth Century Literature,* XXI (1975), 288–304.

Bové, Paul. "The World and Earth of William Carlos Williams: *Paterson* as a 'Long Poem.'" *Genre,* XI (Winter, 1978), 575–96.

Breslin, James E. B. "Whitman and the Early Development of William Carlos Williams." *Publications of the Modern Language Association,* LXXXII (1967), 613–21.

_____. *William Carlos Williams: An American Artist.* 1970; rpr., Chicago, 1985.

_____. "William Carlos Williams and Charles Demuth: Cross-Fertilization in the Arts." *Journal of Modern Literature*, VI (1977), 248–63.

_____. "William Carlos Williams and the Whitman Tradition." In *Literary Criticism and Historical Understanding: Selected Papers from the English Institute*, edited by Philip Damon. New York, 1967.

Breton, André. "En Marge de *Les Champs magnétiques.*" *Change*, VII (1970), 9–11.

_____. *Les Manifestes du Surréalisme.* Paris, 1955.

_____. *Manifestos of Surrealism.* Translated by Richard Seaver and Helen R. Lane. Ann Arbor, Mich., 1969.

Breton, André, and Philippe Soupault. *Les Champs magnétiques.* 1919; rpr., Paris, 1971.

Brooks, Van Wyck. "On Creating a Usable Past." *Dial*, LXIV (1918), 337–41.

Brown, Milton W. *American Painting from the Armory Show to the Depression.* Princeton, 1955.

_____. "Cubist-Realism: An American Style." *Marsyas*, III (1943–45), 138–60.

Brumm, Ursula. *American Thought and Religious Typology.* Translated by John Hoaglund. New Brunswick, N.J., 1970.

Bruns, Gerald L. *Inventions: Writing, Textuality, and Understanding in Literary History.* New Haven, Conn., 1982.

Bry, Doris. *Alfred Stieglitz.* Washington, D.C., 1958.

Caws, Mary Ann, ed. *About French Poetry From Dada to 'Tel Quel.'* Detroit, 1974.

Cheney, Sheldon. "Why Dada?" *Century Magazine* (May, 1922), 22–29.

Clark, Timothy J. *The Painting of Modern Life: Paris in the Art of Monet and His Followers.* Princeton, 1984.

Conarroe, Joel. "The Measured Dance: Williams' 'Pictures from Brueghel.'" *Journal of Modern Literature*, I (1971), 565–77.

_____. *William Carlos Williams's "Paterson": Language and Landscape.* Philadelphia, 1970.

Cooke, Jacob Ernest. *Alexander Hamilton.* New York, 1982.

Cott, Nancy F. *The Bonds of Womanhood: "Woman's Sphere" in New England, 1780–1835.* New Haven, Conn., 1977.

Cushman, Stephen. *William Carlos Williams and the Meanings of Measure.* New Haven, Conn., 1985.

Davidson, Abraham A. *Early American Modernist Painting, 1910–1935.* New York, 1981.

Dewey, John. *Character and Events: Popular Essays in Social and Political Philosophy.* Edited by Joseph Ratner. 2 vols. London, 1929.

De Zayas, Marius. "How, When, and Why Modern Art Came to New York." Introduction and notes by Francis M. Naumann. *Arts Magazine,* LIV (April, 1980), 96–126.

Dickie, Margaret. *On the Modernist Long Poem.* Iowa City, Iowa, 1986.

Dijkstra, Bram. *Cubism, Stieglitz, and the Early Poetry of William Carlos Williams: The Hieroglyphics of a New Speech.* Princeton, 1969.

Donato, Eugenio. "The Ruins of Memory: Archeological Fragments and Textual Artifacts." *Modern Language Notes,* XCIII (May, 1978), 575–96.

Doyle, Charles. *William Carlos Williams: The Critical Heritage.* London, 1980.

Driscoll, Kerry. "Mother Tongue, Mother Muse: *Yes, Mrs. Williams.*" *William Carlos Williams Review,* XI (Fall, 1985), 61–83.

Eddy, Arthur Jerome. *Cubism and Post-Impressionism.* Chicago, 1914.

Emerson, Ralph Waldo. *Selections from Ralph Waldo Emerson.* Edited by Stephen E. Whicher. New York, 1957.

Erenberg, Lewis A. *Steppin' Out: New York Nightlife and the Transformation of American Culture, 1890–1930.* Chicago, 1981.

Fahlman, Betsy. *Pennsylvania Modern: Charles Demuth of Lancaster.* Philadelphia, 1983.

Federal Writers Project. *New Jersey: A Guide to Its Present and Past.* New York, 1939.

Foucault, Michel. *Language, Counter-memory, Practice: Selected Essays and Interviews.* Edited by Donald F. Bouchard. Ithaca, N.Y., 1977.

Fredman, Stephen. *Poet's Prose: The Crisis in American Verse.* New York, 1983.

Freud, Sigmund. *The Interpretation of Dreams.* London, 1953. Vol. V of James Strachey, ed., *The Standard Edition of the Complete Psychological Works of Sigmund Freud.* 24 vols.

———. *Introductory Lectures on Psycho-Analysis.* London, 1953. Vol. XV of Strachey, ed., *The Standard Edition of the Complete Psychological Works of Sigmund Freud.*

Friedman, Martin L. "The Art of Charles Sheeler: Americana in a Vacuum." In *Charles Sheeler.* Washington, D.C., 1968.

———. *The Precisionist View in American Art.* Minneapolis, 1960.

Gilbert, Sandra M. "Purloined Letters: William Carlos Williams and 'Cress.'" *William Carlos Williams Review,* XI (Fall, 1985), 5–15.

Gleizes, Albert, and Jean Metzinger. *Du cubisme.* Paris, 1912.

Graham, Theodora R. "'Her Heigh Compleynte': The Cress Letters of William Carlos Williams' *Paterson.*" In *Ezra Pound and William Carlos Williams: The University of Pennsylvania Conference Papers,* edited by Daniel Hoffman. Philadelphia, 1983.

Green, Jonathan, ed. *"Camera Work": A Critical Anthology.* Millertown, N.Y., 1973.

Grover-Rogoff, Jay. "Hart Crane's Presence in *Paterson.*" *William Carlos Williams Review,* XI (Spring, 1985), 20–29.

Guimond, James. *The Art of William Carlos Williams.* Urbana, Ill., 1968.

Gutman, Herbert G. *Work, Culture, and Society in Industrializing America.* New York, 1976.

Hacker, Louis M. *Alexander Hamilton in the American Tradition.* New York, 1957.

Hartley, Marsden. *Adventures in the Arts.* New York, 1921.

Hartman, Geoffrey. *Beyond Formalism.* New Haven, Conn., 1970.

Hedges, Inez. *Languages of Revolt: Dada and Surrealist Literature and Film.* Durham, N.C., 1983.

Hemingway, Ernest. *A Moveable Feast.* New York, 1964.

Herbert, Robert L., ed. *Modern Artists on Art.* Englewood Cliffs, N.J., 1964.

Hieatt, A. Kent. *Short Time's Endless Monument: The Symbolism of the Numbers in Edmund Spenser's Epithalamion.* New York, 1960.

Hofstadter, Richard. *The Progressive Historians: Turner, Beard, Parrington.* New York, 1968.

Homer, William Innis. *Alfred Stieglitz and the American Avant-Garde.* Boston, 1977.

Janowitz, Anne. "*Paterson:* An American Contraption." In *William Carlos Williams: Man and Poet,* edited by Carroll F. Terrell. Orono, Maine, 1983.

Josephson, Matthew. "After and Beyond Dada." *Broom,* II (July, 1922), 346–50.

———. "The Great American Billposter." *Broom,* III (November, 1922), 304–12.

———. "Made in America." *Broom,* II (June, 1922), 266–70.

Juhasz, Suzanne. *Metaphor and the Poetry of Williams, Pound, and Stevens.* Lewisburg, Pa., 1974.

Jump, John D. *The Ode.* London, 1974.

Kahnweiler, Daniel-Henry. *Juan Gris: His Life and Work.* Translated by Douglas Cooper. New York, 1969.

Kallet, Marilyn. *Honest Simplicity in William Carlos Williams' "Asphodel, That Greeny Flower."* Baton Rouge, La., 1985.

Kasson, John F. *Civilizing the Machine: Technology and Republican Values in America, 1776–1900.* New York, 1977.

Keats, John. *Selected Poems and Letters.* Edited by Douglas Bush. New York, 1959.

Kenner, Hugh. *A Homemade World: The American Modernist Writers.* New York, 1975.

_____. *The Pound Era.* Berkeley, Calif., 1971.

Kermode, Frank. *English Pastoral Poetry.* 1952; rpr., New York, 1972.

Knight, Christopher. "On Native Ground: U.S. Modern." *Art in America,* LXXI (October, 1983), 166–74.

Krauss, Rosalind. "In the Name of Picasso." *October,* XVI (Spring, 1981), 6–22.

_____. *Passages in Modern Sculpture.* New York, 1977.

_____. "Re-Presenting Picasso." *Art in America,* LXVIII (December, 1980), 90–96.

_____. "Stieglitz/*Equivalents.*" *October,* XI (Winter, 1979), 129–40.

Lawrence, Sidney, "Clean Machines at the Modern." *Art in America,* LXXII (February, 1984), 127–41, 166–68.

Lears, T. J. Jackson. *No Place of Grace: Antimodernism and the Transformation of American Culture, 1880–1920.* New York, 1981.

Leavens, Ileana B. *From "291" to Zurich: The Birth of Dada.* Ann Arbor, Mich., 1983.

Levertov, Denise. "The Ideas in the Things." In *William Carlos Williams: Man and Poet,* edited by Carroll F. Terrell. Orono, Maine, 1983.

Levin, Gail. "American Art." In *"Primitivism" in Twentieth-Century Art: Affinity of the Tribal and the Modern,* edited by William Rubin. Vol. II of 2 vols. New York, 1984.

Lieber, Todd M. *Endless Experiments: Essays on the Heroic Experience in American Romanticism.* Columbus, Ohio, 1973.

Lippard, Lucy R., ed. *Dadas on Art.* Englewood Cliffs, N.J., 1971.

_____. *Surrealists on Art.* Englewood Cliffs, N.J., 1970.

Lippmann, Walter. *Drift and Mastery.* New York, 1914.

Lloyd, Margaret Glynne. *William Carlos Williams' "Paterson": A Critical Reappraisal.* Cranbury, N.J., 1980.

Loewinsohn, Ron. "'Fools Have Big Wombs': William Carlos Williams' *Kora in Hell*." *Essays in Literature*, IV (Spring, 1977), 221–38.

MacGowan, Christopher. *William Carlos Williams' Early Poetry: The Visual Arts Background*. Ann Arbor, Mich., 1984.

Maddison, Carol. *Apollo and the Nine: A History of the Ode*. Baltimore, 1960.

Margolis, Marianne Fulton, ed. *Camera Work: A Pictorial Guide*. New York, 1978.

Mariani, Paul. *William Carlos Williams: A New World Naked*. New York, 1981.

Marling, William. *William Carlos Williams and the Painters, 1909–1923*. Athens, Ohio, 1982.

Marx, Leo. *The Machine in the Garden: Technology and the Pastoral Ideal in America*. New York, 1964.

Masheck, Joseph, ed. *Marcel Duchamp in Perspective*. Englewood Cliffs, N.J., 1975.

Maurer, Evan. "Dada and Surrealism." In *"Primitivism" in Twentieth-Century Art: Affinity of the Tribal and the Modern*, edited by William Rubin. Vol. II of 2 volumes. New York, 1984.

May, Lary. *Screening Out the Past: The Birth of Mass Culture and the Motion Picture Industry*. Chicago, 1980.

Mazzaro, Jerome. *William Carlos Williams: The Later Poems*. Ithaca, N.Y., 1973.

Merrill, James. *The Changing Light at Sandover*. New York, 1982.

————. *Late Settings*. New York, 1985.

Miki, Roy. *The Pre-Poetics of William Carlos Williams: "Kora in Hell."* Ann Arbor, Mich., 1983.

Millard, Charles. "The Photography of Charles Sheeler." In *Charles Sheeler*. Washington, D.C., 1968.

Miller, J. Hillis. *The Linguistic Moment From Wordsworth to Stevens*. Princeton, 1985.

————. *Poets of Reality*. Cambridge, Mass., 1965.

————. "Williams' *Spring and All* and the Progress of Poetry." *Daedalus*, XCIX (1970), 415–29.

Miller, James E. *The American Quest for a Supreme Fiction*. Chicago, 1979.

Miller, Perry. *Errand into the Wilderness*. Cambridge, Mass., 1956.

Mitchell, Broadus. *Alexander Hamilton: The National Adventure, 1788–1804*. New York, 1962.

Moore, Marianne. *The Complete Prose of Marianne Moore*. Edited by Patricia C. Willis. New York, 1986.

Moore, Patrick. "Cubist Prosody: William Carlos Williams and the Conventions of Verse Lineation." *Philological Quarterly*, LXV (Fall, 1986), 515–36.

Motherwell, Robert, ed. *The Dada Painters and Poets: An Anthology.* New York, 1951.

Mumford, Lewis. *The Golden Day: A Study of American Experience and Culture*. New York, 1926.

Naef, Weston, and James Wood. *Era of Exploration: The Rise of Landscape Photography in the American West, 1860–1885*. New York, 1975.

Naumann, Francis M. "The Big Show: The First Exhibition of the Society of Independent Artists." Part I, *Artforum*, XVII (February, 1979), 34–39. Part II, *Artforum*, XVII (April, 1979), 49–53.

_____. "The New York Dada Movement: Better Late Than Never." *Arts Magazine*, LIV (February, 1980), 143–49.

_____. "Walter Conrad Arensberg: Poet, Patron, and Participant in the New York Avant-Garde, 1915–1920." *Philadelphia Museum of Art Bulletin*, LXXVI (Spring, 1980), 2–32.

Nelson, William, and Charles A. Shriner. *History of the City of Paterson and the County of Passaic New Jersey.* Paterson, N.J., 1901.

_____. *Records of the Township of Paterson, N.J., 1831–1851*. Paterson, N.J., 1895.

Newhall, Beaumont. *The History of Photography from 1839 to the Present*. Rev. ed. New York, 1982.

Novak, Barbara. *American Painting of the Nineteenth Century: Realism, Idealism, and the American Experience*. New York, 1969.

Panofsky, Erwin. *Meaning in the Visual Arts*. New York, 1955.

Paul, Sherman. *The Music of Survival.* Urbana, Ill., 1968.

_____. "A Sketchbook of the Artist in His Thirty-Fourth Year: William Carlos Williams' *Kora in Hell: Improvisations.*" In *The Shaken Realist: Essays in Modern Literature in Honor of Frederick J. Hoffman*, edited by Melvin J. Friedman and John B. Vickery. Baton Rouge, La., 1970.

Pearce, Roy Harvey. *The Continuity of American Poetry.* Princeton, 1961.

Perloff, Marjorie. "The Invention of Collage." *Collage*. X-XI. New York, 1983, 5–47.

_____. *The Poetics of Indeterminacy: Rimbaud to Cage.* Princeton, 1981.

Pound, Ezra. *Ezra Pound: Translations.* New York, 1963.

_____. *Gaudier-Brzeska.* 1916; rpr., New York, 1970.

_____. *Literary Essays of Ezra Pound.* New York, 1968.

Pultz, John, and Catherine B. Scallen. *Cubism and American Photography, 1910–1930.* Williamstown, Mass., 1981.

Rapp, Carl. *William Carlos Williams and Romantic Idealism.* Hanover, N.H., 1984.

Riddel, Joseph N. *The Inverted Bell: Modernism and the Counterpoetics of William Carlos Williams.* Baton Rouge, La., 1974.

_____. "The Wanderer and the Dance: William Carlos Williams' Early Poetics." In *The Shaken Realist: Essays in Modern Literature in Honor of Frederick J. Hoffman,* edited by Melvin J. Friedman and John B. Vickery. Baton Rouge, La., 1970.

Rosenblum, Robert. *Cubism and Twentieth-Century Art.* New York, 1961.

Rosenthal, M. L., and Sally M. Gall. *The Modern Poetic Sequence: The Genius of Modern Poetry.* New York, 1983.

Rubin, William S. *Dada, Surrealism, and Their Heritage.* New York, 1968.

Said, Edward. *Beginnings: Intention and Method.* New York, 1975.

Sankey, Benjamin. *A Companion to William Carlos Williams' "Paterson."* Berkeley, Calif., 1971.

Sanouillet, Michel. *Dada à Paris.* Paris, 1965.

Sayre, Henry M. "Avant-Garde Dispositions: Placing *Spring and All* in Context." *William Carlos Williams Review,* X (Fall, 1984), 13–24.

_____. "Ready-mades and Other Measures: The Poetics of Marcel Duchamp and William Carlos Williams." *Journal of Modern Literature,* VIII (1980), 3–22.

_____. "The Tyranny of the Image: The Aesthetic Background." *William Carlos Williams Review,* IX (1983), 125–34.

_____. *The Visual Text of William Carlos Williams.* Urbana, Ill., 1983.

Schmalenbach, Werner. *Kurt Schwitters.* New York, 1967.

Schmidt, Peter. " 'These': Williams' Deepest Descent." *William Carlos Williams Review,* IX (1983), 74–90.

Schmidt, Peter *et al.,* eds. "A Descriptive List of Works from Williams' Library Now at Fairleigh Dickinson University." *William Carlos Williams Review,* X (Fall, 1984), 30–53.

Seitz, William C. *The Art of Assemblage*. New York, 1968.

Shattuck, Roger. *The Banquet Years: The Origins of the Avant-Garde in France, 1885 to World War I*. 1958; rpr., New York, 1968.

Shi, David E. "Matthew Josephson and *Broom*: Cultural Nationalism in the Jazz Age." *Southern Review*, XIX (July, 1983), 573–95.

Shuster, George N. *The English Ode from Milton to Keats*. New York, 1940.

Simpson, Louis. *Three on the Tower: The Lives and Works of Ezra Pound, T. S. Eliot, and William Carlos Williams*. New York, 1975.

Slate, Joseph Evans. "Kora in 'Opacity': William Carlos Williams' Improvisations." *Journal of Modern Literature*, I (May, 1971), 463–76.

Snyder, Joel. *American Frontiers: The Photography of Timothy H. O'Sullivan, 1867–1874*. Philadelphia, 1981.

Soupault, Philippe. *Les Dernieres Nuits de Paris*. Paris, 1929.

Stearns, Harold, ed. *Civilization in the United States*. New York, 1922.

Steiner, Wendy. *The Colors of Rhetoric: Problems in the Relation Between Literature and Painting*. Chicago, 1982.

Steinman, Lisa. *Made in America: Science, Technology, and American Modernist Poets*. New Haven, 1987.

———. "Once More, with Feeling: Teaching *Spring and All*." *William Carlos Williams Review*, X (Fall, 1984), 7–12.

Stevens, Wallace. *The Collected Poems of Wallace Stevens*. New York, 1954.

———. *Opus Posthumous*. New York, 1971.

Stieglitz, Alfred. *Georgia O'Keeffe: A Portrait*. New York, 1978.

Stillinger, John. *The Poems of John Keats*. Cambridge, Mass., 1978.

Strand, Paul. "Photography." *The Seven Arts*, No. 10 (August, 1917), 525.

———. "Photography and the New God." *Broom*, III (November, 1922), 252–58.

Susman, Warren. *Culture as History: The Transformation of American Society in the Twentieth Century*. New York, 1984.

Sutton, Walter. "Dr. Williams' *Paterson* and the Quest for Form." *Criticism*, II (Summer, 1960), 242–59.

Tapscott, Stephen. *American Beauty: William Carlos Williams and the Modernist Whitman*. New York, 1984.

Tashjian, Dickran. *Skyscraper Primitives: Dada and the American Avant-Garde, 1910–1925*. Middletown, Conn., 1975.

———. *William Carlos Williams and the American Scene.* New York, 1979.

Terrell, Carroll F., ed. *William Carlos Williams: Man and Poet.* Orono, Maine, 1983.

Thompson, E. P. "Time, Work-Discipline, and Industrial Capitalism." *Past and Present,* XXXVIII (1967), 56–97.

Thompson, Jan. "Picabia and His Influence on American Art, 1913–1917." *Art Journal,* XXXIX (Fall, 1979), 15.

Tichi, Cecelia. *Shifting Gears: Technology, Literature, Culture in Modernist America.* Chapel Hill, N.C., 1987.

———. "Twentieth Century Limited: William Carlos Williams' Poetics of High-Speed America." *William Carlos Williams Review,* IX (Fall, 1983), 49–73.

———. "William Carlos Williams and the Efficient Moment." In *Prospects,* edited by Jack Salzman. New York, 1982.

Tillim, Sidney. "The Ideal and the Literal Sublime: Reflections on Painting and Photography in America." *Artforum,* XIV (May, 1976), 58–61.

Townley, Rod. *The Early Poetry of William Carlos Williams.* Ithaca, N.Y., 1975.

Tsujimoto, Karen. *Images of America: Precisionist Painting and Modern Photography.* San Francisco, 1982.

Turner, Frederick Jackson. *The Frontier in American History.* New York, 1920.

Tzara, Tristan. "Memoirs of Dadaism." *Vanity Fair* (July, 1922), 70, 92, 94.

———. *Oeuvres Complètes.* Edited by Henri Behar. 5 vols. Paris, 1975.

Verkauf, Willy. *Dada: Monograph of a Movement.* London, 1961.

Wagner, Linda, ed. *Interviews with William Carlos Williams: Speaking Straight Ahead.* New York, 1975.

Walker, David. *The Transparent Lyric: Reading and Meaning in the Poetry of Stevens and Williams.* Princeton, 1984.

Wallace, Emily Mitchell. *A Bibliography of William Carlos Williams.* Middletown, Conn., 1968.

———, ed. An Interview with William Carlos Williams, conducted by John W. Gerber. *Massachusetts Review,* XIV (Winter, 1973), 130–48.

———. "Musing in the Highlands and the Valleys: The Poetry of

Gratwick Farm." *William Carlos Williams Review,* VIII (Spring, 1982), 8–41.

_____. "The Satyrs' Abstract and Brief Chronicle of Our Time." *William Carlos Williams Review,* IX (1983), 136–55.

Wallis, Brian, ed. *Art After Modernism: Rethinking Representation.* New York, 1984.

Wasserstrom, William. *The Ironies of Progress: Henry Adams and the American Dream.* Carbondale, Ill., 1984, 184–213.

Weaver, Mike. *William Carlos Williams: The American Background.* Cambridge, England, 1971.

Wescher, Hanna. *Collage.* New York, 1968.

Whitaker, Thomas R. *"Spring and All:* Teaching Us the Figures of the Dance." *William Carlos Williams Review,* X (Fall, 1984), 1–6.

_____. *William Carlos Williams.* New York, 1968.

Whitman, Walt. *Leaves of Grass.* Edited by Emory Holloway. Garden City, N.Y., 1926.

Whittemore, Reed. *William Carlos Williams: Poet From Jersey.* Boston, 1975.

Williams, William Carlos. "America, Whitman, and the Art of Poetry." *Poetry Journal,* VIII (November, 1917), 27–36. Rpr. in *William Carlos Williams Review,* XIII (Spring, 1987), 1–4.

_____. *The Autobiography of William Carlos Williams.* 1951; rpr., New York, 1967.

_____. *The Collected Later Poems of William Carlos Williams.* New York, 1950.

_____. *The Collected Poems of William Carlos Williams. Volume One: 1909–1939.* Edited by A. Walton Litz and Christopher Mac-Gowan. New York, 1986.

_____. "Eight Improvisations." *Antaeus,* XXX/XXXI (Summer/Autumn, 1978), 26–33.

_____. *The Embodiment of Knowledge.* Edited by Ron Loewinsohn. New York, 1974.

_____. "Fourteen Unpublished Letters by William Carlos Williams." Edited by Barbara Herb Wright. *William Carlos Williams Review,* XII (Spring, 1986), 22–38.

_____. *Imaginations.* Edited by Webster Schott. New York, 1970.

_____. *I Wanted to Write a Poem.* Edited by Edith Heal. Boston, 1958.

_____. "Letter to an Australian Editor." *Briarcliff Quarterly,* III (October, 1946), 205–208.

_____. "The Little Red Notebook of William Carlos Williams (1914)." Edited by Emily Mitchell Wallace. *William Carlos Williams Review,* IX (1983), 1–34.

_____. *Paterson.* 1946–58; rpr., New York, 1969.

_____. *Pictures from Brueghel and Other Poems.* New York, 1962.

_____. *A Recognizable Image.* Edited by Bram Dijkstra. New York, 1978.

_____. "Rome." Edited by Steven Ross Loevy. *Iowa Review,* IX (Summer, 1978), 1–78.

_____. *Selected Essays.* 1954; rpr., New York, 1969.

_____. *The Selected Letters of William Carlos Williams.* Edited by John C. Thirwall. 1957; rpr., New York, 1985.

_____. "The Situation in American Writing." *Partisan Review,* IV (1939), 41–42.

_____. *Something to Say: William Carlos Williams on Younger Poets.* Edited by James E. B. Breslin. New York, 1985.

_____. *Yes, Mrs. Williams.* New York, 1959.

Williams, William Carlos, Fred Miller, and Lydia Carlin. "Man Orchid." Introduction by Paul Mariani. *Massachusetts Review,* XIV (Winter, 1973), 67–117.

SELECTED PERIODICALS

Blast. 1914–15.
The Blind Man. 1917.
Broom. 1921–24.
Camera Work. 1903–17.
Dada/Surrealism. 1985–
Contact. 1920–23.
The Dial. 1880–1929.
The Egoist. 1914–19.
The Little Review. 1914–29.
New York Dada. April, 1921.
Others. 1915–19.
Rongwrong. 1917.
TNT. 1921.
391. 1917–24.
transition. 1927–38.
291. 1915.

INDEX